CW00493736

Donald Davidson

Philosophy Now

Series Editor: John Shand

This is a fresh and vital series of new introductions to today's most read, discussed and important philosophers. Combining rigorous analysis with authoritative exposition, each book gives a clear, comprehensive and enthralling access to the ideas of those philosophers who have made a truly fundamental and original contribution to the subject. Together the volumes comprise a remarkable gallery of the thinkers who have been at the forefront of philosophical ideas.

Published

Donald Davidson
Marc Joseph

Michael Dummett
Bernhard Weiss

Thomas Kuhn
Alexander Bird

Robert Nozick
A. R. Lacey

W. V. Quine
Alex Orenstein

Richard Rorty
Alan Malachowski

John Searle
Nick Fotion

Charles Taylor
Ruth Abbey

Peter Winch
Colin Lyas

Forthcoming

Nelson Goodman
Daniel Cohnitz & Marcus Rossberg

Saul Kripke
G. W. Fitch

David Lewis
Daniel Nolan

John McDowell
Tim Thornton

Thomas Nagel
Alan Thomas

Hilary Putnam
Max de Gaynesford

John Rawls
Catherine Audard

Wilfrid Sellars
Willem de Vries

Bernard Williams
Mark Jenkins

Robert Segal
Department of
Divinity and
Religious studies
University of
Aberdeen

Donald Davidson

Marc Joseph

ACUMEN

First published in 2004 by Acumen

Acumen Publishing Limited
15a Lewins Yard
East Street
Chesham
Bucks HP5 1HQ
www.acumenpublishing.co.uk

ISBN: 1-902683-26-9 (hardcover)
ISBN: 1-902683-27-7 (paperback)

British Library Cataloguing-in-Publication Data
A catalogue record for this book is available
from the British Library.

Designed and typeset in Century Schoolbook
by Kate Williams, Swansea.
Printed and bound by The Cromwell Press, Trowbridge.

For Sheila, and the boys

Contents

	Acknowledgements	ix
1	Introduction: Davidson's philosophical project	1
2	Meaning and truth I	12
3	Meaning and truth II	26
4	Radical interpretation	48
5	Interpretation and meaning	77
6	Events and causes	102
7	Action theory and explanation in the social sciences	117
8	The matter of mind	144
9	Conclusion: scepticism and subjectivity	175
	Notes	197
	Bibliography	227
	Index	239

Acknowledgements

I have been fortunate in writing this book to have had the kind assistance of a number of colleagues, friends and students. Before that, my work on Davidson benefited from the support and encouragement of two people who helped to shape my philosophical interests. The first was Professor Sue Larson, who introduced me to Davidson's writings and helped me recognize that the technical issues addressed by the analytic tradition in the philosophy of language have profound implications. The second was the late Bruce Cooper, in whose work I first saw drawn out in detail the connection between Davidson's philosophy of language and action theory, on the one hand, and deep and important issues in moral and political theory, on the other.

I am indebted to the many people who read versions of this book, in part or in whole. They include Jerry Clegg, Hillary Glick, Sheila Alter Joseph, Sue Larson, Elizabeth Potter, John Shand, Maury Silver and Kate Williams as well as the two anonymous reviewers who made many helpful suggestions. I'd also like to thank the students in my philosophy of language and philosophy of mind classes at Mills College for their useful feedback on earlier drafts. Thanks are owed, too, to Professor Akeel Bilgrami for his help in my clarifying some issues that remain unresolved in Davidson's writings. I am also grateful to my publisher, Steven Gerrard, for his patience and assistance in seeing this work through to press. Finally, I owe a debt of gratitude to Professor Davidson, who passed away just as this book was moving through its final prepublication stages. Early on he supplied me with an up-to-date bibliography, which proved to be crucially helpful, and he answered a number of questions that arose as I was completing the book.

Chapter 1

Introduction: Davidson's philosophical project

Donald Davidson ranks as one of the most influential philosophers of the second half of the twentieth and beginning of the twenty-first century. Davidson was trained in the analytic tradition in philosophy, which traces its origins back to Gottlob Frege and Bertrand Russell and continues through the logical empiricists and W. V. Quine, who was Davidson's teacher when he was a graduate student. A central focus of this tradition is the nature of language, and some of Davidson's most significant and widely cited work is his contribution to methodological and substantive debates about fundamental matters in the philosophy of language. Davidson argues that the most fruitful way to answer the basic question "What is it for our words to mean what they do?" is to investigate *theories of meaning* that model the knowledge an interpreter possesses when she understands a speaker's utterances.[1] His work on theories of meaning connects with problems in the metaphysics of mental concepts, and his arguments for the position he calls *anomalous monism* present one of the live options in contemporary philosophy of psychology; at the same time, Davidson's ideas about language and mind have a bearing on the nature of action, and since his earliest published work Davidson has been one of the seminal figures in contemporary action theory. From the complex ties that link these disparate writings there emerges, especially in Davidson's later work, a critique of traditional ideas about truth, scepticism and relativism, and the relation of subjectivity to objectivity. This critique is highly controversial, for Davidson counsels nothing less than "relinquishing what remains of [the] empiricism" that characterized Anglo-American philosophy for much of the twentieth century (Davidson 1990d: 68). In this respect, Davidson's work in philosophy departs from the tradition in novel and exciting ways.

1.1 From Plato to the philosophy of language

Given this brief overview of his work and interests, it is at first somewhat surprising to learn that Davidson began his career working on Greek philosophy – as he ironically puts it, the "bold purpose" of his Harvard PhD thesis is "to try to explain the philosophic meaning and intention of Plato's *Philebus*"[2] – after having majored in classics and literature in college. However, a closer examination of his writings reveals an underlying programme and pattern (evident, no doubt, only in retrospect) and, indeed, one of the attractions of Davidson's work is the breadth and unity of his interests. Alfred North Whitehead, one of Davidson's undergraduate professors at Harvard, famously described European philosophy as a series of footnotes to Plato, and one might characterize the arc of Davidson's career as a more or less systematic working through of a number of the problems Plato left us: the nature of meaning and its connection to truth; the relation of belief to knowledge; the nature of human action; and the place of the human mind in the world order.

Davidson has explained that he began to direct his energies to the topics we associate with him only after participating in research on the theory of rational choice in the mid 1950s.[3] The theory of rational choice, or decision theory, is a modern, formal investigation of the ancient concept of deliberation, the *locus classicus* for which is Aristotle's *Nicomachean Ethics*. According to Aristotle, human behaviour rises to the level of ethical concern when we can say that an agent *deliberately chooses* to engage in that behaviour. This seems right, for it excludes acts we perform under compulsion or due to ignorance; in the former the choice to act is made for us by whoever or whatever compels us, while in the latter we lack understanding of what we seem to have chosen to do. In both scenarios, not having chosen the action our behaviour is not subject to moral evaluation, and we should not be blamed or praised for it.

In his discussion of deliberate choice (*proairesis*), Aristotle identifies as *deliberation* (*bouleusis*) the stage that precedes our making a choice. An agent deliberates over which of several courses of action open to her is likely to eventuate in an outcome she values, and on the basis of that deliberation she chooses to pursue a course of action. In thus constructing a theory of deliberation or rational choice, we model the process of an individual's decision-making: how she chooses to realize her goals through actions in which she is able to engage. A moment's reflection reveals the very wide import of such a theory, as Davidson writes, for its goal "is to throw light on how people make decisions in the circumstances of everyday life" (Davidson 1957: 7).

Davidson has made some contributions to the theory of rational choice, but the most important consequence of his work is the way it led him to ask questions about the nature of action, belief and meaning. To see how reflection on problems in decision theory led Davidson in this direction, consider the case of a researcher, Jane, who offers an experimental subject, Jack, the opportunity either to receive $5 (option A), or to choose to gamble and receive $11 if a tossed coin comes up heads and nothing if it comes up tails (option B). The pattern of Jack's choices, given his beliefs about his chances of tossing a head in option B (e.g. he might believe that the coin is weighted one way or another), is of considerable interest to decision theorists. For example, suppose further that Jack has expressed his preference for option B over option A, and he has also expressed a preference for some third option (option C) over option B; will Jack also prefer option C to option A? That is, is the pattern of his preferences transitive?

An agent's choice behaviour is a function of two independent factors: the strength of his beliefs and the strength of his preferences. In our example, whether Jack chooses option A or option B depends on how likely he believes it is that he will win the money in option B, and it also depends on the value he places on receiving different sums of money. Davidson notes that there is a third factor that plays a role in Jack's deliberation; namely, his interpretation of the words Jane speaks in setting up the situation. If Jane is to succeed in teasing out the relative contributions of Jack's beliefs and desires then, as part of her analysis of Jack's pattern of choices, she has to assume that Jack understands her instructions in setting up the choice scenario, and this supposition is non-trivial.

Davidson's observation runs deeper. Jane is interested in the pattern of her subject's beliefs and values, but her only access to

Jack's attitudes are his words and other actions; she only knows what Jack prefers because he *says* or otherwise *communicates* that he prefers one option over another. Thus Jane, too, must be an interpreter; she cannot begin to construct or test a theory that describes the pattern of Jack's choices unless she already knows enough about his language to interpret his words. If we model this knowledge as a *theory of meaning* or *interpretation*,[4] knowledge of which would suffice for her interpreting Jack's utterances, then we can express the point by saying that the project of constructing a theory of meaning is prior to constructing a theory of rational choice. In other words, *first* she figures out what he means by his words, *then* she analyses the pattern his choices make. This priority is merely apparent, however, for the evidence on which any interpreter bases her theory of meaning for a speaker includes a description of the speaker's attitudes, especially his network of beliefs and desires, and this is given (in part) by rational choice theory. Hence we ought to see Jane as engaged *simultaneously* in two closely related interpretative projects. In light of this, Davidson sets as his goal "a theory where just by noticing what choices a person makes among *sounds* you could figure out what those sounds meant to them, and *at the same time* then figure out what they valued and what they believed" (Davidson 1994c: 210).

1.2 What is and ought to be a theory of meaning?

This goal points to a difference separating Davidson from one of the main traditions in twentieth-century philosophy of language, represented by J. L. Austin, Paul Grice, and P. F. Strawson and, more recently, John Searle, Stephen Shiffer and Brian Loar.[5] These philosophers adopt an *intention-based* approach to semantics, in the sense that they take as fundamental the idea that when a speaker utters a sentence, she intends to produce certain beliefs in her audience by means of that utterance, and what she intends determines what she means.

Grice, for example, identifies speakers' intentions as the vital component in an account of linguistic meaning, and that which distinguishes linguistic meaning from what he calls "natural meaning".[6] By natural meaning, Grice has in mind the relation we express when we say, for example, that certain spots *mean* that a person has measles or that smoke *means* fire; and natural meaning differs from linguistic meaning in that as we cannot argue from "'Those spots meant measles' to any conclusion to the effect that *somebody or other meant* by those spots" that he had measles (Grice 1957: 39, emphasis added).[7] This is important, because the concept of linguistic meaning finds its home in an account of interpersonal communication. Thus, in contrast, we can argue from *an utterance's* meaning that someone had no wish to make a long speech to the conclusion that *someone* (namely, Pericles, in his funeral oration to the Athenians) meant that he had no wish to make a long speech; and this, in fact, is what is important about the utterance. Grice has revised his original proposal under the weight of many counterexamples, but setting aside most of these details we can roughly define Pericles' meaning (in the sense of *linguistic meaning*) that he had no wish to make a long speech as his intending to cause his audience to believe that he had no wish to make a long speech, and his intending to produce that belief by uttering the ancient Greek translation of my English sentence, "I have no wish to make a long speech."

Davidson has remarked on the influence that Grice has had upon his work, especially the view that words mean what their speakers intend them to mean (Davidson 1990d: 311). It should be evident, however, that Davidson cannot directly exploit Grice's insight to construct a theory of meaning since, according to Davidson, "an analysis of linguistic meaning that assumes prior identification of nonlinguistic purposes or intentions will be radically incomplete" (Davidson 1990d: 315–16). Recall that in our hypothetical situation Jane wants a theory of meaning to help her interpret Jack's words. If she follows the path that Grice's analysis suggests, then Jane will interpret Jack's words by appealing to his intentions and beliefs, such as his intention to cause Jane to believe that he prefers option *B* over option *A* and his belief that he can accomplish this goal by saying, "I prefer option *B* to option *A*". In effect, this strategy depends on Jane's knowing details of Jack's psychology prior to her knowing the meanings of his words: *first* she knows Jack's intentions and other attitudes, and *then* she interprets his utterance by fitting his words into an account of his beliefs and desires. Davidson urges, however, that an interpreter's only access to a speaker's attitudes are through his actions and that, more generally, "interpreting an agent's intentions, his beliefs and his words are parts of a single project, no part of which can be assumed to be complete before the rest is" (Davidson 1984:

127). In our example, Jane only knows that Jack prefers option *B* to option *A* by his *saying* that he prefers option *B* to option *A*, or perhaps by his doing something else that indicates the relative strengths of his desires (such as pointing to a card on which the words, "option *B*", are written), where this indicating, too, stands in need of interpretation.

What Davidson seeks, therefore, is akin to David Hume's "science of Man": a unified theory that encompasses the study of thought, language and action (Hume 1978: xv). Is such a "theory of everything" possible? Whatever is actual is possible, hence Davidson would argue that a unified theory is possible; after all, we do manage, in fact, to interpret the words our fellows speak, and *at the same time* we fit those words into our overall picture of their lives. We accomplish these feats, moreover, based on only those resources that Davidson identifies as being available to our hypothetical researcher and experimental subject, including a catalogue of people's utterances and other actions, and the attitudes we can observe in these actions. What Davidson is after, then, is nothing more than making explicit or rationally reconstructing what we all, in effect, already possess in some form.

1.3 Quine and Davidson

The greatest influence on the development of Davidson's philosophy is the work of Quine, his friend and teacher. Quine, in turn, is most deeply influenced by the revolution in modern logic, beginning with Frege, Russell and Kurt Gödel, and by the empiricist tradition running from Locke and Hume through the logical positivists. These two traditions intersect in the person of Rudolf Carnap, who was never Quine's formal teacher, but was his mentor and friend, and the frequent target of his criticism.

By the early 1920s, Carnap came to see the "new logics" that Frege, Wittgenstein and Russell and Whitehead had developed as supplying a key to removing vitiating defects in traditional empiricism. By adopting a symbolic or formal method, these new theories provided that key by indicating the true character of logic and mathematics; in this way, they opened the door to solving "the greatest difficulty" that empiricism had faced – the problem of our knowledge of necessary truths. That true character is that "all the sentences of logic are tautological and devoid of content", and thus the difficulty is removed in recognizing that logical and "mathematical sentences are neither empirical nor synthetic *a priori* [as Immanuel Kant had thought] but analytic" (Carnap 1930–31: 143). In other words, Carnap (with thanks especially to Frege, Russell and Wittgenstein) solved the problem that dogged Hume and J. S. Mill by arguing that our knowledge of the truths of logic and mathematics is no knowledge at all, except in the trivial sense that we know the rules of the languages we speak.[8]

Ironically, though, Carnap's project shared with Kantianism the *anti*-empirical idea that the empirical scientific enterprise is preceded by an a priori investigation of the framework of science. This affinity is easily overlooked, for while Kant identifies that framework with the structure of the human mind, Carnap instead focuses on the framework implicit in a language system.[9] For Carnap this includes logic and pure mathematics, very general statements about the structure of the physical world (e.g. the statement that space-time does, or does not, obey the laws of Euclidean geometry) and the ontology of the theory. The present point, however, is that Carnap and the other logical empiricists retain a very powerful a priori apparatus, even if it is not the a priori apparatus envisaged by Kant.

Quine turns away from Carnap's latent a priorism and returns to a model of philosophizing more associated with Locke and Hume than Kant. Like Locke and Hume, Quine takes the methods and subject matter of philosophy to be continuous with those of natural science. In a different respect, though, Quine is Carnap's faithful student, for he also takes as his project the constructing of an improved empiricism, unflawed by what Quine famously identifies as its twin dogmas: the thesis that *analytic statements* (e.g. "All bachelors are unmarried") are true in virtue of meaning or linguistic convention, independently of matters of fact; and the principle that every *synthetic statement* can be translated into a report about a discrete range of immediate experience. Both claims depend on the idea that one can separate the *meaning* of a statement from its *informational content*, which Quine subjects to an extended critique in a pair of landmark works bracketing the 1950s.[10]

To see Quine's point, consider how a person learns a theory – a theory being a set of sentences closed under logical or evidential relations – that describes the properties of some particular kind of objects, for examples, sets or molecules. We might suppose that her learning takes place in two distinct stages. In the first stage she learns the identity of the objects the theory is about (i.e. sets or molecules), and in the second stage she learns what the theory, with its conceptual resources, says about those objects: what truths about those objects it asserts (such as that for any two sets *A* and *B* there is a set *C* to which they both belong, or that if the molecules of a non-ionic compound are linked by polar covalent bonds, then the compound is water soluble).

This model works to the extent that we have good analogies for introducing the objects of the theory. We might tell the person learning the theory, for example, that the objects spoken about by set theory are like groupings of physical objects, or that a molecule is an object the size of which compares to an amoeba as the size of an amoeba compares to a mastodon. These analogies cannot bear much weight, however, and her grasp of what sets or molecules are – alternatively, her understanding of the words that occur in set or molecular theory – awaits her learning the truths about sets or truths about molecules expressed by the statements of the theory. As Quine says, "our coming to understand what the objects are *is* for the most part just our mastery of what the theory says *about* them. We do not learn first what to talk about and then what to say about it" (Quine 1960: 16). Quine concludes that we cannot separate the meaning of a term, what one would find in a dictionary entry for that word, from information that bears on that term, or the sort of information one would find in an encyclopedia entry under that term; there is no isolatable meaning that attaches to the word "molecule" distinct from the truths of molecular theory.

The point is not merely that the meanings of someone's words are constituted by their context in the language or theory to which they belong. It is, rather, that that context is a *seamless web*. Quine famously illustrates this *holistic* conception with the image of human knowledge as

> a man-made fabric which impinges on experience only along the edges. Or, to change the figure, total science is like a field of force whose boundary conditions are experience. A conflict with experience at the periphery occasions readjustments in the interior of the field. ... But ... no particular experiences are linked with any particular statements in the interior of the field, except indirectly through considerations of equilibrium affecting the field as a whole. (Quine 1961: 42–3)

Because the epistemological bearing that experience has upon any sentence, which Quine identifies as the empirical content of a sentence, is mediated by the theory or language to which it belongs, the meaning of a sentence is distributed across the network of sentences that constitute the language. Quine thus draws from the image of human knowledge as "a man-made fabric" or "field of force" the implication that a sentence means what it does as a nodal point in a network of epistemologically and semantically interrelated sentences, and likewise for terms and other expressions. We have to surrender, therefore, the dogmas that the truth of some sentences ("All bachelors are unmarried") depends all on meaning and not on how things stand in the world and that the meaning of other sentences ("*That's* a molecule") can be identified with a determinate range of experiences, since the content of each statement is dispersed through the theory as a whole.

Davidson describes this observation, and the methods Quine founds on it, as "having saved philosophy of language as a serious subject by showing how it could be pursued without what there cannot be: determinate meanings" (Davidson 2001a: 145). Much more than Quine, however, Davidson uses this observation as a fulcrum with which to move contemporary philosophy of language and mind away from the empirical tradition. Davidson, as we shall see in subsequent chapters, undertakes a radical critique of the notions of meaning and mind, and arrives at a position that stands apart from that of the tradition in which he had his philosophical training.

The reader will find in the following chapters a sympathetic reading of Davidson's philosophy, not because he has the right or final answers to all the outstanding questions that define the contemporary scene in philosophy, but because, first, he offers what few other philosophers do today, namely, an over-arching theory of persons as rational animals. Secondly, this interpretation is undertaken in the spirit of the principle of charity – about which the reader will hear a great deal in what follows – in that the best way to understand a difficult thinker's work is to see it as making the best overall sense we can.

To this end, I begin Chapters 2 and 3 with an account of the assumptions and structure of Davidson's philosophy of language. This involves taking the reader through Davidson's compositionalism and extensionalism and his commitment to adopting a

Tarski-style theory of truth as the model for theories of meaning. This discussion is at times technical, and the reader with a less formal background may wish to proceed from §2.1 directly to Chapter 4, which she may do without too much loss of continuity (although with loss of formal detail). For those wishing to work through the formal details, I emphasize, at the end of Chapter 3, the philosophical importance of the concept of truth for Davidson, and thus begin to give the reader a sense of the bigger picture that embeds Davidson's philosophy of language.

Chapters 4 and 5 turn from elucidating the framework of Davidson's philosophy of language to showing how that framework is to be applied, at least in principle. There are two points I especially emphasize in these chapters. The first is the importance of Ramsey's writings on decision theory for Davidson. Davidson often comes back to Ramsey in his published writings, but that influence receives inadequate attention in other treatments of Davidson's philosophy intended for audiences of non-specialists. The other point is that Davidson's account of meaning rewrites the traditional picture, and this sets the stage for the metaphysical conclusions Davidson comes to, which we shall discover in Chapter 9.

Chapter 6 marks a transition. It introduces the concept of an event, which figures prominently in Davidson's work on mind and action theory. A great deal more could be said about the topic, but since most non-specialists will not have come to the present book with a particular interest in this issue, Chapter 6 serves mainly as a "service chapter" for other parts of the book.

In Chapter 7 I turn to Davidson's action theory, which is a topic on which Davidson's influence has been enormous. I compare Davidson's theory both to Aristotle's account of the practical syllogism and to more recent work influenced by Wittgenstein and represented by Peter Winch. In this chapter, too, I discuss a charge commonly made against Davidson's theory of action and mind: that it leaves the category of the mental as a mere "epiphenomenon" of the physical. I argue that a defence against this charge can be sustained if one bears in mind the systematic structure of Davidson's philosophy.

Chapter 8 takes up the topic of Davidson's philosophy of mind. I set that philosophy in a context that should be familiar to many readers, by comparing Davidson's account of mind with Cartesian dualism; later, I show that Davidson's theory achieves one of the paramount results that any philosophy of mind should achieve, that of showing how we as minded beings (to use John McDowell's apt phrase) belong to the physical world and yet retain our autonomy. Finally, in Chapter 9, I set out the conclusions of Davidson's picture of mind and meaning for traditional views of subjectivity and objectivity, and, more generally, the relation between minded beings and the physical and mental world they occupy.

Chapter 2

Meaning and truth I

In his *Philosophical Investigations*, Wittgenstein compares a natural language, for example, English or German, to an ancient city. Our everyday speech, he says, is like the ancient town centre with its "maze of little streets and squares, of old and new houses, and of houses with additions from various periods", while more recently added idioms (e.g. a specialized scientific vocabulary), like newly constructed suburbs, are regular and predictable in their structure (Wittgenstein 1958: §18). Part of Wittgenstein's point is to stress the complex interrelatedness of different parts of a language, but the image also appeals to him for its implication that mapping a language's structure is no easier than mapping the geography of an ancient city. The merit of this comparison should be evident to anyone who has navigated the back streets of London or Boston.

Davidson is sympathetic to this analogy between finding one's way around a city and within a language, but unlike Wittgenstein (and like Frege) he is persuaded that a language must be amenable to systematic semantic analysis. In this chapter I begin to present Davidson's philosophy of language by examining those formal constraints he takes to be needed if one is going to find one's way within a language. These constraints have the effect of identifying the structure an adequate theory of meaning may take, and in Chapter 3 I focus on Davidson's appropriation of Alfred Tarski's work in the semantics of formal languages as supplying the leading candidate for this structure.

2.1 A first constraint on a theory of meaning

A leading idea of Davidson's philosophy of language is that – subject to a number of qualifications – a compositional theory of truth can serve the purposes of a theory of meaning. This thesis, obviously, stands in need of elucidation, and in the remainder of this section I explain the meaning and motivation of the thesis that a theory of meaning ought to be *compositional* in structure; then, in §2.2 and §2.3, I explore the notion of a *theory of truth* and begin to examine its suitability to play the role of a theory of meaning.

The idea that a theory of meaning ought to be compositional in structure expresses Davidson's commitment to language's being amenable to systematic analysis; and this commitment, in turn, is a legacy of Plato's insight that sentences are semantically complex, which Frege went on to clarify in an exact fashion 22 centuries later. For Plato, the problem of the nature of language arises in the context of the "paradox of false propositions", a problem he inherits from the Eleatic philosophical tradition.[1] Here is the paradox. Consider that when I say that the man Theaetetus sits, I express or mean (let us assume) the fact that Theaetetus sits; but what do I express when I say that he flies? Since Theaetetus does *not* fly, there is no fact that I mean; I have meant something (namely, the fact that Theaetetus flies) that does not exist. But, following Parmenides, we ought to say that what is not, in no way is. We conclude, therefore, that when I say that Theaetetus flies I have not said anything. Yet my words are *not* nonsense; in uttering them I do *seem* to be saying something.

Plato unravels this apparent problem in three steps. First, he distinguishes the *meaningfulness* of a statement from its *being true*; when I say that Theaetetus flies, I say something meaningful, but false. This separation of significance from truth is the *sine qua non* of the philosophy of language.[2] Secondly, Plato contrasts the complexity of a sentence with the simplicity of a *semantic primitive*, a meaningful expression, no proper part of which is itself meaningful. In our example the words "Theaetetus" and "flies" are semantic primitives since each is a meaningful expression – which together compose the semantically *complex* sentence "Theaetetus flies" – but no ingredient of either (e.g. the letters "t", "h", etc. that compose the name "Theaetetus") is itself meaningful.[3] Finally, Plato completes his analysis by identifying the meaning of semantic primitives with assorted objects: for example, the noun "Theaetetus" with the man Theaetetus and the verb "flies" with the property (or Form) of flying. This neatly solves the problem of how a sentence can be both false and meaningful, since it guarantees that an expression is meaningful as long as its parts are; when I say that Theaetetus flies I have spoken meaningfully, since Theaetetus and flying exist, regardless of whether, as a matter of fact, Theaetetus flies. Plato's solution, however, engenders new questions.[4]

Frege clarifies Plato's insights about complex linguistic expressions, and he shows the way to extending those insights in his groundbreaking works on logic and the philosophy of logic. In particular, Frege lays bare the structure of language when he shows in an exact fashion how the sentences of a language result from applying, repeatedly perhaps, some fixed set of rules of composition to symbols drawn from a finite set of primitive symbols.[5] For example, the Arabic numerals are compositional in this sense: starting from a base set containing the simple numerals "0", "1", "2", "3", "4", "5", "6", "7", "8" and "9", we can construct any numeral by applying the rule that affixing a simple numeral to the left of a numeral is a numeral. Thus "639" is a numeral, because it results from applying this rule of composition twice, first stringing together the simple numerals "3" and "9" to generate "39", and then affixing "6" to this result to generate "639".

In the same way any sentence of a compositional language *L* (considered from a syntactic perspective apart from its meaning[6]) can be viewed as having been constructed from simpler expressions according to some fixed set of rules. For example, given the rule for disjunction ("or"),

> If *A* and *B* are sentences of *L*, then their disjunction (*A* or *B*) is a sentence of *L*,

we can compose sentences of unbounded complexity. Given the sentences "Theaetetus sits" and "Socrates stands" (which we suppose to have been constructed from the words "Theaetetus", "sits", "Socrates" and "stands" using other rules), we can construct the sentence "Theaetetus sits or Socrates stands" by applying our rule; and we can go on to construct "Theaetetus sits or Socrates stands, or Plato reclines" by applying the rule again. To spell out the compositional syntax of a language *L*, therefore, one needs only to specify a finite list of words and other syntactic primitives (prefixes and suffixes, case endings, etc.), along with a set of formation rules for combining those basic expressions into complex ones, according to the basic plan laid out by Frege.

With this syntactic framework in place, we can go on to characterize the compositional semantics of a language. Having fully defined the syntax of *L*, we transform that description into a definition of its semantics by specifying a meaning for every primitive expression and an interpretation of each formation rule, thereby showing how the meaning of a sentence is a function of the meanings of its parts.[7] For example, we superimpose upon our earlier syntactic rule the following interpretation:

> If either *A* is true or *B* is true, then their disjunction (*A* or *B*) is true.

To understand a disjunctive sentence, therefore, is a matter of grasping the sentence's semantic structure (e.g. seeing that it *is* a disjunction) and knowing the meanings of the disjuncts. In our example, if I know the meaning of "Theaetetus sits" and the meaning of "Socrates stands", and I understand the structure of the sentence, then I know the meaning of their disjunction.

Most philosophers agree that a constraint on a systematic theory of meaning for a language *L* is that it treat *L* as having a compositional semantic structure.[8] This idea, expressed as the *principle of compositionality*, finds support in the observation (usually credited to Noam Chomsky[9]) that competent users of a language can generate and understand indefinitely many sentences that they have never previously encountered. (For example, you had never heard or read the preceding sentence, and yet you were able to understand it.) To see what is at issue, consider the case of a young child first learning to speak. By the time he is 18 months old, the child will have heard some finite number of sentences. Over the course of the next year or so, he will begin to mimic and repeat his elders' utterances, and before he is 3 years old he will be freely generating grammatical sentences that are not only novel, but also apt to the situations he encounters. How does he manage this *limitless* feat, given the *limited* stimulus to which he has been exposed?

Compositionalists see in this phenomenon a first constraint on a theory of meaning. Unless we can regard the meaning of each sentence as the product of a finite number of operations performed on a finite (albeit extendable) base, the language to which it belongs will be unlearnable; for unless the complex expressions of a language bear systematic relations to one another, no matter how many sentences someone has mastered there will always be others she does not understand. Conversely, if we can regard the meaning of a sentence as a product of its structure and the meanings of its parts, then we can see "how an infinite aptitude can be encompassed by finite accomplishments" (Davidson 1984a: 8).

Thus a *compositional theory of meaning* M_L for a language L will include both an interpretation of each primitive expression of L and an interpretation of each formation rule of L, such that these together determine the interpretation of each complex expression of L. If we think of M_L as an axiomatic theory, then it will contain axioms that enumerate the meaning of each primitive expression, and it will draw upon the interpretations of the formation rules to deliver a list of theorems, one for each complex expression s of L, specifying the interpretation of s. Theories of meaning, or semantic theories, of this sort are familiar from discussions of simple artificial languages, such as the language of first-order logic.[10]

2.2 A second constraint on a theory of meaning

What might a compositional theory of meaning look like in detail? Simon Blackburn suggests that we think of philosophers of language as trying to sort out the relations among a triangle of elements composed of speakers' thoughts, language and the world (Fig. 2.1).[11] Following on from this idea, we might either take the relationship represented by the triangle's base as fundamental and identify the meaning of linguistic expressions with corresponding objects and events in the extra-linguistic world; or we might tip the

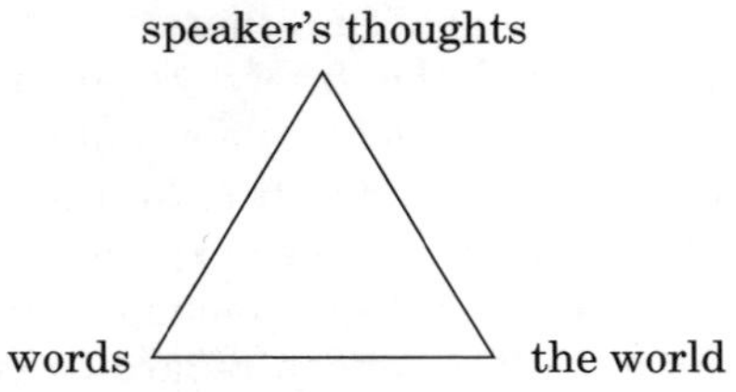

Figure 2.1

triangle and identify the meaning of linguistic expressions with a corresponding mental entity in the mind of the speaker. Either way, we adopt a *relational* or *correspondence theory of meaning*,[12] wherein the meaning of each primitive expression w of a language L is laid down by a rule or axiom of the form

w means m,

where m is the (external or mental) object that w means.

Consider, for example, Russell's correspondence theory of meaning in his early book, *Principles of Mathematics* (1938). Russell's theory identifies the meanings of the parts of sentences with the external objects and relations to which they refer, and it identifies the meanings of sentences with situations composed of those objects and relations. For Russell, then, the meaning of each sentence s is given by the rule,

s means m,

where m is the fact to which the sentence refers. For example, if the terms "Charles I", "died on" and "the scaffold" mean, respectively, the unfortunate king, the relation of dying on and the apparatus on which England's singular regicide occurred; then the sentence, "Charles I died on the scaffold" means the complex entity m, the situation or fact that Charles I died on the scaffold.[13] Russell's theory satisfies the compositionality con-straint, since it proposes that the meaning of a sentence (a fact or situation) is a product of its structure and the meanings of its parts (the objects that compose that fact).[14]

An attractive feature of Russell's early theory is that it treats the verb "means" as generating an extensional context, and the logic of extensional theories is well understood. A context or expression (such as a sentence) is *extensional* in this sense if it satisfies the substitution principle that if we replace one word or phrase in the expression with another that has the same reference, then the reference of the original expression remains unchanged.[15] For example, since the predicate "x ordered the death of y" is extensional and "Cicero" and "Tully" name the same person, if we replace "Cicero" in

Antony ordered the death of Cicero

with "Tully", then the result,

Antony ordered the death of Tully

will refer to the same situation as the original sentence: the fact that Antony ordered the death of that great man. Thus Russell treats meaning as an extensional relation, since, again, if the sentence "Antony ordered the death of Cicero" means an object, namely, the fact that Antony ordered Cicero's death, and "Antony ordered the death of Tully" differs from that first sentence just in its containing an occurrence of the word "Tully" where the first sentence has an occurrence of the name "Cicero", and Cicero = Tully, then the second sentence means the same fact as the first; namely, that Antony ordered the death of Cicero.

The tight connection that Russell forges between meaning and reference, however, can also be a vice. There is an argument, which has its roots in Frege and finds its classic exposition in the writings of Alonzo Church, to the effect that identifying the meaning of a sentence with the situation to which it refers has the intolerable result that all true sentences refer to the same fact. To see this, consider the following sequence of sentences:

(1) Antony ordered the death of Cicero.
(2) $\{x: x = x$ and Antony ordered the death of Cicero$\} = \{x: x = x\}$[16]
(3) $\{x: x = x$ and grass is green$\} = \{x: x = x\}$
(4) Grass is green.

If we assume that (1)–(4) satisfy the substitution principle, and we further assume that logically equivalent sentences have the same reference, then on Russell's early theory of meaning, (1)–(4) all refer to the same fact. If this is right, then clearly something is amiss with Russell's theory.

Here is how the argument works. Sentences are *logically equivalent* just in case the truth of one implies the truth of the other and vice versa; thus two sentences s_1 and s_2 are logically equivalent just in case s_1 and s_2 necessarily have the same truth-value. (For example, "All bachelors are unmarried" and "No bachelors are married" are logically equivalent.) Sentences (1) and (2) are logically equivalent, therefore, since the only way that the set to the left of the identify sign in (2) can turn out *not* to be identical to the set on the right is if Antony did not order the death of

Cicero, that is, if (1) is false. Thus (2) is true (i.e. the two sets are identical) if and only if (1) is true. The same reasoning guarantees that (3) and (4) are logically equivalent. By our assumption, then, that logically equivalent sentences have the same reference, we conclude that (1) and (2) refer to the same fact, and (3) and (4) refer to the same fact.

Next, observe that since Antony *did* order the death of Cicero, the term "$\{x: x = x$ and Antony ordered the death of Cicero$\}$" refers to the set that contains everything; and since grass *is* green the term "$\{x: x = x$ and grass is green$\}$" also refers to the set that contains everything. Thus the terms "$\{x: x = x$ and Antony ordered the death of Cicero$\}$" and "$\{x: x = x$ and grass is green$\}$" have the same reference, and by the substitution principle we can replace one with the other in a sentence without altering the reference of the original sentence.[17] Putting all this together, we observe that (1) and (2) have the same reference, since they are logically equivalent; and, by the substitution principle, (2) and (3) have the same reference, since they differ only in containing different but co-referring terms (namely, "$\{x: x = x$ and grass is green$\}$" in place of "$\{x: x = x$ and Antony ordered the death of Cicero$\}$"); and, finally, (3) and (4) have the same reference, since they are logically equivalent. Given the substitution principle and our assumption about logically equivalent sentences having the same reference, therefore, Russell's correspondence theory of meaning implies that the fact that grass is green is identical to a fact about Roman history. And since the argument can be run for any pair of sentences, we can infer that *all true sentences* mean what one might call the Great Fact or, following Frege, the True; and, similarly, *all false sentences* mean the False.

This argument, which Jon Barwise and John Perry have dubbed "the slingshot" for the combination of its compact size and deadly effectiveness, is (as one might easily guess) not uncontroversial.[18] In particular, they point out that a correspondence theorist who identifies the meaning of a sentence with its reference will find the slingshot unpersuasive because she will be dubious of the assumptions on which the argument rests. Indeed, from her perspective both of those assumptions, the substitution principle and the principle that logically equivalent sentences have the same reference, are baldly question-begging, since each supposes that the references of sentences are insensitive to variations in their subject matter, that is, whether the sentence is about Roman history or the colour of grass. And that supposition is *precisely* the point of disagreement between semanticists like Barwise and Perry, on the one hand, who reject the slingshot's conclusion, and Davidson, on the other, who accepts it.

The slingshot, therefore, leaves us with three options. Following Barwise and Perry in their theory of "situation semantics" (Barwise & Perry 1983), one may drop the substitution principle and Frege's assumption that logically equivalent expressions have the same reference. This permits a sentence's reference to vary with its subject matter and thus underwrites a correspondence theory that identifies meaning with reference, but it comes at the price of revising our logical practices.[19] Barwise, the mathematical logician of the pair, argues for such a departure from standard logical practice; as he puts it, "this way of looking at things shifts attention from truth to information", that is, from a sentence's truth-value (which is insensitive to subject matter) to the information a speaker communicates when she utters it (Barwise 1989: xiv). Davidson, on the other hand, rejects the correspondence theory of meaning and holds to standard first-order logic. Like Barwise and Perry, he wants a theory of meaning to capture the content of speakers' words and thoughts, but he believes that standard first-order logic, combined with other semantic tools and embedded within the sort of approach I will examine in Chapters 3–5, is up to that task.

The third option is to tip Blackburn's triangle and to identify the meaning of a sentence not with its reference or extension, but rather with its intension or Fregean *Sinn*.[20] We find an historical antecedent to this approach in Locke's philosophy of language, which identifies the meanings of linguistic expressions with "the *Ideas* in the Mind of him that uses them" (Locke 1975: III, ii §2). Locke's theory is a correspondence theory, since for him meaning is a relation between words and extra-linguistic objects; but for Locke those objects are mental objects. This move secures the sensitivity to an expression's subject matter that Russell's theory surrenders because the idea associated with an expression is finer-grained than its reference; while the terms

> the set of x such that $x = x$, and Antony ordered the death of Cicero

and

> the set of x such that $x = x$, and grass is green

both refer to the same set, when I think of that set *as* the set (partly) determined by Antony's proscribing Cicero and when I think of it *as* the set (partly) determined by the colour of grass, I have different ideas in mind. To take a simpler example, the term

the morning star

and the term

the evening star

both refer to the planet Venus, but the ideas I associate with those different phrases are different. For example, when I say the former I am thinking *the brightest body in the morning sky*, and when I say the latter I am thinking *the brightest body in the evening sky*, and these are different even though the same object satisfies both descriptions. Locke, therefore, by identifying meanings with ideas supposes that "*w* means *m*" (e.g. "the morning star" means the idea *the brightest body in the morning sky*) violates the substitution principle, and hence he treats meaning as an intensional notion.

Locke's idea-theoretic approach to meaning has few contemporary defenders, but contemporary logical grammarians such as Richard Montague, Jaakko Hintikka and David Lewis follow Locke in defending theories that separate meaning or intension (in the form of abstract, usually set-theoretic objects) from extension or reference. One standard move, for example, is to identify the meaning of a sentence with the set of possible worlds in which it is true. On this construal, then, the sentences

The morning star is the planet closest to earth

and

The evening star is the planet closest to earth

will have different meanings, since in some possible worlds the brightest body in the morning sky is the planet Saturn.[21]

Some of these theories are of considerable interest, but Davidson opposes them and conforms as far as possible to an extensionalist line. Part of Davidson's opposition to intensionalist treatments of meaning is a matter of his patrimony: his work is indebted to

Quine, who is the fiercest contemporary critic of introducing intensional notions into philosophy and logic. Davidson is less dogmatic than Quine about the perils that attend introducing intensions, but Quine's influence does run deep and Davidson prefers extensional over intensional concepts and techniques.

I explore the conception of meaning implicit in Davidson's preference in Chapters 3–5, and I draw out its metaphysical implications in Chapter 9, but here I can briefly sketch a basis for that preference. People acquire a language by observing objects and occurrences in their environment, including especially other people's actions; and when they speak, in turn, what they mean by their words generally reflects the causes that prompt them to utter those words. These causes are usually fairly mundane sorts of natural things and events, such as other people, grass, things' flying or sitting, and the like. This picture of meaning is vague, but it suggests that the psychological achievement of understanding a sentence like "Grass is green" rests on the same (or very nearly the same) natural abilities as knowing that grass is green; and it suggests to Davidson that theories of meaning should eschew the esoteric logical concepts that some intensional theories of meaning invoke and the exotic fauna (possible worlds, transworld identity relations, etc.) whose existence they presuppose. And psychology aside, by eschewing intensional concepts and objects, Davidson positions theories of meaning closer to the *epistemology* of linguistic understanding, in the sense of an account of the way that a speaker's actions and other events are evidence for an interpreter's attributing meaning to the speaker's words.

For Davidson, then, a second formal constraint on theories of meaning is the requirement that they avoid intensional concepts in their technical apparatus (Davidson 1984a: 132).[22] We may add to this, too, the desideratum that the logic of the theory avoid (in the manner of Barwise and Perry) revisionist deviations from standard logic.

2.3 Truth and meaning

Let us begin to look in detail at how Davidson's approach to the philosophy of language emerges under these constraints. We begin by reconsidering the schema "*s* means *m*" (from §2.2) in a more instructive version, namely:

(*M*) *s* means that *p*

where *s* is a sentence in the object language and the schematic letter "*p*" is replaced by the sentence that *s* names or its translation into a metalanguage.[23] One instance of schema *M* is:

(5) "Schnee ist weiss" means that snow is white

which we might call an *M*-sentence. The advantage of schema *M* over its predecessor, "*s* means *m*", lies in the difference between *naming* an object *m* that *s* means and using a sentence *p* to *track* that meaning without reifying it. Schema *M* tracks it in the sense that the schema correlates the sentence *s* on its left-hand side with the non-linguistic condition that *p* (e.g. that snow is white) that we mention on the right, but without treating that correlation as denotation. The virtue of this strategy will emerge further in §4.6 and §5.1, but at present we can observe that it avoids collapsing that condition into the same object for all true sentences (if, *pace* Barwise and Perry, we endorse the slingshot) and without calling into play abstruse mathematical objects like possible worlds.

But what is the logic of this correlation? In other words, assuming that this relationship is not a matter of denotation or reference, what is it? Davidson's answer is that we model the relation "*x* means that *p*" using the well-understood relation between a sentence and its truth-condition. Thus Davidson proposes that in place of schema *M* we work with schema *T*:

(*T*) *s* is true_L if and only if *p*.

A few remarks about schema *T* are in order. First, observe that the sentence "*s* is true_L" (read "The sentence *s* is true in the language *L*) to the left of the connective "if and only if" is made up of the predicate "is true_L" applied to a sentence *s* of the object language *L*. The sentence *s* is here *mentioned* using the name "*s*", and either its translation or the sentence *s* itself is *used* on the right-hand side of the schema.[24] The sentence *s* mentioned on the left is itself used on the right if the metalanguage contains the object language, as in:

"Snow is white" is $\text{true}_{\textit{English}}$ if and only if snow is white,

where *s* = "Snow is white", while if the theory is heterophonic, then a translation of s into the metalanguage is used on the right-hand side of the schema, as in:

"Schnee ist weiss" is true_{German} if and only if snow is white,

where the object language is German, the metalanguage is English and s = "Schnee ist weiss", the English translation of which is "Snow is white".

Secondly, the subscript "L" in the predicate "is true_L" stands in for the name of a particular language, for example, English or German, and this name is an undetachable part of the predicate. In other words, L is *not* a variable. There will be a truth predicate for English sentences, another truth predicate for German sentences, another truth predicate for Urdu sentences and so on.

Thus we need to identify the language for which the truth predicate is being defined. The reason for this complication is that, considered as a sequence of sounds or marks, a sentence may have different truth-conditions in different languages. For example, the sequence of sounds,

em·ped·ə·klēz lēpt,

may either be the English sentence that is true if and only if Empedocles leapt, as he is said to have done, to his death into Mount Etna or – since the German "liebt" and the English "leapt" can be identical vocables – it may be the German sentence that is true if and only Empedocles loves (Davidson 1984a: 98). In selecting one of these truth conditions for the utterance, we determine to which language the sentence belongs; conversely, depending upon the speaker's language, the sentence has either one or the other truth-condition (Davidson 1990e: 295).

Finally, the connective "if and only if" is the familiar biconditional from propositional logic, and therefore schema T is extensional. Thus, if s is true_L if and only if p, and p if and only if q, then s is true_L if and only if q. This marks an advantage of schema T over schema M, since the latter (but not the former) generates an intensional context.

We have thus arrived at Davidson's thesis that, subject to a number of qualifications, a compositional theory of truth can go proxy for a theory of meaning. A *compositional theory of truth* θ_L for a language L comprises a finite list of axioms that specify the reference of each primitive expression of L, plus rules that determine the truth-condition of each sentence of L based on the reference of its parts and its semantic structure. That is, for each sentence s of L, θ_L entails an instance of schema T, called a "T-sentence" or "T-theorem", that states the circumstances that obtain just in case s is true, and in this way θ_L states what is required for the predicate "is true$_L$" to apply to each sentence s of L. In this sense, θ_L defines the concept of truth for that language.[25]

Thus Davidson's idea is that we can use a definition of truth as a theory of meaning (subject, again, to several qualifications), and he quotes Quine in support: "in point of meaning ... a word may be said to be determined to whatever extent the truth or falsehood of its contexts is determined" (Quine 1976a: 82, quoted in Davidson 1984a: 24). Davidson readily concedes that his idea has a long history in the analytic tradition, for example, in Frege and the early Wittgenstein. To see its attraction for Davidson, observe that instances of schema M are *interpretive* in this sense: that anyone who knows them knows what an utterance of s says about the world. If someone knows that "Ein Schwan ist weiss" means that swans are white, then she knows that a speaker says that swans are white when he utters the sentence "Ein Schwan ist weiss." Like M-sentences, T-sentences assign to every sentence s of L an interpretation in the metalanguage, and thereby they directly relate each s to the circumstances that make it true. Davidson's claim, then, is that (subject to qualifications we discuss in Chapter 5) T-sentences are also interpretive: anyone who knows the theorems of a truth theory for a language L knows what the sentences of L say, and with this information she can understand L-speakers and their utterances.

Chapter 3

Meaning and truth II

In Chapter 2 we saw that, under pressure from several constraints, a compositional theory of truth emerges as the leading candidate for supplying the outline for a theory of meaning. We continue our discussion of truth and meaning in this chapter, focusing on Alfred Tarski's groundbreaking work on semantics as the model for compositional truth theories[1] and on Davidson's discussion of the applicability of Tarski's work to natural languages.

3.1 Tarski's theory of truth

As a mathematician and logician, Tarski's focus is somewhat specialized, at least considered from our current vantage point in the philosophy of language. He is especially interested in the semantic paradoxes (e.g. the liar paradox: "This sentence is false") and also in the relation between the set of sentences of a specified formal language that *are true* and the set of sentences belonging to the language that *can be proved*. (Intuitively, these two classes should bear some close relation to one another.) Tarski's results are of considerable importance to mathematical logicians; one of those results is that while we can define the metalogical concept of *being provable in L* (i.e. *being* $provable_L$) in the language L itself, we cannot, on pain of contradiction, define in L the concept of *being* $true_L$. Hence the concepts of *being* $provable_L$ and *being* $true_L$, although closely allied in some way, are not equivalent.

In the course of his work, Tarski applies mathematical logical methods to the concept of truth, and he shows how to construct a compositional truth theory for a formal language. *Formal languages* are characterized by our being able to describe their structures exactly and exhaustively in purely syntactic terms; we cannot give the same treatment to natural languages because of their ambiguity and imprecision. This feature of natural languages, however, which hinders our efforts to describe and analyse them formally, also accounts for their expressive power. Another difficulty that natural languages present to formal analysis is that many common grammatical constructions, like statements of indirect discourse ("Galileo said that the earth is flat") or attributive adjectives and adverbs ("Mickey is a large rat"), are quite complicated from a logical point of view, despite their being effortlessly employed and understood by native speakers. Consider, for example, that while we cannot infer that Mickey is large from "Mickey is a large rat", or that Dumbo is small from "Dumbo is a small elephant" – a large rat, in the scheme of things, is something small, while a small elephant is something large – we can infer that Jesse is black from "Jesse is a black dog." Prima facie this last sentence has the same grammatical form as the first two, but the possibility of drawing an inference from it, while parallel inferences from the others are invalid, means there must be an underlying logical difference in their semantic interpretations.

Tarski's treatment of theories of truth for formal languages falls into two parts. He first lays out two conditions that a theory of truth ought to satisfy, and then he shows how to construct a theory that meets these conditions. The first adequacy condition requires that the theory is *formally correct*, in the sense that it avoids inconsistency and other technical problems. We shall have something to say about this in §3.2, where we look at Davidson's extension of Tarski's methods. The second adequacy condition requires that the theory is *materially adequate* and is familiar from our discussion so far. Recall from Chapter 2 the constraint that a theory of meaning for a language L should entail an interpretation of each sentence s of L, based on the semantic structure of s and the interpretation of its parts; Convention T, which is Tarski's term for the condition of material adequacy, parallels this demand by stipulating that a theory of truth is acceptable only if it entails instances of schema T,

(T) s is true_L if and only if p,

for every sentence *s* of *L*, where "*p*" is the sentence that *s* names or its translation into the metalanguage.[2]

Having developed a standard against which to measure the adequacy of theories of truth, Tarski goes on to construct a theory that meets his criteria. His construction begins with a description (or what amounts to a definition) of a formal language that lays out the language's syntax and its semantics. The specification of its syntax lists each primitive expression of the language, including the language's basic logical vocabulary (the connectives of sentential logic such as negation, conjunction, etc.; the quantifier symbols; variables, and auxiliary symbols such as parentheses) and its basic *non*-logical vocabulary (singular terms and expressions for properties and relations), if it has any. Having exactly identified the simplest expressions of the language, the description continues with a complete and precise recursive definition of its sentences; given the set of simple sentences as a basis, it characterizes the class of all sentences of the language as those expressions that can be generated according to specified modes of composition from that basis.

Tarski's object language is the language of elementary set theory, but to illustrate his procedure let us instead focus on the language *G* that consists of the sentential connectives "~" and "&", the existential quantifier "∃", individual variables drawn from the list $x_1, x_2, x_3, \ldots$, a one-place predicate "ist ein englisch Monarch", a two-place predicate "starb auf" and the left and right parentheses "(" and ")" as auxiliary symbols.[3] Next, we recursively define the sentences of *G*. The simple or *atomic sentences* of *G* are any expression constructed in accordance with the following rule:

> A one-place predicate preceded by one variable, or a two-place predicate preceded by one variable and followed by one variable, is an atomic sentence.

Thus the atomic sentences of *G* are all of the form "x_i ist ein englisch Monarch" or "x_i starb auf x_j", for $i, j = 1, 2, 3, \ldots$. A *sentence* of *G*, then, is any expression constructed in accordance with the following rules.

(a) Atomic sentences of *G* are sentences.
(b) If *A* is a sentence of *G*, then ~*A* is a sentence of *G*.
(c) If *A* and *B* are sentences of *G*, then (*A* & *B*) is a sentence of *G*.

(d) If A is a sentence of G, then $\exists x_i\,(A)$ is a sentence of G.
(e) Nothing else is a sentence of G.

Finally, we introduce the notion of a closed sentence. First, we define the *scope of a quantifier* as the shortest complete sentence to the right of the quantifier. For example, the scope of "$\exists x_1$" in

> $\exists x_1$(x_1 ist ein englisch Monarch) & $\exists x_2$(x_2 ist ein englisch Monarch & x_1 starb auf x_2)

is the expression "(x_1 ist ein englisch Monarch)", and the scope of "$\exists x_2$" is "(x_2 ist ein englisch Monarch & x_1 starb auf x_2)". Notice that while both "x_1" and "x_2" fall within the scope of "$\exists x_2$" – that is, both occur in the smallest complete sentence to the right of the quantifier – the quantifier binds only "x_2". In general, the occurrence of a variable is *bound* if and only if it falls within the scope of a quantifier formed from that variable (as "$\exists x_2$" is formed from "x_2"); if the occurrence of a variable is not bound, then it is said to be *free*. Thus "x_1" is free in "$\exists x_2$(x_2 ist ein englisch Monarch & x_1 starb auf x_2)", for although "x_1" falls within the scope of "$\exists x_2$", the quantifier is not formed from "x_1". Finally, a sentence that contains no free variables is called a *closed sentence*, and a sentence with at least one free variable is an *open sentence*. Thus "$\exists x_1$(x_1 ist ein englisch Monarch)" is a closed sentence, but "$\exists x_2$(x_2 ist ein englisch Monarch & x_1 starb auf x_2)" is open.

With these syntactic preliminaries in place, we describe the concept of satisfaction in terms of which we then define "being true". The reason we begin with satisfaction instead of truth – or, rather, satisfaction$_G$ instead of truth, since we are talking specifically about the satisfaction and truth predicates that apply to sentences of the language G – is that our definition of "being a true sentence of G (i.e. being true) will piggyback on our recursive definition of "being a sentence of G", and that definition has the atomic sentences of G as its basis; however, atomic sentences are all open, and open sentences are neither true nor false – only closed ones are. Hence the need for a detour through the concept of satisfaction$_G$, which does apply to open sentences.

Here is the idea. A sentence with a dangling pronoun (e.g. the English sentence "He is a king of England", where the antecedent or deictic reference of "he" is unspecified) is incomplete in the sense that, not knowing who *he* is, we cannot judge the sentence to be true or false. Indeed, the concepts of being true and false do not apply to it. We *can* say that the sentence "He is a king of England" is true *of* something, namely, Charles I; or that the sentence "He died on it" is true *of* the ordered pair of things <Charles I, the scaffold>; or that the sentence "She succeeded him and preceded (a different) him as English monarch" is true *of* the ordered triple things <Anne, William III, George I>. The notion of being true *of* something is just what Tarski means by *satisfaction*; in place of saying that "He died on it" is true of <Charles I, the scaffold>, we say that the ordered pair satisfies the open sentences "x_1 died on x_2" and "x_1 starb auf x_2".

In general, an n-member sequence of objects $<o_1, o_2, \ldots, o_n>$ satisfies an m-place open sentence $A(x_1, x_2, \ldots, x_m)$, for $m \leq n$, if and only if $A(o_1, o_2, \ldots, o_m)$, that is, if and only if the open sentence $A(x_1, x_2, \ldots, x_m)$ is true of the first m members of $<o_1, o_2, \ldots, o_n>$. If $n > m$, in other words, if there are leftover o_is in the sequence, then we just ignore these extra objects as irrelevant to deciding whether the sequence satisfies the open sentence; only the o_is that correspond to free variables in $A(x_1, x_2, \ldots, x_m)$ matter.

To describe the semantics of *G*, we define the satisfaction$_G$ conditions for the atomic sentences of *G* explicitly and then define satisfaction$_G$ for the rest of the sentences of *G* recursively.

(i) A sequence $<o_1, o_2, \ldots, o_n>$ satisfies$_G$ "x_j ist ein englisch Monarch" just in case o_1 is an English monarch.

(Remember that the rest of the o_is do not matter, since there is only one free variable in the open sentence.)

(ii) A sequence $<o_1, o_2, \ldots, o_n>$ satisfies$_G$ "x_i starb auf x_j" just in case o_1 died on o_2.

(Again, the rest of the elements of the sequence do not matter.)

(iii) A sequence $<o_1, o_2, \ldots, o_n>$ satisfies$_G$ $\sim A$ just in case it does not satisfy$_G$ A.

In other words, $\sim A$ is the negation of A.

(iv) A sequence $<o_1, o_2, \ldots, o_n>$ satisfies$_G$ $(A \,\&\, B)$ just in case $<o_1, o_2, \ldots, o_n>$ satisfies$_G$ A and $<o_1, o_2, \ldots, o_n>$ satisfies$_G$ B.

And, finally,

(v) A sequence $<o_1, o_2, \ldots, o_n>$ satisfies$_G$ $\exists x_i\,(A)$ just in case a sequence $<o_1', o_2', \ldots, o_n'>$, which differs from $<o_1, o_2, \ldots, o_n>$ in at most the ith position, satisfies$_G$ the result of dropping the quantifier from the original open sentence.

This last clause calls for some comment. We want to say that the sentence

(1) $\exists x_2(x_1$ died on $x_2)$

is true of any sequence of objects that starts with Charles I – for example, the sequence <Charles I, the *Titanic*> – since what (1) says is that there is something such that Charles I died on it. Of course, the "something" is not the *Titanic*, but that does not matter because "x_2" is not free in "$\exists x_2(x_1$ died on $x_2)$". Again, (1) says that there is something such that Charles I died on it, and this is true since the something on which Charles I died does exist, even though, again, that "something" is not the *Titanic*. We secure this by clause (v), which requires that there is a sequence (namely, <Charles I, the scaffold>), the second member of which *is* the thing upon which Charles I died. Thus <Charles I, the *Titanic*> satisfies "$\exists x_2(x_1$ died on $x_2)$" since there is a sequence <Charles I, the scaffold> that differs from <Charles I, the *Titanic*> in only the second position, and <Charles I, the scaffold> satisfies "(x_1 died on x_2)".

To complete the description of the semantics of *G*, we emphasize once again that the objects in a sequence corresponding to "missing" variables in an open sentence have no effect on whether the sequence satisfies the sentence. Thus <Charles I, the scaffold, the Eiffel Tower> satisfies$_G$ "x_1 starb auf x_2" because the open sentence contains only two free variables, and the first two objects in the sequence <Charles I, the scaffold, the Eiffel Tower> satisfy$_G$ it; in general, then, it is satisfied by *any* sequence <Charles I, the scaffold, …> as long as the first member of the sequence died on the second. Similarly, every sequence <Anne, …> satisfies$_G$ "x_3 ist ein englisch Monarch" since the sentence contains only one free variable, and hence nothing that follows Queen Anne in the sequence makes any difference to satisfying the open sentence. What about the *closed* sentence "$(\exists x_1)x_1$ ist ein englisch Monarch"?

What sequences satisfy a sentence with no free variables? Following the pattern of the previous cases, we should say that it is satisfied by *every* sequence regardless of its composition, since no members of the sequence make any difference to satisfying the sentence. It is satisfied by any and every sequence, or by none:

(2) A sequence $<o_1, o_2, \ldots, o_n>$ satisfies$_G$ "$(\exists x_1)\ x_1$ ist ein englisch Monarch" if and only if any sequence satisfies$_G$ "x_1 ist ein englisch Monarch",

that is, if and only if *something* is an English monarch. This, then, is the definition that Tarski adopts for being true$_G$: a closed sentence is true if it is satisfied by *all* sequences, and it is false if it is satisfied by *none*. Replacing talk in (2) of *satisfying* the sentence "$(\exists x_1)\ x_1$ ist ein englisch Monarch" with reference to its being *true*, we obtain:

(3) "$(\exists x_1)\ x_1$ ist ein englisch Monarch" is true$_G$ if and only if something is an English monarch.

This completes the description of the semantics of *G* and, as (3) illustrates, the theory satisfies Convention *T*.

3.2 Tarski-style theories of truth and natural language

In using Tarski's formal methods to study natural languages, Davidson departs from Tarski in two important respects. First, Davidson takes Tarski's apparatus for defining *truth* and uses it to elucidate the concept of *meaning*. Davidson writes that it

> only gradually dawned on me that while Tarski intended to analyse the concept of truth by appealing (in Convention T) to the concept of meaning (in the guise of sameness of meaning, or translation), I have the reverse in mind. I considered truth to be the central primitive concept, and hoped, by detailing truth's structure, to get at meaning.
>
> (Davidson 1984a: xiv)

We return to this point in §5.4.

Secondly, in looking to lay bare the semantic structure of *natural*, as opposed to *formal*, languages Davidson undertakes a project that Tarski had considered and rejected as presenting the semanticist with "insuperable difficulties" (Tarski 1983: 164). These difficulties are two-fold: natural languages are indefinitely plastic and never quite finished, and hence they cannot be exactly and exhaustively described (for example new words are forever being coined); and even if we were to take a "snapshot" of a living natural language at a given time, many common linguistic forms resist assimilation to the methods available to the extensional logician.

A different sort of problem that natural languages present is that their very richness can lead to paradox. Consider, for example, that the descriptive vocabulary of English (or Polish, Urdu, etc.) is rich enough for us to compose *one* English sentence that describes the properties of *another* English sentence; thus we can say in English that the English sentence "Theaetetus flies" contains fifteen letters. We can even construct a sentence that is *self-referential* in the sense that it describes itself, such as the sentence "This sentence contains thirty-eight letters." This is a problem, because it means that we can say something like:

(4) "This sentence is true" is false

or more simply

(4′) This sentence is false.

Sentences (4) and (4′) formulate the liar paradox: if (4) is true then it is false, and if it is false then it is true. No consistent theory of truth can be formulated for a language that permits construction of (4), which is to say that no consistent theory of truth can be formulated for a natural language.

Davidson's response, if not quite to dismiss these two problems with natural languages, is at least to suggest that they are not insuperable. His discussion of Tarski's second worry is the least satisfactory. He concedes that it "deserves a serious answer", and he adds, "I wish I had one" (Davidson 1984a: 28–9). After making several unhelpful observations he proposes in the end that we separate those features or parts of natural language that permit construction of the liar paradox, and write our truth definition for what remains. It is far from evident that this tactic will work, however, or whether (as Davidson avers) "most of the problems of general philosophical interest arise within" the rump of a natural language that remains after we set aside what amounts to the elementary set-theoretic apparatus needed for constructing self-referential statements (*ibid*.: 29).[4]

Davidson's treatment of Tarski's first worry is more interesting. As we shall see in §5.3, Davidson believes that an interpreter is always, in effect, working with a snapshot of a speaker's language. Or, rather, that what we ordinarily describe as a particular natural language, such as Chinese or Cherokee, is like a smooth curve drawn through the many idiolects different speakers speak in different contexts and at different times.[5] What there really is are these many idiolects; and what we call *the* natural language that every Cherokee speaker shares is a grouping together of idiolects that bear more similarity (by some standard) to one another than to another idiolect we place in a different group (collected together by a parallel standard). An interpreter's work, on this view, is always directed at the totality of an agent's verbal behaviour and dispositions during some bounded period of time.

Granting this point, there remains the difficulty of the multiformity of colloquial linguistic structures. On this point, Davidson is optimistic.

> It is certainly reasonable to wonder to what extent it will ever be possible to treat a natural language as a formal system ... Still, a degree of optimism is justified. Until Frege, serious semantics was largely limited to predication and the truth-functional compounding of sentences. By abstracting quantificational structure from what had seemed a jungle of pronouns, quantifiers, connectives, and articles, Frege showed how an astonishingly powerful fragment of natural language could be semantically tamed. Indeed, it may still turn out that this fragment will prove, with ingenuity, to be the whole. Meanwhile, promising work goes on in many directions.
>
> (Davidson 1984: 51)

Frege's achievement was to invent formal methods that exposed the semantic patterns that lay hidden beneath the pronouns, quantifiers (e.g. "every", "some", "none") and connectives ("if ... then", "or" and so on) of colloquial discourse. Quantificational and truth-functional structure is only the beginning, though, and the semanticist of natural language also confronts demonstrative terms ("this", "that") and tenses ("was"), adjectives and adverbial modifiers ("Mickey is a *large* rat"), empty singular terms ("Santa Claus") and so on; and he has to find a way to model, with his theoretical apparatus, reported speech ("Galileo said that the earth moves"), contrary-to-fact conditionals ("If Al Gore were president, there would be a Tennessean in the White House"), modality ("It is possible that there is intelligent life on other planets") and so on. If he is successful, he will describe for each of these constructions its semantic structure or logical form,[6] which we all (usually) recognize intuitively, but which may be obscured under the unsystematic thicket of linguistic devices that speakers have at their disposal. In the remainder of this section and the next, I examine Davidson's proposals for treating demonstratives and reported speech, and later, in §6.1, I discuss his work on adverbial modification. In §5.2 I examine metaphorical speech, which presents students of natural language with a somewhat different set of problems.

It is easy to see why demonstratives are absent from the formal languages traditionally studied by mathematicians and logicians. The sentence "$\sim\exists y \forall x(x \in y)$" of Zermelo–Frankel set theory is true just in case there is no universal set in the domain of pure sets, and it remains true regardless of the circumstances of its utterance. Contrast this with the natural language sentence,

(5) That is white,

uttered on two separate occasions: once at time t_1 when the speaker points to a patch of snow, and again at t_2 when she indicates a plot of grass. On these two occasions (5) has separate truth-conditions: in the first instance it is true if and only if snow is white, and in the second it is true if and only if grass is white. To apply Tarski's methods, therefore, we have to recognize that truth and meaning are properly properties of the situated production of a sentence-token by a speaker at a certain time, that is, they are properties of an *utterance*, not a *sentence*, which (considered as a type) is the same in the two utterances of (5).

To represent its semantic properties, we define *an utterance* to be an ordered triple consisting of a sentence-token, a time and a speaker. Truth and meaning are thus properties of such a triple, and when we construct a Tarski-style theory of truth for a language L we want it to imply T-theorems such as

> "That is white" is true_L when spoken by x at t if and only if the object indicated by x at t is white.

This T-theorem captures two distinct demonstrative elements. First, the object-language pronoun "that" refers to the object the speaker indicates when she makes her utterance; we model its contribution to the utterance's truth-condition by explicitly referring on the right side of the T-theorem to that object. Second, the object-language verb "is" is conjugated in the present indicative tense and refers to the time the speaker performs her utterance. We represent this indexical feature by repeating the time variable "t" on both sides of the T-theorem. Most sentences, even if they lack a demonstrative pronoun or adverb ("that", "this", "here", "now", "today", "tomorrow", "yesterday"), or indexical word ("I", "you", "she", "he", "it"), contain a demonstrative element in the tense of the sentence's main verb.[7]

3.3 The logical form of indirect discourse

Let us turn, then, to indirect or reported speech. Given the sentence

(6) The earth moves,

and the fact that D.D. was born on the earth in 1917, we can make the substitution

(6′) The planet on which D.D. was born in 1917 moves,

and the substitution principle guarantees that (6′) is true if and only if (6) is. This works, too, if we embed (6) in complex sentences such as:

(7) Galileo is Italian and the earth moves,

or

(8) It is false that the earth moves.

We can make the substitutions

(7′) Galileo is Italian and the planet on which D.D. was born in 1917 moves,

and

(8′) It is false that the planet on which D.D. was born in 1917 moves,

and the sentences match up as materially equivalent pairs. But the logical form of these embeddings differs from the form of:

(9) Galileo believed that the earth moves,

since we cannot make the substitution:

(9′) Galileo believed that the planet on which D.D. was born in 1917 moves.

For while he believed that the earth moves, it is surely false that Galileo (who died in 1642) believed that the planet on which D.D. was born almost 300 years later moves. This anomalous behaviour infects a wide class of sentences, the problem being localized in a set of transitive verbs ("believes", "desires", "says") that typically take as their subjects a term that refers to a person and as their objects a subordinate noun clause that describes the content of that person's belief, desire, statement and so on ("that the earth moves").

The philosophy of language is thick with proposals for treating this anomaly, and indeed Frege's discussion of the problem in his article "On Sense and Meaning" (1980) is a founding document of the modern period in the field. Frege famously proposed that the words occurring in the content clause of (9) (i.e. "the earth moves") refer not to their usual *Bedeutungen*, but to what is customarily their *Sinne*. This solves the problem, for although "the earth" and "the planet on which D.D. was born in 1917" have the same reference, they differ in their intensions, and thus we cannot use the substitution principle to infer "Galileo believed that the planet on which D.D. was born in 1917" from (9).[8] Frege thus saves the substitution principle, but at the price of tolerating a different anomaly, namely, that one and the same expression has different semantic properties in different contexts (i.e. the term "the earth" sometimes refers to the planet earth, and sometimes it refers to the sense a speaker associates with it). And this violates the spirit of the Fregean principle that underlies the compositionality constraint of §2.1, that natural languages are amenable to *systematic* semantic analysis. "Language is the instrument it is", Davidson writes, "because the same expression with ... semantic features unchanged, can serve countless purposes" (Davidson 1984a: 108). Otherwise, no matter how many uses of an expression someone masters, there will be others she may not understand; in Frege's treatment of the propositional attitudes, in particular, it may be necessary to posit an endless hierarchy of senses to serve as the references of the nested content sentences in, for example, "Einstein believed that Newton believed that Galileo believed the earth moves."

Davidson offers a counter-proposal that meets both the compositionality and extensionality constraints, and also avoids the anomalousness that vitiates Frege's theory. It comes, though, at the price of some grammatical novelty. Focusing on statements of indirect discourse, such as:

(10) Galileo said that the earth moves,

Davidson proposes that the word "that" occurs in (10) as a *demonstrative* pronoun and not, as our grammar books tell us, as a *relative* pronoun; and thus that the direct object of "said" is this demonstrative, and not the subordinate noun clause "that the earth moves". In fact, under analysis this noun clause disappears and becomes two separate expressions: the demonstrative "that", which completes the open sentence "Galileo said x", and the *grammatically independent sentence* "The earth moves." This new sentence is the demonstrative's referent; or, rather, its referent is my *utterance* of my sentence, "The earth moves", which follows my utterance of the sentence "Galileo said that." Thus Davidson proposes that, from a logical point of view, (10) is composed of *two separate utterances*:

(11) Galileo said that. The earth moves.

In other words, the *grammatical* connection between "the earth moves" and "Galileo said that" is severed and replaced by the same *deictic* relation that connects snow and my pointing to snow and saying "That is white".

More properly, (11) should be:

(11′) Galileo said something that meant the same as my next utterance. The earth moves.

This qualification is needed, since the utterance to which "that" refers in (11) is *my* utterance of a sentence in *my* language, which I use to report the content of an utterance Galileo made in *his* language. As Davidson sometimes puts it, Galileo and I are *samesayers*; what he and I mean, when he performs his utterance and I perform mine, is the same. Thus (10) is "really":

(10′) Galileo samesaid that the earth moves.

Finally, then, a careful semantic analysis of (10) should look something like this:

(12) There exists some utterance x performed by Galileo, and x has the same meaning in Galileo's idiolect as my next utterance has in mine. The earth moves.

Thus when we construct a Tarski-style theory of truth for English, we want it to imply T-theorems such as

(13) "Galileo said that the earth moves" is $\text{true}_{English}$ when spoken by a at t if and only if there exists some utterance x performed by Galileo at time t', where t' is earlier than t, and x has the same meaning in Galileo's idiolect as an utterance of "the earth moves" has in a's idiolect.

This proposal, sometimes referred to as Davidson's *paratactic theory*, calls for several remarks.

It is easy to be misled by the role that samesaying plays in Davidson's account, and to suspect that he (not very discretely) sneaks in an intensional notion. After all, samesaying relates different speakers who have uttered synonymous sentences, and Quine was supposed to have banished synonymy from semantics in "Two Dogmas of Empiricism" (Quine 1961). However, this objection rests on a confusion of the limitations of semantic analysis. To see this confusion, recall from §3.1 that in our semantical analysis of the language *G* we interpreted the predicates "ist ein englisch Monarch" and "starb auf" using the concepts of "being an English monarch" and "dying on", without defining those concepts. In effect, we assumed familiarity with those concepts *before* we undertook to interpret *G*, and in this sense those concepts do not belong to the logical apparatus of the semantical theory. Rather, it *presupposes* them. Or, to take a different example, if

(14) Das ist ein Walross,

is a well-formed German sentence, then a semantical theory for German is materially adequate only if it entails a *T*-sentence like:

(15) "Das ist ein Walross" is true_{German} if and only if that is a walrus.

However, we do not expect our theory of meaning to define or explain what walruses are, beyond specifying that all and only walruses satisfy the open German sentence "*x* ist ein Walross". In this sense, the concept of being a walrus does not belong to the apparatus of the semantical theory proper, it is presupposed by it.

Just as we take for granted the concept of being a walrus when we interpret (14) by (15), so, too, we presuppose the concept of two speakers *v* and *x* being samesayers (with respect to their utterances *u* and *w*) when we interpret "Galileo said that the earth moves" by (13). Hence the idea that *v* and *x* are samesayers (with respect to *u* and *w*) when

(16) *u* has the same meaning in *v*'s idiolect as an utterance of *w* has in *x*'s idiolect,

is not a technical or theoretical concept of semantics in the way that, for example, the notions of satisfaction_L, truth_L, and an *n*-membered sequence of objects are. Certainly, when someone invokes samesaying to interpret my statement that Galileo said that the earth moves, she exposes internal structure that had been merely implicit in my utterance. In particular, she locates in my statement argument places for not only the original speaker (Galileo) and the reported utterance *w* ("the earth moves") but also the original speaker's original utterance (Galileo's "Eppur si muove") and the current speaker of the reported utterance (me). But that internal structure is already present in my utterance before she undertakes to interpret me and is not an artifact of her interpretative enterprise, as, for example, the notion of $\text{satisfaction}_{English}$ is. The concept of samesaying belongs to the common-sense background my interpreter and I share; it is not part of a specialized toolkit she carries with her as a semanticist.

The paratactic theory gains support from several quarters. First, it neatly piggybacks on the etymology of English and other Germanic languages: the "that" of indirect discourse did apparently develop from its demonstrative use, and similar stories can be told for Scandinavian languages and classical Greek, although not for Romance languages. In support, Davidson cites the *Oxford English Dictionary* (Davidson 1984a: 106).[9] More importantly, Davidson's proposal captures the logical form of indirect discourse in extensional terms, locating the intensionality of the locution in the vocabulary (i.e. the semantic primitives) of the object language where, on Davidson's construal, it belongs.

Like every attempt to describe the semantic structure of indirect discourse, however, Davidson's theory has attracted objections.[10] Consider, for example, that if (11) differs from (10) just in being a bit more logically perspicuous, then the semantic properties that characterize (10) should carry over into (11). But consider

(17) Every boy believes that he is a nice fellow.

This sentence permits two different semantic interpretations: that every boy believes *of one particular boy* that that boy is a nice fellow, and that every boy believes that *he himself* is a nice fellow. But when we gloss (10) along the lines suggested by (11), that is,

(18) Every boy believes that. He is a nice boy,

it seems clear that this can be interpreted only in the first way. This objection, which is James Higgenbotham's,[11] weighs against seeing the pronoun "that" as a demonstrative. In response, Davidson could make a partial strategic retreat and concede that in paraphrasing (10) as (11) he is already regimenting the sentence in preparation for its semi-formalization as (12); and in regimenting natural language some of the semantical structure is always lost. How serious this loss is, and whether the objection is fatal, depends on how central the phenomenon of ambiguity is to natural language or whether Davidson can find other resources to reintroduce into the sentence(s) the lost structure.

A second question, which goes to the heart of Davidson's unified approach to language and mind, is whether the paratactic theory can be extended to the other propositional attitudes, such as belief and desire. For while we can infer:

There exists an utterance u such that Galileo performed u,

from "Galileo said that the earth moves", we cannot infer:

(19) There exists an x such that Galileo believed x,

from "Galileo believed that the earth moves." This disanalogy arises because, while Davidson treats samesaying as a two-place relation between a speaker and an actual utterance (indicated by a deictic "that"), he has argued elsewhere that belief is a *state* of a believer, not a relation between a thinker and an object.[12] More generally, Galileo had many beliefs he never verbalized – so there are no corresponding utterances to satisfy (19) – or even consciously entertained, so there are no thoughts (in the sense of conscious mental episodes or events) that satisfy it. For example, Galileo believed that the earth was larger than his fist, but we may assume that he never *consciously* thought it. Davidson's response to this criticism is to suggest that *were* Galileo to speak his mind on the matter, he *would* utter a sentence that means the same as the utterance I perform following my assertion "Galileo believes that". This, though, involves us in "some delicate assumptions about the conditions under which such a subjunctive conditional [were, would, etc.] is true" (Davidson 1984a: 167), and it presupposes an extensional analysis of such locutions. At present, though, Davidson has none to offer, and nor are the prospects especially bright.

3.4 The structure and meaning of truth

Before we examine, in Chapter 4, Davidson's further appropriation of Tarski's methods, it is worthwhile to pause in order to ask exactly what Tarski accomplishes in his work. Mathematically, the results of that work are plain to see; our question regards their *philosophical* import.

Six years before Tarski published his original article,[13] Frank Ramsey set out the germ of what has become known as the *redundancy theory of truth*. It is evident, Ramsey observes, that

It is true that Caesar was murdered

means the same as

Caesar was murdered;

and similarly

It is false he was murdered

means the same as

He was not murdered.[14]

In general, asserting that a sentence *s* is true is equivalent to asserting *s*, and asserting that *s* is false is equivalent to asserting the negation of *s*. On the basis of these and similar examples, the redundancy theory concludes that whatever we can say with a truth predicate we can express more economically without it, and thus the predicates "is true" and "is false" are empty, in the sense that they do not represent any genuine properties of utterances or sentences.

One estimation of Tarski's work is that it validates the redundancy theory. On this reading, Tarski's achievement is to show in formal detail how the truth predicate is (as Quine puts it) a "device of disquotation", that is,

(27) "Snow is white" is $\text{true}_{English}$

means the same as the quoted sentence, without the quotation marks:

(28) Snow is white.

Sentences (27) and (28) are familiar as instances of the left- and right-hand sides of schema *T*, and thus efforts to link Tarski to the redundancy theory centre on the *T*-sentences; if all there is to truth is exhibited by the *T*-sentences, then the prima facie triviality of

"Snow is white" is $\text{true}_{English}$ if and only if snow is white

runs as deep as truth itself. In requiring that a theory of truth for a language *L* entail a *T*-sentence for each sentence of *L*, and in showing how to meet this requirement, Tarski completely captures the content of the concept of truth.

This cannot be right, however. Intuitively, Tarski demonstrates how to sort the sentences of a given language into two classes, one that includes all and only the true sentences, and another that contains all and only the false ones, but describing his achievement this way (i.e. as sorting the sentences into the class of *true* ones and the class of *false* ones) *relies* upon rather than defines the intuitive notion of truth. The reason for this is that while he defines the predicates "is $\text{true}_{English}$", "is true_{Urdu}", "is $\text{true}_{Chinese}$" and so on, and these lay bare the compositional structures of English, Urdu, Chinese and so on in the sense of showing how certain properties of a sentence depend on its internal structure and certain properties of its parts, without our intuitive notion of truth there is no basis for identifying those structures as the *semantic* structures of English, Urdu, Chinese and so on or calling those predicates *truth* predicates. This may be somewhat hard to see since "is $\text{true}_{English}$" is obviously the truth predicate for English, but that is precisely the point; it is *obvious* that a Tarski-style construction defines a truth predicate because we know what truth looks like, and we bring this knowledge to bear when we work through Tarski's construction. The point is analogous to Socrates' complaint when Meno begins to list examples of virtue instead of saying what virtue itself consists in: "even if they are many and various, yet at least they all have some common character which makes them virtues" (*Meno* 72c6–8). Meno has trouble seeing what Socrates is up to, and this, again, is because he already knows (or recollects, as Plato would say) what every virtuous act shares; Socrates, however, wants him to articulate just *this* information, which lays stored up in Meno's soul.

Like Meno, Tarski does not identify the "common character" that is shared by the relativized truth predicates[15] for English, Urdu, Chinese and so on, but, unlike Plato, Davidson denies that

that character is amenable to Socratic definition. In this respect Davidson sympathizes with defenders of the deflationary theory of truth,[16] who reject efforts to define truth in more fundamental terms, such as correspondence or coherence. Correspondence theorists look for a metaphysically satisfying explanation of truth in terms of the correspondence between statements and some sort of extra-linguistic entity, like a situation or fact; while coherence theorists propose that a statement's being true consists in its coherence or consistency with a body of other beliefs. Each of these efforts has its idiosyncratic faults,[17] but they share the common flaw of trying to define an explanatorily fundamental concept in more basic terms. As Davidson puts it, truth belongs to the class of "the most elementary concepts we have, concepts without which ... we would have no concepts at all" (1996: 264). We should not expect that truth be definable in the way that Socrates and Plato had expected to define virtue.

The deflationist, however, faces a dilemma. On the one hand, he agrees with the redundancy theorist in emphasizing the role that *T*-sentences have in saying what there is to be said about truth. (A difference is that deflationists have a more sophisticated treatment of generalizations, such as "Everything he said is true.") On the other hand, unlike the redundancy theorist, he believes that there *is* something to be said about truth. (The redundancy theorist thinks that the *T*-sentences say all there is there to say, which is nothing.) But the *T*-sentences, as we have observed, capture at most the concept of truth relativized to a language, and not truth *simpliciter*. Paul Horwich negotiates the deflationist's dilemma by proposing that the relativized truth predicates, which apply to utterances or sentences, reflect an *un*relativized concept that applies to *propositions*, taken as abstract objects expressed by a speaker's utterances. Thus Horwich proposes that standing behind schema *T* is something of the form:

(*P*) <*p*>is true if and only if *p*,

where enclosing a sentence within angled brackets ("<", ">") produces an expression that refers to the proposition corresponding to that sentence (Horwich 1990: 19n.3). The truth predicate in schema *P*, then, expresses the unrelativized, intuitive concept of truth, which we model when we use Tarski's schema *T* to define the truth predicate of some particular language.

Although Davidson avoids them, propositions are a common device to which philosophers of language resort. Depending on what story one tells about properties, however, it is not clear that they can help here. For aside from nominalistic worries, it is necessary to characterize *which* abstract objects propositions are, and one answer (deriving from Frege's characterization of thoughts, or the *Sinne* of sentences) is that a proposition is that for which the question of truth arises (Frege 1967: 20). But if we identify propositions as those objects that are either true or false, then we cannot, without circularity, take schema *P* to define the concept of truth, since it presupposes the notion of a proposition and the notion of a proposition, we have just said, is defined in terms of the concept of truth. There are other ways to characterize propositions, however, and some of these (such as defining propositions as sets of possible worlds) may avoid this circularity.

Davidson looks in another direction for the content of the concept of truth, and he finds it a rather more interesting concept that the deflationist. Davidson proposes that we reveal the common character of truth$_{English}$, truth$_{Urdu}$ and so on, by looking within, on the one hand, to the laws of logic (following Frege), and looking without, on the other, to the position that a theory of truth occupies in a unified account of language, thought and action. "The problem of how to relate truth to human desires, beliefs, intentions, and the use of language – [this] seems to me the right one to concentrate on in thinking about truth" (Davidson 1990e: 280; see also Davidson 1996: 276–7). Thus for Davidson truth takes its position alongside allied notions like meaning, belief and action as a fundamental explanatory concept, but one that, as such, does not permit a Socratic definition.

To see what this means, consider that when a scientist has described a phenomenon in the most basic terms available to her, she is left with explaining that phenomenon by relating different aspects of the phenomenon to one another. Ideally, the explanation captures these relations by invoking a few simple concepts and then investigating the connections among these concepts. This is exactly what physicists do, for example, when they describe quantum phenomena in terms of the "flavours" of subatomic particles and the types of "colour" charges that quarks can have; the content of these notions is given by the mathematical equations that relate the terms of the theory to one another. This is why descriptions of quantum phenomena sound absurd to the layperson, who, lacking the mathematics, cannot grasp the internal structure of the theory; that internal structure, however, *constitutes* the theory. To take an easier example, this is also the method followed by decision theorists when they describe the structure of a person's actions and attitudes. To understand someone's actions, the decision theorist looks at his preferences or the choices he makes, and considers how his choices relate to his beliefs about different events and the relative values he places on the occurrence of those events. In pursuing this investigation, the decision theorist does not reduce or define the concepts of action, preference, belief and value in any simpler terms (just as the quantum physicist does not define "quark" or "lepton" in simpler terms, since there are none.) Instead, she illuminates the concepts of choice and action by first developing a mathematical theory of preference, which imposes certain formal constraints (for example, the relations of transitivity and asymmetry) on the terms of the theory (such as "belief" and "value"). Then she imposes additional empirical constraints on the theory, and thereby relates that formal structure to the pattern made by her subject's actual choices and actions. If all goes well, the theory optimally fits her evidence about the subject's actions, and we shall say that the theory is true of the subject's choice behaviour.

Davidson believes that we should find in this methodology a model for the role that truth plays in a theory of meaning. A Tarski-style theory of truth is a formal structure that relates the concepts of truth, satisfaction and reference; when combined with empirical constraints, which I shall describe in Chapter 4, that theory, if it fits the evidence available to an interpreter, explains an individual's or community's speech behaviour. In explaining that behaviour, an interpreter brings the logico-linguistic structure elucidated by Tarski into contact with other philosophically interesting concepts, especially belief, desire and action. As a result, we clarify the relations among important philosophical ideas; "even if," as Davidson puts it,

> we cannot hope to define concepts like truth, virtue, probability, belief, action, or intention in terms of more basic concepts ... there is legitimate philosophical work to be done in relating these concepts to one another in as clear a way as we can. (Davidson 1990b: 32)

Chapter 4

Radical interpretation

In Chapter 3 we saw that a Tarski-style theory of truth for a language diagrams the semantic structure of the language. As with any mathematical theory, however, that structure can be fitted on to *any* system of objects that satisfies the conditions expressed by its axioms. Consider, for example, a simple theory *K* that one might set up to describe the pattern of relations among the lengths of assorted objects. *K* would contain an axiom of the form,

(1) If *Rxy*, then not *Ryx*,

which, when we assign the interpretation "is longer than" to "*R*", says that if some object *x* is longer than an object *y*, then *y* is not longer than *x*; under this assignment, (1) expresses that length is asymmetric. Notice, however, that at least in so far as it contains (1), *K* could have been a theory of time rather than length, if we had assigned to "*R*" the interpretation "is earlier than" and taken "*x*" and "*y*" to range over events; under *this* assignment, (1) says that if an event *x* is earlier than an event *y*, then *y* is not earlier than *x*. Time, like length, is asymmetric.

We begin to convert a mere formal diagram into a theory of truth when we assign semantic concepts (truth, satisfaction and reference) to its predicate constants, but unless we show that the theory's *T*-sentences correctly assign truth-conditions to sentences from a language that someone actually speaks, we have failed to supply the theory with an empirical interpretation. For

Tarski, figuring out whether a theory of truth is adequate in this sense is not an issue; the object languages he studies are all familiar mathematical languages, hence he can see right away whether the *T*-theorems get the truth conditions right. Moreover, since Tarski's goal is to define a language's truth predicate, he can harmlessly move back and forth between the object-language sentences he studies and the metalanguage sentences (on the right-hand side of the *T*-sentences) that translate them. Because Davidson's goal is to examine the concept of meaning, rather than truth, he cannot take the notion of translation – which, in effect, is just synonymy across two languages – for granted as part of the apparatus of his theory. Davidson, therefore, needs to look beyond Tarski in developing a framework for deciding when a theory is empirically adequate.

In this chapter we turn from our elaboration of the formal theory to the problem of its empirical interpretation. If a theory of truth can do the work of a theory of meaning or, as Davidson prefers, a theory of *interpretation*, then the formal theory will lay out the internal structure of an interpreter's understanding of a speaker's language; in looking at the empirical application of that theory, we examine the evidence upon which an interpreter constructs her theory and thus trace the path from that evidence to her theory of interpretation. Officially, Davidson speaks in terms of confirming that a given theory correctly describes the semantics of someone's language, but for the most part he follows Quine's example and examines an interpreter's constructing *in vivo* a correct theory of truth for a speaker's utterances. Again following Quine, Davidson assumes that the interpreter, in constructing her theory, works under the constraint that she has no prior knowledge of the language or special access to the attitudes of its speakers.

4.1 Ramsey's analysis of choice behaviour

Davidson often cites work by decision theorists, especially Frank Ramsey,[1] to illustrate the problem of relating the formal apparatus of a Tarski-style truth theory to actual speech behaviour. Nostalgia for his own youthful research aside, Davidson revisits these writings because he finds in Ramsey's work on teasing apart and tracking the relative contributions that an agent's desires and beliefs make to her choice behaviour, not only an analogue to a central problem in the theory of interpretation, but also a solution that is "strikingly similar" to the methods he endorses (Davidson 1990e: 318). Quine, rather than Ramsey, was the immediate influence on the development of Davidson's philosophy, but the clarity of Ramsey's work illuminates Davidson's account, and it sheds light on how Davidson situates his own work in the tradition.

Ramsey develops an empirical theory of decision-making by showing us how to fit the formal apparatus of the probability calculus on to the pattern of agent's actions and attitudes. Having made this connection we can use that apparatus to explain a person's behaviour by relating his actions to his beliefs and desires; we can interpret his actions as being caused by his believing certain conditions to be more or less likely – Will it rain this afternoon? Will the share price of Microsoft climb or fall? Will the Yankees make it to the Series next year? – and his desiring certain ends (that he not get caught unprepared in wet weather, that he not lose money playing the stock market, that he purchase a large-screen television in time to watch his team vie for the championship and so on).

Ramsey infuses empirical content into the probability calculus by showing how to interpret it as a theory describing degrees of what he calls "partial belief". What he means by this is that there are some statements one may feel certain about, for example, that the sun will rise tomorrow, and others that one may feel less than certain about, such as the correct route to take to town when standing at an unfamiliar crossroads. According to Ramsey, we do not have to be satisfied with describing these certainties and less-than-certainties in terms of intensities of feeling that can be known and distinguished through introspection; we can, he argues, interpret the degree to which someone believes that *p* (e.g. that the correct route is to the right) in terms of "the extent to which [one is] prepared to act on it" (1931c: 169). In a review of Ramsey's article, Russell felicitously summarizes an illustration of a degree of belief:

> Suppose I come to a fork in the road, and I think I ought to keep to the right, but am not sure. If I see a person some distance off across the fields, I shall [cross the field to] ask his opinion if the distance is small or if I feel considerable doubt; but if the distance is great or my doubt small, I shall not

> think it worthwhile to go and ask him. Thus the number of yards I am willing to go out of my way can be used to measure my degree of doubt. (1931: 480)

In fact, Ramsey's position is a stronger. He takes it that the number of yards the traveller is willing to go out of his way to ask for directions *is* his degree of doubt (and, inversely, his degree of belief), given some suitable standard of measure: the degree of belief an agent reposes in a statement that *p* is the strength of his disposition to choose a course of action that, were it the case that *p*, would realize his desires, whatever they may be. Analogously, the strength of an agent's desire that *q* is the strength of his disposition to select a course of action that, were his beliefs (whatever they may be) true, would bring it about that *q*.

Part of the difficulty facing the decision theorist is that since belief and desire are individuated by their respective roles in disposing an agent to behave in certain ways, it is difficult *in vivo* to tease apart the relative contribution of each attitude in causing an agent's actions. So how does one measure an agent's attitudes? Ramsey's solution lies in making multiple observations of an agent's expressing his (ordinal) preferences[2] among outcomes or gambles he is offered, under the assumption that he acts consistently to maximize the likelihood of his realizing his desires. This strong assumption that the agent's behaviour is *rational* permits us to extract from his simple choice behaviour a rich structure describing his beliefs and desires, which we can, in turn, bring to bear in constructing explanations of the agent's actions. Note that we *assume* that he behaves rationally as a constraint on our interpretation of his actions: our describing the agent's behaviour as rational does not depend on our *finding* evidence that his actions form a coherent pattern. Rather, we *presuppose* that he is rational; indeed, we have to make this supposition, for it is this assumption that sustains our project of finding an intelligible pattern in someone's actions and utterances.

Ramsey's wedge into an agent's mental economy is the observation of the agent's being indifferent between pairs of gambles he is offered. Suppose, for example, that Jack prefers to take a course on logic than on aesthetics, and that he is offered the following two options:

- *Option 1*: If a red card is selected from a deck he will take logic, while if a red card is not selected he will take aesthetics.

- *Option 2*: If a red card is selected from a deck he will take aesthetics, while if a red card is not selected, he will take logic.

If Jack expresses indifference between options 1 and 2, then the relative values he assigns to the two possible outcomes in option 1 (taking a logic course, taking an aesthetics course) reverse the values he assigns to the outcomes in option 2 (taking an aesthetics course, taking a logic course); if this is the case, then we can, as it were, subtract out those desires and solve for his degree of belief. From his indifference we infer that he assigns a probability of ½ to the statement that a red card will be selected, in the sense that he believes it equally likely that a red card will be selected as a black card. If this is right it explains Jack's indifference between having his preferred outcome (that he enrols in a logic course) tied to a red card's being drawn or its not being drawn. Having made this assignment, it is in principle easy to assign degrees to some of his other beliefs and to calibrate the strengths of his desires *as long as we assume that the agent's actions and attitudes form a coherent pattern*. Given the statement that a red card will be selected, to which he assigns a probability (½) midway between certainty (probability = 1) and perfect disbelief (probability = 0), we offer him further gambles to identify a statement to which he assigns probability ¾, which is the mid-point between certainty and his degree of belief that a red card will be selected; and *mutatis mutandis* to identify a statement to which he assigns probability ¼, which is the mid-point between perfect disbelief and his degree of belief that a red card will be selected. A similar set of offers, resting on our knowing that he assigns the probability of ½ to the statement that a red card will be selected, reveals the scale of his desires.[3]

4.2 Evidence for interpretation

Ramsey develops an empirical interpretation of the probability calculus by *inter alia* assuming that people behave rationally; making this assumption, he can exploit information gleaned from observations of an agent's simple choice behaviour to generate a detailed picture of his mental economy. Davidson's project, like Ramsey's, involves introducing empirical substance to a mathematical theory (a Tarski-style theory of truth); and like Ramsey, too, Davidson succeeds by exploiting observations of people's behaviour to infer a structure that, in turn, can be used to interpret their words.

In setting out the empirical situation facing an interpreter in terms that parallel the decision theorist's situation, Davidson identifies observations of an agent's overt behaviour as the evidence upon which the interpreter fashions her theory of interpretation. This focus on overt behaviour means that the interpreter's evidence will consist in fairly superficial descriptions of what a speaker says and does, for example, it will consist in events described as his making certain verbal noises in such-and-such circumstances. Davidson says in an early article that the "theory [of meaning will] be specifically semantical in nature, while the evidence [will] be in non-semantical terms" (Davidson 1984a: 142), but later he recognizes this as overly restrictive and concedes that the evidence will mention notions closely allied to meaning, including especially attitudes such as belief. What he wants to exclude as evidence, rather, are putative *detailed* accounts of speakers' beliefs or intentions, for example, that in making certain verbal noises the speaker intended to ask his interlocutor to shut the window. (As we shall see shortly, Davidson describes the semantic information available to an interpreter as *non-individuative* in character.) Davidson's parsimony here is motivated by his conviction that the fine structure of a speaker's attitudes are unobservable – like the meanings of his words and unlike the sounds he is observed to make, which are open to public scrutiny – hence the project of elucidating that structure belongs to the same unified project encompassing the interpretation of his words, "no part of which can be assumed to be complete before the rest is" (*ibid.*: 127). Again, there is a parallel with Ramsey; the decision theorist simultaneously infers her subject's beliefs and preferences based on nothing more than her observing his choice behaviour.[4]

Davidson's account of an interpreter's evidence is an emendation of Quine's approach, where Quine takes an explicitly behaviourist approach to the matter: "In psychology one may or may not be a behaviorist, but in linguistics one has no choice" (Quine 1990: 38). For Quine, an interpreter's evidence consists in her observing a speaker's *prompted assent* and *dissent* when that speaker (of a language hitherto unknown to the interpreter) is queried about a hypothetical translation, into the interpreter's home language, of one of his utterances. In the next section I shall flesh out this picture, but the present point is that Quine takes prompted assent and dissent to be behaviours of a speaker that can be described without mentioning his mental states.

Davidson is less sanguine about the prospects for a behaviouristic reduction, and he presents his own, less austere account of the evidence for testing the interpreter's hypothesis. Like Quine, Davidson allows that interpreters have immediate access to recurrent sound patterns produced by speakers under observable circumstances, but he also believes (unlike Quine) that they observe speakers' *holding sentences true* (or *false*). Davidson does not have an argument that shows that an interpreter's evidence is richer than what Quine is prepared to allow, except, perhaps, that unless one accepts "frankly intensional attitudes towards sentences, such as holding [or preferring] true", the interpretive project cannot get off the ground; because we do understand our fellows and "despair[ing] of behaviourism", we assume that we have this access (Davidson 1984a: 231).

Jane Heal observes that any theory of radical interpretation should be applicable to giant octopuses or super-beings emerging from their spaceships as well as to newly encountered human beings. If we consider such non-human cases, however, then it is obvious that identifying a creature's stance as a case of its holding a sentence true presupposes that we distinguish voluntary from involuntary behaviour, and linguistic from non-linguistic conduct. In making these distinctions, though, we become involved in "making rich hypotheses about the contents of [its] beliefs and purposes", hence "Davidson's proposed radical interpretation starts in a place which is either not available or is not radical" (Heal 1997: 184). In other words, Heal argues that Davidson's evidential base for radical interpretation either does not include detailed information about the subject's mental states – in which case the evidence is too weak to achieve its purpose – or it does include that information, in which case "radical interpretation" begins to look more like a Gricean picture of understanding.

This objection rests on an error, although it is one that is easy to make since Davidson is less than clear about the point. Heal mistakes the choice to interpret someone's (or something's) behaviour – that is, the choice to treat that behaviour as an *action* – as putting forward a *hypothesis*, which it is not, much like

Kierkegaard's leap of faith that God exists is not a hypothesis. Rather, choosing to interpret a creature's behaviour (and thus treating it, for example, as voluntary) is deciding to adopt a postulate that makes the project of interpretation (or theistic belief) possible, without that choice's being *justified* by some body of information, known in advance of the interpretation, about the subject's behaviour or mental state (or about the structure or origin of the cosmos).

> The only way to tell if [anything] ... has beliefs, intentions, desires, and the ability to perceive and interact with the world as a person does, is to attempt to interpret [its] behaviour ... in the same way we do the behaviour of a person. (Davidson 1990b: 26)

This is how it has to be; if we are going take a creature's behaviour as evidence for attributing some attitude to her, then perforce we are *already* treating her as a rational agent and her behaviour as reasonable, and therefore voluntary and purposive. We cannot so much as begin to wonder whether an occurrence is someone's intentional action until we assume that she holds something true, and that she performs some actions on purpose.

Alternatively, one might say that choosing to interpret a creature's behaviour is justified, but by the fruitfulness of the consequences of that choice (i.e. its descriptive success in explaining the subject's behaviour) and not based on behavioural evidence already on hand. Putting the matter this way shows that a Davidsonian interpreter (unlike a fideist) keeps open the option of abandoning the postulate, if it turns out to be barren. And it brings out, too, the similarity between Davidson's account and Daniel Dennett's idea that when we decide to interpret the behaviour of a complex system by attributing propositional attitudes to it, we do so because it is a "tactic" we expect to "pay off" (Dennett 1978: 6).[5] Therefore, when we interpret beings emerging from a silver saucer-shaped ship (rather than trying to explain their movements ethologically), we treat them as rational agents, not based on any experience, but rather in anticipation that by treating them as such we maximize our understanding of their behaviour.

To hold a sentence *s* true is to believe *s*. Therefore, in amassing her evidence for a theory of interpretation for a speaker, an interpreter appeals to facts about a speaker's mental states. Davidson maintains that in liberalizing Quine's strictures he has not, however, given away the semantic store. The reason for this is that although we attribute a mental state to a speaker when we describe him as holding a sentence true, we can make the attribution *without knowing the content of that state* or, what comes to the same thing, we can describe him as holding a sentence true *without our knowing what that sentence means*; the state of holding a sentence true is an attitude toward an *un*interpreted sentence. Thus I may know that Cheng holds some sentence *s* of Chinese true, even if I do not know what *s* means, because I perceive that in uttering *s* he intends to express a truth, even though, again, I do not know what that truth is. In this way the attitude of holding true is *non-individuative*, in the sense that in attributing it to a speaker we do not have to specify (i.e. individuate) the *content* of that attitude. Because it is non-individuated, Davidson avoids the objection he raises against Gricean theories of meaning, that they "smuggl[e] into the foundations of the theory concepts too closely allied to the concept of meaning" (Davidson 1984a: xiii; see §1.3).[6]

Because he takes this liberalized stand, Davidson escapes some of the more severe criticism levelled against his theory. Stephen Mulhall, for example, characterizes the world of a Davidsonian interpreter as one "radically devoid of significance", in which a person's experience of other people's humanity is a "theoretical construct out of brute data"; and given this characterization, Mulhall assimilates Davidson's philosophical stance to (now widely discredited) sense-datum theories of knowledge.[7] However, since Davidson includes speakers' holding sentences true within their purview, it is false that Davidsonian interpreters face a world *radically* devoid of significance. Interpreters perceive *that* there are meanings associated with speakers' utterances, although they do not know what those meanings are.

Still, though, one might wonder whether the slender thread by which Davidson's account avoids this criticism does not falsify the transaction between speakers and their auditors. In conversation with our fellows, it certainly *seems* that we perceive more than their bare movements and sounds, or even their non-individuative attitudes towards uninterpreted sentences; it seems, indeed, that we do not so much *infer* the significance of someone's utterance from its sound and surrounding circumstances, as much as we *perceive* the recognizable thoughts of the speaker in his words. As

McDowell puts it, in learning a language we acquire a perceptual capacity that makes *immediately* "available to our senses ... [new] facts about what people are saying", in the sense of facts about the *meanings* of their words (McDowell 1998a: 333). On this alternative picture, the world accessible to perception is rich in thoughts and meanings.[8]

Davidson has described possessing a language as analogous to "having eyes and ears ... all three are organs [with] which we come into direct contact with our environment", but he does not intend the analogy to extend to the idea that we perceive meanings with a "language organ" (Davidson 1997f: 18). More to the point, perhaps, Davidson concedes that the way he sets up the problem, the details of which I shall describe in §4.3, is somewhat artificial: "I do not think we normally understand what others say by consciously reflecting on what they mean or ... by summoning up what we take to be the relevant evidence" (1994b: 3).

Nevertheless, Davidson urges that we reveal "the philosophically important aspects of communication" when we examine linguistic understanding under the most austere circumstances in which it can occur, which is the programme he follows, in Quine's footsteps. Certainly, there may as a matter of empirical fact be other resources that interpreters exploit when they understand their fellows; but Davidson worries that in investigating the question of how people, in fact, go about understanding the speech of others, we give into the temptation "to speculate about arcane empirical matters that neither philosophers nor psychologists know much about" (*ibid.*).[9] McDowell concedes that trying to set out the details of actual linguistic transactions would be exceedingly complicated; it would, for example, have to take into account "one's ... conception of the world, including a conception of oneself as a person among others" (McDowell 1998a: 333). Switching traditions, it would require, so to speak, an account of one's being-in-the world.[10] But McDowell worries that *failing* to distinguish between interpreting a speaker of a radically alien language (in which case an interpreter has only those resources Davidson permits) and understanding the words of a speaker of a familiar language, we miss what is "essential". Davidson disagrees; in showing that "the theoretical possibility of communication" remains under those more austere circumstances we show what is, and what is not, "an essential constituent in meaning" (Davidson 1994b: 10). "The point of the theory", Davidson emphasizes, "is not to describe how we actually interpret, but to speculate on what it is about thought and language that makes them interpretable".[11] Davidson's goal is a metaphysics of meaning, thought and action, not a phenomenology.

4.3 Radical translation

Davidson happily avows that his project is shaped by the influence of Quine,[12] who presents his reflections on language in the context of a thought experiment he dubs "radical translation". In radical translation a linguist observes a speaker's verbal behaviour, where the language of that behaviour is wholly unknown to her, and her task is to construct a translation manual that maps the speaker's language onto her own. Because the speaker's language is (as far as she knows) unrelated to her own, the linguist cannot rely on, for example, the existence of cognate words to facilitate her translations, nor can she fall back on the intuitions that a Tarskian theory builder relies on when he decides straightaway whether his translations are correct. Her evidence consists entirely in her observations of overt features of the speaker's actions and his relation to his environment.

The linguist begins to construct her translation manual by focusing on utterances that coordinate with conspicuous features of the situation she shares with her subject. We may suppose, to take Quine's famous example, that a rabbit scurries in front of the linguist and the alien speaker, who then says "Gavagai!" Taking this as her initial evidence, the linguist construes the utterance holophrastically (that is, as a one-word sentence expressing a single, complete thought), deferring consideration of how it may decompose and how its parts may individually refer to details of the environment. She sifts through the features of the complex state of affairs that embeds the alien's speech behaviour and reasons that were she in the subject's position of a rabbit's crossing her path in good light and in full view, she would be disposed to assert, "Lo, a rabbit!" On the assumption, then, that the alien speaker's verbal dispositions are related to his local environment (via *his* sensations) as her own dispositions are, or would be, related to her own (via *her* sensations) – an assumption that Davidson terms "the principle of correspondence" (2001a: 211) – the linguist tentatively translates the alien speaker's "Gavagai!"

with her own "Lo, a rabbit!" This initial hypothesis is strengthened on further occasions of rabbits' presenting themselves to the speaker and his uttering "Gavagai", and occasions of no rabbits (but squirrels, perhaps) making themselves known to the speaker and his not uttering the sentence. For additional support, the linguist moves from being a mere chronicler of behaviour to an experimental scientist; she prompts speakers of the alien language by querying, "Gavagai?" and records their assent or dissent.

How does the linguist recognize signs of native assent and dissent? The alien speaker volunteers "Gavagai!", and the linguist, in turn, queries "Gavagai?" and records his response. The linguist thereby generates a first working assumption: whatever the native says in response to her query she correlates with her own "Yes". If her hypothesis about which alien vocable signals assent fails in future trials to describe a reasonable pattern of native behaviour, "the linguist may decide to discard that hypothesis and guess again" (Quine 1960: 30; see also Quine 1990: 39).

"Gavagai" can serve the linguist as her entering wedge into the alien speaker's language because its truth-value is especially sensitive to the occasion of its use, permitting her to infer its meaning from the subject's volunteering the sentence on that occasion, or from his assent or dissent when queried. "Gavagai", in this sense, is an *occasion sentence*, a category Quine defines as a sentence "true on some occasions, false on others" (1990: 3). Unlike a *standing sentence*, for example, "All men are mortal", to which a speaker will assent every time, statements such as "There's a rabbit", or "It's getting cold", will elicit agreement only if, on that occasion, there is a rabbit in the speaker's vicinity or a drop in temperature.

"Gavagai" is, further, an observation sentence in Quine's terminology. *Observation sentences* are that subset of occasion sentences to which "speakers of the language can agree outright on witnessing the occasion" (Quine 1990: 3). As Quine sometimes puts it, what separates observation sentences ("That's a rabbit") from *non*-observation occasion sentences ("That's a bachelor") is that a speaker's holding a non-observation sentence true depends on his possessing *collateral information* about the scene he witnesses. A subject's prompted assent to the query "Is that a bachelor?" draws upon much more than his observing the bachelor's face; it draws on "stored information [about the indicated man's marital status] and none on the prompting stimulation except as needed for recognizing the bachelor friend concerned" (Quine 1960: 42).[13] Given the empiricist dictum that the meaning of a sentence is the difference to experience that its truth would make, Quine identifies the meaning of an observation sentence with its *stimulus meaning*, which he defines as the patterns of sensations that dispose a speaker to assent to it.[14] The meaning of observation sentences, therefore, unlike the meaning of other occasion sentences and standing sentences, narrows to a single point.

But herein lies a problem for Quine. On the one hand, observation sentences are drawn upon as an entry into language precisely because their meaning is wholly focused on the occurrent situation, and therefore they are poised to do much of the work in Quine's account of radical translation. This identification also subserves the epistemological character of Quine's reflections: "I am interested in the flow of evidence from the triggering of the senses to the pronouncements of science" (Quine 1990: 41). Thus, going epistemological, Quine locates his project within the traditional problematic of describing how our beliefs ("the pronouncements of science") connect to the world; and as an empiricist, he identifies the connector as sensory experience (variously described as the triggering of the senses, impacts at nerve endings, neural intake, surface irritations, etc.) and observation sentences as the point at which sensations get taken up into science and, more generally, the body of our beliefs.

On the other hand, though, Quine is a holist. He is, therefore, committed to saying that the meaning of an observation sentence – like any other sentence – is dispersed throughout the network of sentences that compose the theory to which it belongs. To be sure, sense experience is "peculiarly germane" to observation sen-tences, but he remarks in "Two Dogmas of Empiricism" that "this relation of 'germaneness' I envisage as nothing more than a loose association reflecting the relative likelihood, in practice, of our choosing one statement rather than another for revision in the event of recalcitrant experience" (1961: 43). Indeed, if observation sentences are going to export empirical content to sentences lying in the interior of the linguistic network, they *must* bear systematic evidential and grammatical relations to those interior sentences; these relations flow in both directions, however, hence holism implies that observation sentences are infected with theory.

Quine proposes to relieve the tension between his holism and his empiricism by describing observation sentences as "Janus-faced":[15] from the perspective of the radical translator or child learning a first language, an observation sentence is holophrastically keyed to its stimulus meaning irrespective of its systemic role and collateral information, while from the point of view of one who already has command of a language it is grasped in its role in the network of interrelated sentences.

Davidson offers a different resolution: dropping observation sentences from their privileged role as the radical translator's entering wedge and therewith residual commitment to empiricism.[16] He agrees with Quine that sentences containing terms indicating objects or observable features of a speaker's local environment – that is, Quine's observation sentences, which Davidson terms "perceptual sentences" (Davidson 1997f: 24) – play an important and early role in interpretation. But their playing this role cannot be a matter of a *principled* privilege because *pace* Quine the pattern of sensory experience associated with an observation sentence, which Quine identifies as its stimulus meaning, does not exhaust the sentence's meaning.

> Someone with no understanding of physics could easily come to utter the sentence "There goes an electron" as the streak appears in the cloud chamber, while having little idea what an electron is. Understanding the sentence depends on prior theory, without which the content [of the sentence] would be totally unlike what we think of as [its] meaning. But isn't theory, in a sense that extends theory to cover tacit understanding, ... always needed for the conditioning of sentence to circumstance to yield the right content? Only someone knowledgeable about sailing ships could recognise on sight that he sees a brig and not a brigantine, though he might use the words in the right situations. (*ibid*.: 24)

One may be trained to classify selectively some objects as electrons or brigantines, but unless those utterances ("There goes a brigantine!") are situated against a background of dispositions to utter other physical or nautical sentences, we should not say that the speaker *recognizes* an electron or brigantine, or that he understands the words. But the difference between using words in the right situations *without* understanding – in our example, identifying one case as like another without understanding what those cases are cases of – and using words in the right situations *with* understanding does not rest on the existence in the latter of an event in the brain or *res cogitans*. Rather, let us assume that a speaker utters the sentence "There goes an electron" when presented with a certain range of stimuli, and that he dissents from the sentence in the absence of any such stimulation. Construing the speaker's utterance holophrastically, we correctly describe him as using the sentence "There goes an electron" as a label to distinguish between two types of events. However, if we cannot credit him with some background of atomic theory – and hence cannot credit him with the ability to use the word "electron" correctly in sentences other than "There goes an electron" – we ought not to say that his utterance distinguishes some of those events as instances of *electrons' being present*. For to classify something as *an electron's being present* is to identify it as the presence of something that falls under the concept of *being an electron*; and no one can classify something under *this* concept unless he knows what an electron is. And he does not know what an electron is unless he knows some fragment of physical theory, for, as we saw in §1.3, there is no principled distinction between grasping a concept and understanding a theory.

This point is reminiscent of Aristotle's claim that although a child might perform the right action, at the right time, and in the right manner – in other words, perform an action that bears all the external marks of virtue – that action is not virtuous because it is not part of an integrated virtuous life. Missing in both instances are further dispositions to act (to act virtuously in the ethical case, and to perform speech acts in the linguistic case) that characterize both moral virtue and understanding a language.

4.4 Charity I: the principle of coherence

Davidson's rejection of observation sentences and the epistemological project that embeds them is reflected in the form of the hypotheses a radical interpreter puts forward when she approaches her task. Beginning with observations such as:

(2) Kurt belongs to a community of speakers of a common language, call it *G*, and he holds "Das ist ein Kaninchen" true_G on Saturday at noon, and there is a rabbit visible to Kurt on Saturday at noon,

and eliciting additional evidence bearing on *G*-speakers' verbal behaviour in relation to their environment, she infers that

(3) if x is a *G*-speaker, then x holds "Das ist ein Kaninchen" $true_G$ at t if and only if there is a rabbit visible to x at t.

This inference will be subject to the vagaries to which empirical research is always subject, but having gathered an adequate sample of instances of *G*-speakers holding "Das ist ein Kaninchen" $true_G$ when and only when rabbits cross their paths, she takes (3) to be confirmed and she takes (3), in turn, as evidence that (partly) confirms the Tarski-style truth theory implying the *T*-sentence:

(4) "Das ist ein Kaninchen" is $true_G$ when spoken by x at t if and only if there is a rabbit visible to x at t.

pp 209-10

Notice that in reconstructing Kurt's language, the radical interpreter refers to neither her own words nor to the speaker's sensations. A radical interpreter thus takes an explicitly semantic turn: unlike a Quinean radical *translator*, Davidson's radical *interpreter* relates speakers' sentences to the world by assigning them objective truth-conditions mentioning situations and objects in their shared world. In this sense, Davidson's focus is *interpretation* rather than translation.[17] Of course, the interpreter *uses* sentences of her home language to make these assignments but, as we saw in §2.3, this does not vitiate the theory; the interpreter's sentences are directed upon extra-linguistic reality, hence using them to assign meaning to the speaker's sentences has the effect of relating those words to that same extra-linguistic world.

In using her own propositional resources to track the relation between speakers' utterances and the extra-linguistic world, an interpreter exports her *logical standards* and *theory of the world* to alien speakers and thinkers. In the remainder of this section we explore the first half of this methodological observation, which Davidson calls the *principle of (logical) coherence*, and in the following section we turn to a second, parallel principle of interpretation, the *principle of correspondence*. Taken together, these canons of interpretation are known in the literature as the *principle(s) of charity*.[18]

Davidson's focus on truth and kindred notions leads him to emphasize the importance for an interpreter of identifying a coherent logical structure in the sentences of an alien speaker. A radical interpreter's first step, then, in approaching an unfamiliar language will be to look for the best way to fit our logic, to the extent required to get a theory satisfying Convention *T*, on to the new language; this may mean reading the logical structure of first-order quantification theory (plus identity) into the language, not taking the logical constants one by one, but treating this much logic as a grid to be fitted on to the language in one fell swoop (Davidson 1984a: 136). Finding the logical constants and the patterns they induce in the alien speaker's language, the interpreter begins to fit that language into the mould of a Tarski-style theory of interpretation.

This first move is crucial. If an interpreter can locate logical patterns in an individual's speech behaviour, then she can expect information she has gleaned from her observations of his behaviour to ramify quickly into a detailed picture of the structure of his language. The interpreter can exploit the apparatus of first-order logic to move from the thin evidence of observations such as (2) to results such as (3) and the Tarski-style theory of interpretation to which (4) belongs. In this respect, there is an analogy between Davidson's invoking the coherence principle and Ramsey's imposing the constraint that an agent acts consistently to maximize the likelihood of his realizing his ends. In both cases, an observer uses evidence drawn from an agent's simple behaviour to extract a detailed picture of his mental economy or language, and in both cases she achieves this end by imposing strong, normative constraints on the agent's behaviour: in decision theory, that he act rationally to maximize the likelihood of his achieving his desires, and in semantics, that he reason in accordance with logical laws. Again, in both cases, the powerful methodological constraint that a theorist ought to see her subject as rational is a first step in locating in his behaviour the structure described by the formal theory (the probability calculus in the decision theory case, and a Tarski-style theory of interpretation in the language case) and, conversely, it is a first step in giving empirical bite to the formal theory.

Identifying a coherent logical structure in a speaker's sentences is crucial, too, because unless we attribute beliefs to a subject, there is nothing to interpret. We cannot, however, attribute beliefs to him and at the same time suppose that he assents to obvious logical falsehoods, for example, that *p* and not-*p*. Of course, everyone is guilty of occasional irrationalities, but when a system *regularly* violates logical laws we cannot make enough sense of it to assign truth-conditions and other semantic properties to its elements, that is, we cannot treat it as a language or system of beliefs. The reason is that we cannot *first* identify the meaning of a sentence someone utters and *then* locate that sentence's position in the network of logical relations it bears to other sentences he believes, because the structure of that network partly constitutes its meaning. Someone's utterance could not plausibly be interpreted to mean that it is about to rain unless her words, if conjoined to the statement that if it rains then pours, entailed that it is about to pour (Davidson 1985c: 251).

The point is that having a truth-value partly characterizes or defines the concepts of sentencehood and belief, and denying the rule of *modus ponens* makes a muddle of the notions of true and false. To paraphrase Frege, the laws of truth (i.e. the principles of logic) explain the concept of truth, and a sentence (or, more precisely, an utterance) is precisely that for which the question of truth arises. One can, therefore, no more interpret someone as uttering a meaningful sentence, or having thoughts, if he consistently flouts logical norms, than one can see someone as playing baseball if he runs the bases backwards. Certainly, we cannot catalogue in advance the degrees and kinds of logical error that render someone's behaviour uninterpretable, but the more extravagant the inconsistency we ascribe to an agent, the more difficulty we have in identifying the contents of his beliefs and meanings of his sentences.

Davidson stresses that what is at issue here is *internal consistency*. What matters is not what we may call the reasonableness or irrationality of one or another belief or statement against a background of objective facts. If someone commits a gross factual error, he may be excused if that error makes sense from his point of view: in other words, if we can rationalize the error by making adjustments to other beliefs we attribute to him. What we cannot make sense of, though, is error that causes an obvious or pervasive failure in the network of a speaker's beliefs "according to principles held by the agent himself" (Davidson 1985c: 348), although putting the point this way is misleading. Davidson says later in the same article that agents "can't *decide* whether or not to accept the fundamental attributes of rationality: if they are in a position to decide anything, they have those attributes" (*ibid.*: 352). The real point is that a speaker cannot consistently and *knowingly* contradict himself:

> no one can believe a proposition of the form (*p* and not-*p*) while appreciating that the proposition is of this form ... This is why I have urged ... that it is only by postulating a kind of compartmentalization of the mind that we can understand, and begin to explain, irrationality. (*Ibid.*)

A necessary condition for interpreting a subject's behaviour, therefore, is the disclosure of "a degree of logical consistency in the thought of the speaker" (Davidson 2001a: 211). Finding such coherence is neither a charitable assumption nor an empirical hypothesis about the intellectual capacities of a subject, nor is it a "commonsense [rule] of thumb that might, like all common sense, sometimes offer bad advice".[19] It is, rather, "the foundation of intelligibility on which all interpretation rests" (Davidson 1990e: 320), because the basic norms of rationality are a *condition* on speaking a language and having thoughts. Failure to locate sufficient consistency in an individual's behaviour means there is *nothing* to interpret: if "we fail to discover a coherent and plausible pattern in the attitudes and actions of others we simply forego the chance of treating them as persons" (Davidson 1980a: 222).

4.5 Charity II: the principle of correspondence

We see the role of the second charity principle when we reflect on Davidson's thought experiment. The problem the radical interpreter faces is that *ex hypothesi* she neither knows what a speaker's sentences mean nor has direct access to his attitudes and their contents. Both of these factors have a bearing on making sense of his verbal behaviour, however, for what sentences a speaker utters or holds true depends simultaneously on his beliefs and the meanings of those sentences; as Davidson puts it, a speaker's holding a sentence true is a "vector of two forces": what he believes about the world and what meanings his words have (just as an agent's choice behaviour is the sum of his beliefs and values) (Davidson 1984a: 196). To solve this problem of too many unknowns, therefore, the radical interpreter performs her own thought experiment; she projects herself into her subject's shoes and assumes that he *does* or *would hold true* what she, were she in his position, *would hold true*. In this way the interpreter neatly solves her problem of lacking access to the contents of her subject's attitudes, for she *knows* what *she would believe* and hence she knows what her subject believes *if* he believes what she thinks he ought to believe in his situation. The principle of correspondence, then, is the methodological injunction that an interpreter affirm the *if*-clause.

It is at this point that Davidson builds a subjunctive component into a theory of interpretation. Following the lead of a Quinean radical translator, a Davidsonian interpreter constructs her theory on the assumption that her subject's verbal dispositions *vis-à-vis* his environment match her own. This allows her to interpret not only a speaker's actual utterances, but also his unrealized dispositions to perform other utterances. This is crucial, since any one utterance can be interpreted (as we shall see in Chapter 5) only if a host of other utterances are simultaneously interpreted, and many of these will remain merely potential utterances. Moreover, the knowledge that we attribute to someone when we credit him with knowing a language is, in effect, a complex disposition to intend to mean various things by one's words, and most of this disposition never gets realized.

The principle of correspondence has struck many critics as resting on an overly generous estimation about human capacities for judgement or convergence in attitudes, and it does stand in need of clarification. Why should it not be the case that someone else's "perceptual bad luck and intellectual frailty" (Bennett 1985b: 601) make most of his beliefs false according to my standards, or that evolution has condemned him fruitlessly to "think and speak, a large proportion of the time, about alchemy, astrology or historical materialism" (Heal 1997: 187), subjects that I recognize as empirically empty?[20]

These expressions of concern are mistaken, though, for the necessity of charity does not rest on optimistic empirical assumptions that may turn out to be wrong. Its necessity lies, rather, in the fact that "the only, and therefore unimpeachable, method available to the interpreter" is to interpret her subject's words with an eye towards "the events and objects in the outside world that cause the sentence to be held true" by the speaker (Davidson 2001a: 150). Too much "perceptual bad luck" severs the link between those events and objects and the sentences he holds true, and it is precisely this link – that is, that his utterances truly describe, for the most part, those external circumstances – that permits an interpreter to use her observations of his situated utterances and attitudes to construct a theory of interpretation. In short, if certain types of speakers' utterances and attitudes are regularly conjoined with identifiable features of their situations (e.g. *G*-speakers' holding "Das ist ein Kaninchen" true$_G$ at *t* when and only when they see a rabbit at *t*), and if those utterances are regularly true, then we can begin to use those identifiable features to interpret their words; but if speakers' words are usually false, then the contexts of their utterances afford us, their would-be interpreters, no evidence. Finding that persistent (and unexplainable) perceptual frailty dogs our interlocutor's mental lives, therefore, is just not an option if we are to make sense of their utterances and other behaviours.

The concern that an interpreter thinks or speaks "a large proportion of the time" about pseudoscience does point to a genuine need for clarification. First, the principle that an interpreter assumes maximal agreement between her beliefs and her subject's beliefs applies especially to speakers' *perceptual* beliefs and sentences. These are the points of immediate causal contact between external events and objects and speakers' attitudes and utterances, and they are the hinge on which the project of interpretation turns. It is here, therefore, that a theory of interpretation can least concede that a subject errs most of the time. In contrast, an account that attributes to a speaker false *theoretical* beliefs and sentences may be sustained without doing too much violence to the assumption that he is rational, because the evidence for those attributions is mediated by a more extensive fragment of intervening theory. This greater distance between cause (features of the speaker's situation) and effect (sentences held true) supplies extra degrees of freedom in explaining how the speaker might reasonably believe something his interpreter counts as false. I shall return to this point in a moment.

Secondly, speaking of "proportions" of beliefs or about interpreters' "maximizing" or "optimizing"[21] agreement between themselves and their subjects suggests that it makes sense to count a person's beliefs, which is impossible. (For example, how many beliefs do I have about Abraham Lincoln?) It is better, therefore, if we drop this pretense and embrace the interpreter's thought experiment, wherein she is enjoined to attribute to her subject those beliefs she would hold were she in his shoes; that is, she attributes to him those beliefs he *ought to hold*, where the force of the "ought" is the normative standard of rationality – that he believes what makes most sense for him to believe. This has the effect of replacing the standard of maximum agreement between interpreter and subject with the goal of maximizing the *intelligibility* of the subject, which we achieve by attributing to him those beliefs that make for the most coherent or consistent overall pattern, taking into consideration everything we know about his behaviour and his attitudes.

This is surely improvement, since we not only eliminate the impression of numerical precision, but we also, by routing our attributions to an agent through (what we know of) his belief set, make those attributions sensitive to the particularities of his situation. Thus the ideal offered by the principle of correspondence is properly read as the counsel that we make sense of a speaker's sentences by assuming he means by his words something that it makes sense for him to mean by those words, even if it turns out that we in *our* (actual) position do not hold true some of the sentences he in *his* position holds true. An interpreter will still export to her subject's mental economy a great deal of her own worldview, but if there are grounds for attributing to him a set of beliefs that includes at least one, and perhaps many more, false beliefs, then she should do so if what she knows about him and his situation makes it more reasonable than not for him to have those beliefs.

In deciding what it is most reasonable for him to mean by his words, we bring to bear our best understanding of how people arrive at and justify their conceptions of the world, hence Davidson describes the "methodology of interpretation [as], in this respect, nothing but epistemology seen in the mirror of meaning" (1984a: 169). We make use of whatever we know about an agent's personal history and his psychology, and we also (implicitly, perhaps) rely upon general canons of inductive and deductive inference and decision theory; much of it, though, comes down to simple common sense in thinking about how a speaker is situated in his local environment and how that bears on his beliefs. Richard Grandy illustrates this with his example of Paul, who arrives at a party and, observing a man holding a martini glass filled with a clear liquid, asserts "The man with a martini is a philosopher." Knowing that the only man holding a martini glass in Paul's range of view is drinking water and is not a philosopher, and also knowing that the party's singular philosopher is drinking a martini out of sight in the garden, we maximize the intelligibility of Paul's remark – given what we know about the relation between people's utterances and the scenes they directly observe – by understanding him as having said something false.[22]

4.6 Indeterminacy of interpretation

This methodology yields powerful constraints on admissible translations and interpretations, nevertheless, Davidson endorses Quine's claim that there will be many equally adequate but mutually inconsistent translation manuals (or theories of interpretation) for a given language. This thesis of the *indeterminacy of translation* (or *interpretation*) takes two forms, but they share a common origin in the mismatch between the surfeit of resources a translator brings to her task and the poverty of her evidence for one or another translation manual. Quine draws from the indeterminacy of translation a sceptical conclusion that confirms his suspicion about meanings; Davidson, while following Quine through the arguments, stops short of Quine's scepticism and draws a different moral from the indeterminacy thesis.

Here is what Quine means by the indeterminacy of translation, and why he sees it as infecting the translator's task. Recall that a radical translator begins to map a speaker's language onto her own by focusing on his observation sentences (Davidson's perceptual sentences). Observing the speaker assent to a sentence s_L (of his language) where she, in his position, would assert sentence s_H (of her home language), the translator assigns to s_L the same stimulus meaning she assigns to s_H: the translator takes them to be *stimulus-synonymous*. In this way she translates a set of the speaker's observation sentences, and this is her wedge into the speaker's language. She then begins to map the logical structure of L by next identifying the words for the truth-functional constants, for example, having translated the L-sentences that correspond to her H-sentences "There's a rabbit" and "There's a squirrel", she identifies the word in L that means conjunction by identifying an utterance in L that fits the pattern that her sentence, "There's a rabbit *and* there's a squirrel" makes in her language.

To extend her translation manual beyond this fragment, the translator requires additional resources. She therefore postulates what Quine calls "analytical hypotheses" that serve as her apparatus for *inter alia* segmenting observation sentences into their components, such as individual non-logical words. This permits her to construct a scheme showing how the speaker's theoretical sentences share words and phrases with observation sentences, and how, thereby, they inherit their empirical content from the observation sentences.[23] With these hypotheses in place, then, she can begin to translate his non-observation sentences with non-observational sentences of her language.

Ex hypothesi the analytical hypotheses are not backed by any direct behavioural evidence. A set of analytical hypotheses is confirmed, rather, as long as the observation sentences it implies are consistent with the observation sentences verified in experience. Indeterminacy arrives on the scene, then, because different sets of analytical hypotheses may generate identical claims about a speaker's verbal behaviour while assigning different translations to a sentence.

We may suppose, for example, that translation manual M_1 assigns the word "rabbit" to the native vocable "ga", while a second translation manual M_2 assigns "undetached rabbit parts" to it. "Rabbit" and "undetached rabbit parts" are stimulus-synonymous in the translator's home language, but they have quite different references, and hence M_1 and M_2 generate stimulus-synonymous but incompatible translations for the native's "Gavagai!": M_1 translates "Gavagai!" as "Lo, a rabbit!" while M_2 translates it as "Lo, undetached rabbit parts!" Because the translator assents to both "Lo, a rabbit!" and "Lo, undetached rabbit parts!" under the same stimulus conditions – a rabbit is present when and only when undetached rabbit parts are – there can be no behavioural evidence for assigning one, rather than the other, translation to the native's utterance. The problem thus arises because of the richness of the translator's language; *in principle* she always has several options in translating his sentence, and this guarantees that her choice of translation manuals (or theories of interpretation) is indeterminate.

Notice that what is going on here is that the interpretation of *individual terms* (e.g. our hypothetical native vocable "ga") is indeterminate. This is because the interpreter's evidence for her developing theory takes the form of information about the *complete sentences* to which a native speaker does or would assent. In effect, Quine's theory of radical translation lends support to Frege's *context principle* – the thesis that it is only within the context of a sentence that a word has meaning – since it makes no sense to speak of translating individual words, apart from translating the sentences in which the words occur. Traditionally, saying that a word had this or that meaning (or translation) was construed as its standing in some sort of special relation, for example, reference, to an extra-linguistic object; Quine's thought experiment shows, however, that truth is the more fundamental semantic property, in the sense that it is closer than reference to the evidence afforded by the behaviour of subjects. Again, an interpreter's entering wedge into a speaker's language is her witnessing his assent to (holophrastically construed) observation sentences. Reference and satisfaction come into play when we begin to systematize that evidence, and it becomes useful and necessary to posit within language an "internal" structure to account for the "external" form we observe. That structure, though, is *merely* an explanatory device, since there is no independent evidence for one structure or another (e.g. that "ga" refers to rabbit or undetached rabbit parts), apart from its delivering the right "external" form. Hence for Quine, reference and satisfaction are theoretical notions whose contents are exhausted by this systematic role; and this is the root of the species of indeterminacy that Quine calls the *inscrutability* or *indeterminacy of reference*.

Davidson illustrates the indeterminacy of reference with this analogy.

> If you have the axioms that define some system of measurement, whether of weight, temperature, or subjective probability, you can represent the structures so defined in numbers in endless ways. ... With weight, an arbitrarily chosen positive number is assigned to some particular object; relative to that assignment, the numbers that measure the weights of all other objects are fixed. You get an equally good way of keeping track of weights by multiplying the original figures by any positive constant. ... Just as endless sets of numbers allow us to keep track of the same complex structures in the world, so our sentences can be used in endless ways to keep track of the attitudes of others, and of what they mean. (1999a: 596)

The metric system of weights is related to the imperial system by a simple linear transformation, and the same goes for the Fahrenheit and Celsius temperature scales: from a temperature of n°F we derive the corresponding temperature in degrees

Celsius by subtracting 32 and dividing by 1.8. This simple relationship reflects the fact that the number that a temperature scale assigns to something's thermal state simply codes the position that state has in a system of physical relations. Analogously, a translation manual codes the relative positions of sentences in a system or structure of sentences, using an interpreter's own sentences; from a translation of "Gavagai!" by M_1, therefore, we derive a corresponding translation according to M_2, if we correlate occurrences of the terms "rabbit" and "undetached rabbit parts". Since, then, M_1 and M_2 are different but equivalent schemes for representing a single, invariant structure of native sentences; and if, according to M_1, a speaker's utterance of "Gavagai!" at time *t* is true; then that utterance comes out true, too, according to M_2, just as if something is n°F at *t*, then it is also (n – 32)/1.8 °C at *t*.

To see how the indeterminacy of reference differs from a second species of indeterminacy, consider the following example from Davidson:

> I find that I very often disagree with other people over whether to call the color of some object green or blue. The disagreement is consistent: there is a fairly definite range of cases where I say green and they say blue. We can account for this difference in two ways: it may be that I (or most other people) are wrong about the color of certain objects, or it may be that I don't use the words "blue" and "green" in quite the way others do. There may be no way to decide between these two accounts; by making compensatory adjustments elsewhere in one's interpretation of my sentences and beliefs, one can accommodate either story. But on one account my pronouncements about colors are false, while on the other they are true. (1997a: 119)

The indeterminacy of terms is generated, as we said, because the evidence for a translation manual comes at the level of sentences. But this is not quite right, for the radical translator does not test her translations one by one (or, if she is a radical interpreter, she does not test her *T*-sentences one by one); rather, what goes before the tribunal of evidence is *a translation manual* (or *theory of interpretation*) *for the entire language*. This means that in the case of complete sentences, too, there is slack between evidence and an individual hypothesis, and we can alter the translation of any one *sentence* as long as we make complementary changes elsewhere.

Nevertheless, the two forms of indeterminacy *do* differ, because in this second form the perturbations caused by adopting one hypothesis (that a speaker is wrong about the colour of certain objects) or the other (that he does not use colour terms in the way others do) are more profound. Davidson traces this second form of indeterminacy to holism combined with a rejection of the analytic–synthetic distinction; having blurred the distinction between information and meaning, our translation of a speaker's words for "blue" and "green" enjoys an extra degree of freedom. We can translate his colour words one way (according to, say, M_3), and charge him with a false belief, or we can cover his disagreement with other people by assigning a different meaning to his words (following M_4). In effect, we expand the range of acceptable translation manuals by casting our hermeneutical net more widely, as we simultaneously translate his words and chart his attitudes; in one case we hold meaning constant across different speakers and attribute to them different beliefs, while in the other we assign them different meanings but the same beliefs. Because the difference between M_3 and M_4 has to be matched by compensatory changes in speakers' beliefs, this second form of indeterminacy is non-trivial, unlike the indeterminacy that afflicts the choice between Fahrenheit and Celsius temperature scales. There is no easy way to calibrate the two translation manuals, although there is a complicated way, and this reflects the fact that M_3 and M_4, considered together with their complementary assignments of content to speakers' beliefs, supply empirically equivalent methods for interpreting single, invariant structure of native sentences.

These arguments for indeterminacy are essentially sceptical arguments, and Quine draws from them the sceptical conclusion that there is "no fact of the matter"[24] whether someone's words mean that he sees a rabbit, or that he sees undetached rabbit parts; or that someone does, or does not, mean what others do by his words "blue" and "green". Quine embraces the sceptical conclusion as congenial to his behaviourism, that "all there is for semantics to be right or wrong about" is "dispositions to behavior" (1990: 101), and no set dispositions to behaviour, however codified, can fix a determinate translation for a speaker's sentences.

Davidson endorses the indeterminacy arguments, and he praises Quine for having "saved the philosophy of language as a serious subject by showing how it could be pursued without what there cannot be: determinate meanings" (Davidson 2001a: 145). He rejects Quine's behaviourism, however, and the sceptical conclusion he draws from its conjunction with the indeterminacy thesis: that there are no semantic facts. In place of Quine's semantic nihilism, Davidson reconceives meaning, as given by a theory of meaning, as a core concept in a unified theory of an agent's actions and attitudes.[25]

Holism implies that in assigning a certain meaning to a single utterance, an interpreter has already chosen one of a number of competing theories of interpretation to interpret his overall language. Choosing that theory, in turn, presupposes that she has identified in the speaker's utterances, actions and attitudes a pattern or structure that she takes that theory to describe at least as well as any other. Herein lies the indeterminacy of interpretation, then, for that theory does *only* at least as well as any other; in other words, others do equally well. There is, therefore, no more an objective basis for choosing one theory of meaning over another than there is for preferring the Fahrenheit to the Celsius scale for temperature ascriptions.

This conclusion, however, has no sceptical implications, for, by assumption, each theory or system of temperature ascriptions does equally well at describing *the same structure*. And for Davidson, it is that structure to which we refer when we speak of a speaker's meaning: "what a speaker means is what is invariant in all correct ways of interpreting him" (Davidson 1999a: 81). Whether there is a "fact of the matter" about the contents of a speaker's intentional states (including his meaning this or that by his words), therefore, is really a question about the reality of that pattern or, better, whether there are objective grounds for saying that that pattern exists. And that pattern, whether it is the pattern of a speaker's meanings and attitudes, or the pattern made by a system's energy states, is as real as patterns can be – patterns are properties of systems of objects. The objectivity of patterns depends on whether there are objective criteria for attributing those properties to their objects; the sceptical conclusion would follow, therefore, only if there were no such criteria. The arguments for the indeterminacy of interpretation do not prove *that*, however, for the indeterminacy thesis emerges from a thought experiment that involves imposing powerful logical and empirical constraints on a relatively rich body of data. (Those data are rich, in as much as they include descriptions not only of an agent's bodily movements, but also some of his attitudes; but they are only *relatively* rich, since those attitudes are non-individuative.) And those constraints, together with the data, do supply objective criteria for attributing patterns of properties to subjects and their actions and attitudes, albeit patterns that permit competing descriptions. The proper moral to draw from the indeterminacy arguments, therefore, is that there are no such things as *meanings*, understood as determinate objects or values that could be identified apart from considering the complex of an agent's actions and attitudes. This is quite different from any form of semantic scepticism or nihilism; it is, rather, a more modest and at the same time a more interesting conclusion, that the way that much of the philosophical tradition has conceived meaning is wrong-headed.[26] In its place, as we shall see in the following sections, Davidson offers a vision of meaning grounded in the interactions between interlocutors and their shared environment.

Chapter 5

Interpretation and meaning

We are now in a position – or almost in a position – to ask a key question about Davidson's philosophy of language; namely, how can we know whether a theory of meaning that meets the desiderata of Chapter 2, and is constructed along the lines set out in Chapters 3 and 4, can play the role Davidson identifies for it as part of a unified theory of interpretation? I turn to this question in §5.4. First, I need to say more about the way Davidson reconceives the concept of meaning in light of his account of interpretation; and we need to see, too, what further knowledge someone brings to bear when she employs a theory of interpretation to make sense of a speaker's utterance.

5.1 Holism and meaning

Davidson writes at one point that "to give truth conditions is a way of giving the meaning of a sentence", but he immediately modulates his thesis as the claim that knowing a truth theory for a language "amounts, in one good sense we can give to the phrase, to understanding the language" (1984a: 24). The difference is important. Holism implies that the meaning that any one *T*-theorem attributes to a sentence is bound up with the semantic assignments the theory makes to other expressions of the language, and these interdependencies run deeper than the observation that to interpret "Schnee ist weiss" it might be helpful first to know the meaning of "Das ist weiss." Combining the context principle, that a word's meaning is its contribution to the meaning of the sentences in which it occurs, with the principle that the meaning of a sentence is a function of its structure and the meanings of its parts, it follows that the interdependence of sentences through their sharing of words bears on the *constitution*, and not merely our *knowledge*, of a sentence's meaning. It thus makes no sense to speak of any one sentence's having meaning apart from the interpretation of a substantial fragment of the language. Hence, Davidson writes, while "Frege said that only in the context of a sentence does a word have meaning ... he might have added [in the same vein] that only in the context of the language does a sentence ... have meaning" (1984a: 22). A salutary consequence of this result is that it subverts the all-too-easy feeling, in looking at the *T*-sentences one by one, that they are all trivial; and, conversely, it is precisely this interconnectedness of meanings that makes the project of interpreting someone's words tractable.

A second consequence is that if language is holistic in this fashion, then there is no such thing as meaning in the sense that traditional conceptualists like Aristotle or Locke, or contemporary semantic atomists like Jerry Fodor, contend; namely, some discrete quantum that an interpreter grasps when she understands a speaker's words.

For Aristotle, words symbolize affections (*pathemata*) of the soul, where these states are representations or likenesses of objects. (These representations are the concepts of "conceptualism".) Because the mechanism by which a mental state represents an object involves the mind's being directly related, in a certain way, to that object, semantic relations are *punctate* in the sense that "one thing could bear [a semantic relation] to the world, even if nothing else did" (Fodor & Lepore 1992: 32).[1] Locke's theory of meaning differs in essential ways from Aristotle's, but like Aristotle Locke grounds meaning in a discrete quality or entity, which he famously calls an *idea*, the presence of which in a speaker's mind is caused by his relation to whatever the idea represents.[2] Thus Aristotelian and Lockean philosophies of language both treat a speaker's meaning as something fixed and determinate in his mind; in this way, meaning something by one's words is like holding a coin in one's pocket, and having a conversation is a matter of a speaker's somehow arranging that a typewise identical but tokenwise different "coin" appears in his interlocutor's pocket.

As Davidson reconceives it, however, meaning something by one's words is more like buying something on credit than it is having a penny in one's pocket. When we explain a person's commerce with others as a credit transaction, we *inter alia* treat him as participating in a money economy, and thence explain his actions in terms of economics, rather than biologically or ethologically. Explaining his actions as economic behaviour, in turn, is a matter of describing and evaluating the pattern of his actions and interactions (his obtaining products or services from other people) in terms of prices and values. Someone fixes his roof, and we explain this relationship by mentioning economic concepts (such as *price*) and non-economic ones (like *being a roof*); we relate these to one another so that they satisfy economic principles, such as that the value he places on having his roof fixed equals the price he is willing to spend to have it repaired; and we say that he spends part of his credit balance to pay the roofer. Notice, now, that his act of purchasing a new roof on credit – as opposed to his paying for it by handing over coins or paper money – cannot be described *as such* without embedding it in a more inclusive account of his economic actions and relations. Further, that description neither relies upon any hypostatized vehicle to carry the value of goods and services he receives, nor supposes that that value is determinate beyond what is implicit in the pattern made by the complex relationship he bears to the seller and to the assorted (non-monetary) objects and events involved in their interaction. Measuring his credit in dollars, pounds, euros or pesos makes no difference to our explanation, since that pattern is invariant under such a change.

Understanding a person's sentences likewise involves discerning patterns in her actions, but no hypostatized meanings. When we interpret someone's words we treat her as a rational agent, and we explain her behaviour in terms of reasons rather than biology. Explaining her behaviour as the actions of a rational agent, in turn, consists in describing and evaluating the pattern her actions, especially her utterances, make in terms of psychological, semantic and other concepts. She utters the vocables "Das ist ein Kaninchen", and we explain her behaviour by bringing into play concepts like belief, intention and truth, as well as the concept of *being a rabbit*; we relate these concepts to one another in accordance with charity and other principles, for example, that people's beliefs are usually true and that they generally assert what they believe; and we explain that she means that the object she is pointing to is a rabbit. In explaining her actions in this way or as having that meaning, we set those actions in the context of the information we have of her psychology, history and situation in the world; and we avoid positing any "meaning entities". And as in the buying-on-credit example, we do not suppose that what she means by her words is determinate beyond what we can discern in the pattern made by her situated behaviour. Finally, there will be a degree of indeterminacy in how we interpret her, but the difference between saying she meant that something is a rabbit, and that it is undetached rabbit parts, comes out as trivial: the pattern of her situated behaviour is invariant, and seeing that pattern is what understanding her speech behaviour amounts to.

Fodor's analysis of meaning is more sophisticated than Locke's, and his theory differs from Aristotle's, too. Like these earlier thinkers, however, Fodor argues that words inherit their meanings from corresponding mental states, and these mental states, in turn, represent the (external) objects that cause them. One difference, not germane to our present subject, is that Fodor believes that these mental representations are symbols in a mental language; thus Fodor speaks of mental symbols in a "language of thought" where Locke envisages non-linguistic ideas. Essentially, for Fodor, a mental representation R in Kurt's language of thought means a rabbit if and only if (a) whenever he sees a rabbit, Kurt thinks R, and (b) he only thinks R when he sees a rabbit.[3] An immediate consequence of this conception is that Fodor, like Aristotle and Locke, treats each word's meaning as capable of existing in isolation from other meanings.

Fodor complements his positive, non-holistic account of meaning with arguments that directly attack holism, some of which appear in his book on holism with Ernest Lepore.[4] This is not the place to rehearse these arguments, but we can get a sense of his opposition if we consider an intuition that seems to drive it. This intuition is the idea that if holism is true, and the meaning of a person's words depends on their systematic role in her language, then no two people ever speak the same language. But

> then a certain standard picture of how communication ... work[s] would seem to be in jeopardy. This picture is that the linguistic and theoretical commitments of speaker and hearer can overlap partially to any degree you like ... This

> would seem to be essential to reconciling the idea that languages have an interpersonal, social existence with the patent truth that no two speakers of the same language ever speak exactly the same dialect of that language.
>
> (Fodor & Lepore 1992: 10)[5]

According to holism, the meanings you intend to associate with your words are constituted by their role in your *total* idiolect, and the meanings I associate with your words are constituted by their place in the *complete* theory of meaning I formulate for your language using my language. Given, then, the differences between our respective idiolects, and the contingencies that afflict interpretation, it is inconceivable that your intentions and my theory should overlap at all, and therefore it is inconceivable how the holist can explain the possibility of communication and the social character of language.

Davidson meets this charge by rejecting the "standard picture" of language and communication that informs the philosophies of both Fodor and his conceptualist forebears. This picture treats linguistic understanding, in effect, as an interpreter's decoding the message a speaker has encoded in a language they partially share, in the sense that the rules an interpreter uses to decode and thus map a speaker's words onto her ideas are the inverse of the conventions the speaker uses to map onto his words the meanings he intends to communicate. Thus two people can converse with one another to the extent that their "linguistic and theoretical commitments ... overlap", and holism poses a threat since it writes into these rules – which are supposed to function as encryption/decryption conventions used to encode/decode ideas into words and vice versa – the idiosyncrasies of a speaker's idiolect. Davidson rejects two key elements of this picture: that languages are systems of shared conventions and, more generally, that interpretation and conversation consist in encoding and decoding meanings into words. As we shall see in §5.3, Davidson's rejecting the first element does not imply, as should be obvious from what we have seen so far of Davidson's philosophy, that meaning is somehow private.

The present point is that as Davidson reconceives it, interpreting a person's utterances is not a matter of matching his words and sentences with discrete ideas, mental representations or any other sort of meaning-bodies. As we have seen, when someone interprets a speaker's utterance, she bases that interpretation on an account she constructs of his actions and attitudes; and she partly bases that construction, in turn, on her interpretation of his utterances. Thus her interpretation is one element in an overall picture she draws of his life as a rational animal, and in this picture the presence or absence of some mental entity in the speaker's mind plays no role. The goal of interpretation, rather than decoding a message that originates hidden in a speaker's mind, is to make what David Wiggins calls "total sense" of a speaker: an "interpreter's linguistic efforts are part of the larger effort to interact successfully with others, to coordinate one's efforts with theirs (where appropriate), to make sense of them, and so on" (Wiggins 1997: 18). The goal of interpretation is not to map meanings onto a speaker's words, but to understand the role his utterance of those words plays in his life, which, in her being his audience, intersects with the life of the interpreter. In this interaction a semantic theory is one tool an interpreter uses to think systematically about the pattern of an agent's actions, and to find order in the multiplicity and multiformity of his utterances and other actions. Our interest in the concept of meaning, therefore, is the role attributions of meaning play in explanations (making "total sense") of people's behaviour.

As we urged at the end of the preceding section, this thesis is not a sceptical thesis, in as much as the concept of linguistic meaning retains a central role in any account of human action. It does entail, though, repudiating a traditional notion of "the" meaning of a word or sentence as a discrete quantum of information that speakers and their interpreters communicate to one another. This follows from the indeterminacy arguments, together with the observation that what matters is never the interpretation of an isolated utterance, but rather the relation that utterance bears to the complex situation that embeds it. And that relation can no more be described in isolation from the rest of his life than can we treat someone's credit purchase in isolation from a network of other economic events. Thus Davidson, as the editors of a recent volume on his philosophy put it, "replace[s] talk of meanings with talk of interpretive theories of speakers" (Kotatko *et al*. 2001: ix).

5.2 First meaning, metaphor and use

Davidson's account of the role that a theory of truth-cum-meaning plays in understanding a speaker's utterances needs further qualification. Consider that when Shakespeare's Fool chides Lear that he has "mad'st thy daughters thy mothers" by dividing his kingdom between Goneril and Regan, the Fool says something that is literally false: Goneril and Regan – Cordelia is not included in this company – remain Lear's daughters, of course, *not* his mothers. Of course, this literal-minded criticism of the Fool misses the significance of his wise and clever reproof, namely, that when Lear unburdened himself of his crown he surrendered his claim to authority in his family and in Britain. The point here is that if we interpret the Fool's words only by citing the *T*-sentence of the Fool's English,

> "Thou mad'st thy daughters thy mothers" spoken by Lear's Fool at I.iv.163–4 is $\text{true}_{\textit{English}}$ if and only if Lear made his daughters his mothers,

then we miss the *metaphorical* or *figurative* force of the Fool's utterance, which is an intrinsic feature of his speech act. There are a host of different accounts of metaphor, and Davidson has his own; more generally, we should observe that a Davidsonian theory of interpretation for a language captures only part of what Shakespeare's audience understands when the Fool chides Lear. It captures the *literal*, or as Davidson prefers, the *first meaning*,[6] of the speaker's words, and there is more to an audience's grasp of what the Fool is up to than their grasp of his literal meaning. This is the case not just for figurative language, for there are myriad uses to which speakers put their sentences: to issue commands, ask questions, tell jokes, say something ironical, hurl an insult and so on. The point is that the total significance of these speech acts exceeds the content that any theory of first meaning attributes to what speakers say.

A standard way to capture this further component of meaning is to single out *pragmatics* as a branch within linguistics or the philosophy of language. As distinct from semantics,[7] pragmatics is an account of the uses to which speakers put language to achieve their purposes, including especially purposes other than to communicate truths about the world (although pragmatics involves the study of these purposes, too). Pragmatics typically refers to the contexts in which a speaker uses a certain form of words, where these circumstances may stray far from language, for example, they may mention rules that a community uses to license a group of people to issue orders of a certain sort in a given circumstance. It describes the properties those words have in virtue of their being used in those contexts, especially properties that bear on the effects those uses have upon the speaker's audience, which, again, may stray far from linguistic effects, such as having the audience perform some (non-linguistic) actions.

Hilary Putnam describes the meaning of an expression as supplying a "coarse grid laid over [its] use", and Higgenbotham usefully reverses this figure to describe the relation between the subject matters of semantics and pragmatics.[8] The first meanings considered in semantics are a core of meaning that belongs to a speaker's words, and the use to which he puts those words (reversing Putnam's image) is a grid he lays over that meaning to specialize it, for example, to use those words with that meaning to make a promise or ask a question. A particular use (promising, ordering, asking, etc.) is the *illocutionary act* that a speaker performs in executing a given *locutionary act*: the making of certain sounds intended as having some definite (first) meaning.[9] Equivalently, we may speak of different *illocutionary forces*, for example, of asserting, commanding, querying and so on, attaching to some given locutionary act. Thus there may be typewise-identical locutionary acts, to each of which someone attaches a different illocutionary force, as when the prosecuting barrister and jury foreman each utters the sentence "She is guilty", which is true just in case the indicated person (i.e. the accused standing in the dock) is guilty. In uttering the sentence, the prosecuting barrister *accuses* her, while by his utterance of the same (i.e. typewise-identical) sentence, the foreman *convicts* her. More generally, we can describe the locutionary content shared by a set of semantically related speech acts – for example, "The door is shut", "Is the door shut?", "Please shut the door", "Would that the door be shut" and so on – by representing the first meaning common to each utterance as a truth condition,

(1) "The door is shut" is $\text{true}_{English}$ at time *t* if and only if the door is shut at *t*,

assigned by a Davidsonian theory of meaning. Different forces, then, are laid over (1) to arrive at the different speech acts ("The door is shut", "Is the door shut?", etc.). Conversely, we can imagine the common core represented by (1) as being abstracted from several speech acts by factoring those acts into their forces and locutionary contents. A *complete* theory interpretation for a speaker, therefore, necessarily incorporates some account of force, and it describes how interpreters discern in an utterance both the first meaning associated with the locutionary act performed in that utterance and the illocutionary force that attaches to that locutionary act.[10]

Davidson's main contribution to pragmatics is a negative one. He agrees that a competent interpreter grasps more than the literal meaning of a speaker's words; this much is evident from considering the Fool's metaphor. A theory of interpretation, therefore, will need to include a pragmatics of force in addition to a theory of meaning modelled on a Tarski-style theory of truth. Davidson denies, however, a common claim among philosophers of language: that it is possible to construct a theory that shows how a speech act's force systematically derives from linguistic and non-linguistic conventions to which speakers and their interpreters are party. For example, there might on such a view – which, again, Davidson rejects – be a convention such that (i) if a speaker does not possess some information, and (ii) his audience will not provide that information unless asked, then a sentence the speaker utters in the interrogative mood is a question.[11] In general, for each type of illocutionary act a theory of force specifies a conventional setting or set of circumstances under which a speaker's uttering a sentence in a given grammatical mood (indicative, imperative, interrogative, etc.) constitutes a speech act with a corresponding illocutionary force (assertion, command, query, etc.).

Davidson grants that there are discernible patterns in the ways that speakers make assertions and ask questions, but he denies that a speech act has its force in virtue of *conventions* that speakers follow in performing their actions. It is surely true that speakers often employ particular grammatical forms when they ask questions and express wishes, and interpreters exploit these facts to formulate rules of thumb for figuring out what illocutionary force attaches to speakers' locutionary acts. However, speakers just as often contravene such rules and yet, as Davidson puts it, they "get away with it", that is, their audiences recognize the illocutionary force they intend their utterances to have. A speaker may, for example, utter a sentence in the interrogative mood, "Did you see the ugly tie Fred was wearing?" and intend by his words *to assert* that Fred's tie is ugly, not query his co-worker about her attention to Fred's choice of neckwear. And as long as there are sufficient clues in the speaker's behaviour or the context of his utterance, he will get away with it, that is, his interpreter will understand him.

Or, to vary the example, suppose that a speaker *does* intend to ask a question by uttering an interrogative, and moreover that he intends to realize this intention by respecting a convention he shares with his audience. As long as his audience believes that he intends to respect the convention, and to utter a question by that respectful utterance, all goes well. However, if his audience does not discern his intention to perform a conventional act, then the convention and his respecting it are idle. Thus what matters is not so much his respecting the convention as his audience's discerning that he intentionally conforms to the convention as a means to his realizing his intention to ask a question; he could have employed some other means to that end and, as long as his audience discerned that he intentionally engaged in that behaviour (whatever it was) as a means to realizing that illocutionary intention, he would have got away with it. It turns out, then, that the particular means – conforming to a convention, or whatever – he selects as his means for realizing his illocutionary intention is not important. What is important, rather, is that his audience discerns the intentions that lie behind his utterance; as long as they do discern that he intentionally does something, and that doing that is his way of asking a question or making a promise, a speaker will succeed at whatever speech act he wants, everything else being equal. Unless, indeed, speakers can get away with it, without their audiences' sharing their conventional practices, radical interpretation would be impossible.

The same point can be made without appeal to radical interpretation. Liars and poets typically represent themselves (or their characters, if they are dramatic poets) as making honest assertions as a matter of course, and in so doing their verbal behaviour may satisfy all the conventional criteria of assertion. *Ex hypothesi*, though, they are *not* sincerely asserting. Consider, for example, a play that contains

> a scene in which there is supposed to be a fire. (Albee's *Tiny Alice*, for example.) It is [the actor's] role to imitate as persuasively as he can a man who is trying to warn others of a fire. "Fire!" he screams. And perhaps he adds, at the behest of the

> author, "I mean it! Look at the smoke!", etc. And now a real fire breaks out, and the actor tries vainly to warn the real audience. "Fire!" he screams, "I mean it! Look at the smoke!"
> (Davidson 1984a: 269–70)

To make his fictive warning convincing, the actor will exploit any conventional devices available to him, but having represented himself while in character as commanding "Run for your lives!", he cannot rely upon the grammatical form of an imperative or other conventional device to alert the audience when he steps out of character. Certainly, the audience *will* discern the difference – discern, in the one case, that he intends to warn them, and in the other that he intends merely to entertain them – even if they smell no smoke; but no formal roadmap or device is of any use to the audience unless they know what he is up to, that is, unless they discern his intentions in his exploiting those devices.

These remarks apply to our earlier discussion of metaphor in the following way. A common thought among philosophers and literary theorists is that when an interpreter grasps a speaker's metaphor, they locate in his words a second or metaphorical sense in addition to or displacing the first meaning of his words. When an author of Genesis writes that "the Spirit of God moved upon the face of the waters", for example, the metaphor works (on this view) because the reader interprets "face" in its *second* sense, in which animals, clocks *and* waters satisfy the open sentence "*x* has a face", rather than its first sense, in which only animals and clocks satisfy it. And because, presumably, we share some convention with the author we know to assign to his words this second meaning in addition to or in place of their first meaning. An advantage of this treatment of metaphor is that it creates a sense in which a sentence containing a metaphor is true: one might say, metaphorically true.

This description perhaps captures the mechanism underlying neologism, where a new meaning is given to old words, but it misses what is most striking about metaphor. To see this, consider the case of a *dead metaphor*, which is akin to neologism. Suppose that clocks were at first said to have faces only figuratively, but that this first sense of "face" – in which it refers only to the front part of animals' heads – was eventually displaced by a second sense in which the word means the front part of animals' heads *or* the front part of clocks. This sort of thing often occurs, and it is one way that a natural language grows. In using a living metaphor ("the face of the waters"), though, unlike using a dead one ("the face of the clock"), an author is not so much doing something *linguistically* new or novel as he is using an old word or phrase to provoke his audience to see something – water, or a foolish old man – in a different light.

To say that the effect of metaphor is to provoke one's audience is pat, but Davidson's urging us to seek the mechanism of metaphor in pragmatics rather than semantics is not. His idea is that metaphor is akin to an illocutionary force that attaches to someone's words, and that as in the cases of assertion, query and so on, an audience has to discern that the speaker or author intends his words to be taken metaphorically. One significant clue they will depend on, to figure this out, is their perceiving a tension between the literal meaning of those words and what they take him (or his character) to believe. To understand the Fool's words as a metaphor, we the audience have to see the tension between the literal meaning of his sentence, "Thou mad'st thy daughters thy mothers", and his not really believing (of course) that Lear has, in fact, made his daughters his mothers. Recognizing this strain – again, that the Fool intentionally says something he believes to be false – is the key to our interpreting his utterance as his clever way of remarking upon the foolishness of Lear's action. If we do not grasp the first meaning of his words, the Fool fails to perform a successful locutionary act; and if we fail to see that he says something he does not believe, then his utterance just leaves us confused. We are left wondering "How can he assert *that*?" when the point is that he is not *asserting* that sentence: he is, rather, speaking metaphorically.[12] Perceiving the tension between his meaning and his beliefs, we become the co-conspirators with the Fool that we need to be, if he is going to get away with his metaphor. The point, then, is that our joining him and his getting away with it depend precisely on our keeping the first meaning of his words in full view, and at the same time discerning what he wants to get away with.

5.3 Communication without conventions

Davidson thus denies that conventions play a philosophically important role in pragmatics, and this negative thesis has a semantic counterpart in his denial that "there is no such thing as a language, not if a language is anything like what most philosophers and linguists have supposed" (Davidson 1986c: 446). The qualifying clause – "not if a language is anything like what most philosophers and linguists have supposed" – is crucial, the point being that most philosophers and linguists, but *not* Davidson, agree that "First meanings are governed by learned conventions. The systematic knowledge or competence of a speaker or interpreter is learned in advance of occasions of interpretation and is conventional in nature" (*ibid.*: 436). Davidson therefore rejects any role for conventions in semantics, just as he did for pragmatics.

Critics have attacked Davidson's statement as linguistic nihilism and as inconsistent with his own earlier writings on theories of truth-cum-meaning. Michael Dummett, for example, wonders how an investigation of linguistic phenomena can

> lead to the conclusion that there is no such thing as a language. Oppressive governments, such as those of Franco and Mussolini, attempt to suppress minority language; under such regimes teachers punish children for speaking those languages in the playground. In India, crowds demonstrate against the proposal to make Hindi the sole official language. Bretons, Catalans, Basques and Kurds each declare that their language is the soul of their culture. The option does not seem to be open to us to declare that such governments and such peoples are under an illusion that there is anything they are suppressing or cherishing. (1986: 465)

And Ian Hacking ponders the implications of Davidson's apparent linguistic nihilism ("there is no such thing as a language") for the philosophy of language. "Is there no longer language for there to be philosophy of? … True-in-*L* is at the heart of Davidson's philosophy. What is left, is there no such thing as an *L*?" (Hacking 1986: 447).

While Davidson's thesis is radical, however, it is also carefully modulated and not nihilistic. First, his thesis leaves room for the existence of what Ferdinand de Saussure calls "*parole*", the use of articulate signs by a speaker or writer in her interaction with an audience, and it is this that the philosophy of language studies.

> It is only by employing such concepts as word and sentence that we can give a systematic description of the linguistic

> aspects of linguistic behavior and aptitudes. ... The main point of the concept of a language ... is to enable us to give a coherent description of speakers, and of what speakers and their interpreters know that allows them to communicate.
> (Davidson 2001a: 109)

The concepts of language, sentence, word and so on can be suitably defined as certain sorts of abstract objects and structures, but until an interpreter gives one of those structures empirical content by using it to explain an agent's behaviour, it is of no more philosophical interest than any other mathematical object.[13] The apparent novelty that Davidson introduces into his philosophy, when he says "there is no such thing as a language", is that the theory an interpreter constructs when she explains a speaker's utterances is always a work in progress, and this point was always implicit in Davidson's methodology. An interpreter approaches her subject with a theory based on what she knows in advance about the speaker; as she observes his situated interactions with herself and their surroundings, she acquires new evidence she can use to revise her theory of interpretation and replace it with a new and improved one; and each time she returns to interpret him anew she tailors her theory to his current linguistic behaviour.[14]

Secondly, Davidson's iconoclasm is consistent with the existence of a language, considered as a set of social practices codified by a system of conventions (Saussure's *la langue*), and with the value many communities associate with their native tongues. We can say that two speakers, but not a third, share a language in this sense if the idiolects of the first two, but not the third, tend to converge in their using typewise-similar sound patterns to express similar thoughts; "and once this idea is properly tidied up it is only a short and uninteresting step to defining the predicate 'is a language' in a way that corresponds, as nearly as possible, with ordinary usage" (Davidson 1994b: 3). Thus Breton, for example, can be defined as a smooth curve drawn through the idiosyncratic linguistic habits of members of a certain population in north-western France. Apart from the moral, social and political significance that attaches to partitioning groups of people based on their linguistic habits, however, there in nothing *philosophically* important about this notion of a language. This is why Davidson starts with idiolects and takes a common language to be an abstraction from them, where other philosophers start with a common language and define a speaker's idiolect as her idiosyncratic departures from the norm.

In place of a common language defined by a set of conventions, Davidson presents a picture of speakers getting away with their locutionary acts that parallels his account of illocutionary force. If a speaker intends to mean that snow is white by his uttering the sentence "Schnee ist weiss", and his audience understands him to have meant that snow is white by his utterance, then he means and communicates to his interlocutors that snow is white by saying "Schnee ist weiss." The keystone of this picture is that a speaker gets away with his locutionary act if his audience discerns the intention behind his utterance, that is, if they come to believe that he intends the sounds he makes to mean what, in fact, he intends to mean. What speakers' words mean just is what they intend them, and what they are understood, to mean.

> Meaning ... gets its life from those situations in which someone intends ... that his words will be understood in a certain way, and they are. In such cases we can say without hesitation: how he intends to be understood, and was understood, is what he, and his words, literally meant on that occasion .... Thus for me the concept of "the meaning" of a word or sentence gives way to the concepts of how a speaker intends his words to be understood, and of how a hearer understands them. (Davidson 1994b: 11–12)

Davidson arrives at this conclusion by reflecting on "misuses" of language.

> We may smile at someone who says "Lead the way and we'll precede", or, with Archie Bunker, "We need a few laughs to break up the monogamy". ... [but] what is interesting is that fact that in all these cases the hearer has no trouble understanding the speaker in the way the speaker intends.
> (Davidson 1986c: 434)

These verbal miscues are *malaprops*, which Hacking's "old *Concise Oxford*" defines as instances of "a ludicrous use of a word, esp[ecially] in mistake for one resembling it" (Hacking 1986: 449). The humour in Davidson's examples is inessential, though; the point is that when Archie Bunker utters the sentence "We need a few laughs to break up the monogamy", he intends his words to mean that we need a few laughs to break up the monotony, and we understand him to mean that we need a few laughs to break up the monotony. He intends to means this, and we understand him to mean this, therefore, he does mean *this*, despite the fact that by the standards or conventions of English, he says something *else*. Indeed, were we to interpret his utterance otherwise, we would *mis*understand him. Communication can succeed, not only in the absence of conventions, as in radical interpretation, but also despite them.

Adopting the perspective of the speaker, if I assert a proposition, I want my interlocutor to know that I am asserting something, and I want her to know the content of my assertion; and the same goes, *mutatis mutandis*, if I want to ask a question or issue a command. I want her, in other words, to recognize in my utterance both its intended illocutionary force and its intended locutionary content. Therefore, if I want to assert a proposition, it behoves me to adopt a strategy that maximizes the likelihood that my audience will successfully discern the force and first meaning I intend to attach to my speech act. Exploiting shared conventions is one such strategy. If there are conventions to which we are both party, and if, therefore, each of us connects certain linguistic forms with certain forces and meanings, then as long as she knows that I intend to act in accord with those conventions she will know what I mean by my words, and communication will proceed easily. And given the premium that communication places on speed and efficiency, there is often considerable pressure to pursue this course. At most, though, the existence of conventions is a happy circumstance, and communication is possible, if somewhat less effortless, in their absence. This last point is implicit in Davidson's approach to meaning from the start and, indeed, it is already present in Quine's account of radical translation; for unless we can translate or interpret a speaker's words without being party to the linguistic or other conventions that surround his verbal behaviour, radical translation and interpretation are impossible.

An attractive feature of this conception of language, as Bjørn Ramberg puts it, is its "exorcis[ing] the ghosts of reification from [our] thinking about communication" (1989: 2). Quine began this process in *Word and Object* when he purged Platonic and Lockean meanings from semantics, and Davidson carries the project further and rids the philosophy of language of additional detritus from the tradition. This detritus includes the notion of a language as a repository of meanings, which Davidson replaces with an emphasis on the communicative interactions between speakers and their interpreters.

> The sole source of linguistic meaning is the intentional production of tokens of sentences. If such acts did not have meanings, nothing would. There is no harm in assigning meanings to sentences, but this must always be a meaning derived from concrete occasions of which sentences are put to use. (Davidson 1993c: 298)

Sentences are put to use by speakers who want to communicate with their interpreters, who, in turn, use their own sentences to track the meaning they associate with speakers' utterances. On the one hand, then, the point about there being "no harm in assigning meanings to sentences" is a bit of hyperbole, since in practice the *only* way for interpreters to make sense of speakers involves assigning meanings to sentences; on the other hand, though, that reference to harm alludes to the real threat that a reified conception of language poses to the philosophy of language.

One reason some philosophers think of languages as systems of conventions that speakers are obliged to follow is to capture the (putative) normativity of meaning. To see their point, suppose a man Bert says that he suffers from arthritis in his thigh, and that he makes this complaint sincerely. Then Bert makes a mistake: he uses the term "arthritis" in a way that is inconsistent with its meaning, since arthritis is a disease that afflicts joints only, and not muscles or ligaments. Now suppose, too, there is a second man $Bert_2$, who resembles his twin in every respect, except that his linguistic community associates with the vocable "arthritis" *our* concept of, say, twarthritis, which *is* a disease of the joints, muscles and ligaments. When $Bert_2$ complains about an arthritic pain in his thigh, then, he makes no mistake. What this shows according to Tyler Burge is that languages are constituted by the conventions of a speaker's linguistic community; for if they were not, and each speaker associated his own idiosyncratic concepts with his words, then there would be no grounds to convict Bert, and to absolve $Bert_2$, of a mistake. And since, intuitively, that is exactly what we want to do, Burge argues that Bert's (and $Bert_2$'s) language is governed by his community's norms, and it exists in advance of and apart from Bert's linguistic behaviour.

There is a second, deeper worry lurking in the idea that languages are reified systems of norms. Suppose that before 1 January 2001 Bert had used the word "arthritis" only to describe diseases of the joints, even when he had occasion to talk about pains he felt in his muscles; but after that date he speaks of arthritic pains in his joints *and* muscles. Should we say (a) that Bert associates *one* concept with the word "arthritis" in the twentieth century, and later he associates a *different* concept with it in the twenty-first? Should we say, in other words, that in the new millennium Bert puts a *new* meaning on an old vocable? Or should we say (b) that his concept has *not* changed, where that concept is (and was) defined as follows:

- If t is before 1 January 2001, then o satisfies "x suffers from arthritis" at t if and only if o suffers from a disease of the joints at t;
- If t is on or after 1 January 2001, then o satisfies "x suffers from arthritis" at t if and only if o suffers from a disease of the joints or ligaments at t.

If this is what Bert means (and meant), then the apparent change in his usage is *merely* apparent, that is, he continues to use the same word with the same (peculiar) meaning.

The deeper worry, then, is whether there *is* a difference between scenarios (a) and (b), for that putative difference makes no difference to any fact about Bert's behaviour. Worse, if Bert should (apparently?) change what he means by "arthritis" at some time in the future – to describe, say, male-pattern baldness – then we could always devise a further, odder concept to accommodate *that* use. If the difference between these conceptual scenarios makes no difference to anything Bert does or says, so the sceptical argument runs, and there is no fact that he meant either one or the other, then we should say, too, that he meant *neither* one. In his famous study of Wittgenstein's private language argument, Saul Kripke cites the *Philosophical Investigations* to make this point.

> This was our paradox: no course of action could be determined by a rule, because every course of action can be made out to accord with the rule. The answer was: if everything can

> be made out to accord with the rule, it can be made out to conflict with it. And so there would be neither accord nor conflict here. (Wittgenstein 1958: §201, quoted in Kripke 1982: 7)

A correct use of the word "arthritis" cannot be determined by a concept Bert intends it to express, since *any* use he makes of it can be understood to accord with some concept we can interpret him to have intended; and if every use can be understood to accord with some concept, then every use can equally be understood to conflict with a concept; and hence there is neither accord nor conflict, nor any concept he intends to express. The only way out of the sceptical paradox, Kripke argues, is, once again, to appeal to the standards of his linguistic community.[16]

Davidson resists this sceptical conclusion by rejecting the assumption that drives it; namely, that languages are systems of norms codified by a community's conventions. In practice, the exigencies of easy communication coerce people to speak more or less as their fellows do, but this has nothing to do with the nature of meaning *per se*, which Davidson identifies with the invariant pattern a speaker's situated utterances and other actions make. Since that pattern is *ex hypothesi* the same whether Bert means arthritis or twarthritis, we can, everything else being equal, attribute to him either concept in pursuit of making the best overall sense of his linguistic and non-linguistic behaviour. That explanation may attribute to him a linguistic or conceptual mistake, or it may not, just as in §4.6 there were two ways to accommodate Davidson's idiosyncratic use of certain colour words; choosing one or the other will entail making compensatory adjustments elsewhere to our theory of interpretation for Bert, and consequently everything else will probably *not* be equal. But that choice carries no philosophical weight.

5.4 Meaning and interpretation

We are now ready to ask whether a theory of meaning, constructed according to the procedure outlined in Chapter 3, can play the role in a theory of interpretation that Davidson gives it. If someone knows the *T*-sentences for a speaker's language, can she relate his words to the world, on the one hand, and what she knows or believes about his attitudes, on the other, to make sense of his utterances? Is a Tarski-style theory of truth – adapted, revised and employed as a theory of meaning in the manner Davidson recommends – empirically adequate?

For Tarski, Convention *T* supplies the criterion for whether a theory of truth is empirically adequate, namely, that a theory θ "gets it right" just in case θ entails an appropriate *T*-sentence for every sentence of the object language. The way Tarski formulates his famous criterion, however, forecloses our using it to test the empirical adequacy of a theory of truth θ, if we want to press that theory into service as part of a theory of interpretation. For, as we saw in §3.1, in requiring that for every sentence *s* of *L*, an acceptable θ imply an appropriate theorem of the form

(*T*) *s* is true_L if and only if *p*,

where "*p*" is the *translation* of *s* into the metalanguage, Tarski builds into Convention *T* a reliance on a pretheoretical notion of *synonymy* or *sameness of meaning*. In appropriating Tarski's work, therefore, Davidson has needed to reconfigure its basis.

> While Tarski intended to analyse the concept of truth by appealing (in Convention T) to the concept of meaning (in the guise of sameness of meaning, or translation), I have the reverse in mind. I considered truth to be the central primitive concept, and hoped, by detailing truth's structure, to get at meaning.[17] (Davidson 1984a: xiv)

Dispensing with translation, Davidson shifts the conceptual load away from meaning on to truth, and rewrites Convention *T* to require that

> an acceptable theory of truth must entail, for every sentence *s* of the object language, a sentence of the form: *s* is true if and only if *p*, where "*p*" is replaced by any sentence that is true if and only if *s* is. Given this formulation, the theory is tested by the evidence that T-sentences are simply true; we have given up the idea that we must also tell whether what replaces "*p*" translates *s*. (*ibid*.: 134)

Note the key difference. Where Tarski employs the *intensional* notion of translation (synonymy across languages), Davidson substitutes the *extensional* criterion that the *T*-sentences "are simply true". The claim, then, is that as long as we can demonstrate that a theory meets this revised – and considerably weaker – criterion, we shall have shown that its *T*-sentences are interpretive and have shown, too, that it can do its duty in a theory of interpretation.

The difficulty Davidson faces is that meaning is a richer notion than truth. Recall, for example, Russell's theory of meaning from §2.2. We described the extensionality of Russell's account as an advantage of the theory, since its being extensional greatly simplifies the theory's background logic; having opted for a coarse grained treatment, though, the theory cannot distinguish between the meanings of materially equivalent sentences. This immediately has a bearing upon the *T*-sentences that a Davidsonian theory of meaning generates, because they, too, cannot distinguish materially equivalent sentences.

To see this, suppose we have a theory θ_1 that entails

(*T*) "Schnee ist weiss" is true_L if and only if snow is white.

If θ_1 is empirically adequate in the sense that it generates a true *T*-sentence for every sentence of the object language *L* (i.e. it satisfies Davidson's revised Convention *T*), then there is a theory θ_2 exactly like θ_1 except that in place of the interpreting condition on the right-hand side of (*T*) there appears a materially equivalent but non-synonymous metalanguage sentence, yielding:

(*S*) "Schnee ist weiss" is true_L if and only if grass is green.

If (*T*) is true, it follows that (*S*) is also true, for the following reason. The sentences "Snow is white" and "Grass is green" are materially equivalent, that is,

(2) Snow is white if and only if grass is green,

because they have the same truth-value; both are, as a matter of fact, true. The inference from (*T*) to (*S*), then, has the following form: *p* if and only if *q*, and *q* if and only if *r*, therefore, *p* if and only if *r*. That is, "Schnee ist weiss" is true_L if and only if snow is white; and snow is white if and only if grass is green; therefore, "Schnee ist weiss" is true_L if and only if grass is green. Thus θ_2 satisfies Davidson's revised Convention *T*, although it does not satisfy Tarski's original Convention *T*. Again, θ_1 and θ_2 differ in their assigning different interpretations to "Schnee ist weiss", but Davidson's revised Convention *T* cannot discriminate between them because the sentences that express those interpretations on the right-hand sides of (*T*) and (*S*) are alike in truth-value, and the "if and only if" connective is extensional. The point is that when it comes to distinguishing between sentences, truth is too coarse a filter to distinguish between materially equivalent sentences with different meanings.

In light of this problem, Davidson has further revised Convention *T*. He now maintains that the criterion for whether the theorems of a theory of meaning are interpretive

> is that the totality of T-sentences should ... optimally fit evidence about sentences held true by native speakers. ... A T-sentence ... can be used to interpret a [speaker's] sentence, then, provided we also know the theory that entails it, and know that it is a theory that meets the formal and empirical criteria. For if the constraints are adequate, the range of acceptable theories will be such that any of them yields some correct interpretation for each potential utterance.
>
> (Davidson 1984a: 139)

Let us take the several ideas crowded in this passage one by one. Recall how the process of interpreting another's sentences proceeds. Beginning with the evidence of a speaker's holding certain sentences true in situations that both he and his interpreter witness, the interpreter infers that the speaker holds those sentences true *if and only if* those situations exist; she (the interpreter) makes this inference based on the patterns she observes in his behaviour, together with the methodological principle that in the simplest cases sentences that speakers are caused to hold true by the occurrence of some event are usually about that event (where she discerns that an event causes a speaker to hold a sentence true in much the same way that she perceives any causal relation). At this initial stage of theory formation, an interpreter treats a speaker's utterances holophrastically, but to make progress beyond his perceptual sentences she adopts analytical hypotheses that segment his sentences into individual morphemes. These hypotheses, then, are adopted as postulates of her evolving theory of interpretation, and she derives further *T*-sentences, including especially *T*-sentences for the standing sentences of the speaker's language (i.e. those sentences that, unlike perceptual sentences, are not directly keyed to the speaker's immediate situation). As she continues to observe the speaker's actions, her theory of interpretation evolves to take into account new evidence as it presents itself.

What emerges from this picture is that when someone knows the *T*-sentences that interpret a language *L*, she knows those *T*-sentences *as theorems* of a theory of interpretation; she knows the complete theory to which they belong (since interpretation is interpretation of large chunks of speech behaviour, not utterances one by one), and she knows *that* the theory entails them (since, again, she knows individual *T*-sentences as consequences of a theory that applies to whole languages, or large fragments of language, not to utterances one by one). This is important for two reasons. First, an interpreter initially treats a speaker's sentences holophrastically, but to make any progress she has to rely on the way the postulates of her theory of interpretation systematically apportion semantic properties to the *parts* of his sentences; and this is true even of his perceptual sentences, once they are brought under the aegis of the theory. Davidson posits, then, that "what Tarski assumed outright for each T-sentence can be indirectly elicited by a holistic constraint" (Davidson 1984a: 139); namely, that what we lose by using a coarse-grained extensional criterion we (partly) recapture in as much as a theory of meaning *simultaneously* interprets infinitely many sentences in the form of infinitely many *T*-sentences. In other words, a theory of meaning comprises not only a correlation between *sentences* mentioned on the left-hand side of its *T*-sentences and their interpreting condition on the right, but also the assignment of reference and satisfaction conditions to the *terms* and *predicates* into which object-language sentences decompose. These assignments matter because as they ramify through the entire theory, deviant assignments can be expected in the long run to contradict the evidence provided by speakers' verbal behaviour. Hence, although the criterion stated in terms of truth does not prima facie filter out (*S*), because the standing sentence "Schnee ist weiss" *is* true just in case grass is green, assigning grass to the term "Schnee" and the property of being true just in case *x* is green to the open sentence "*x* ist weiss", will raise red flags, because those assignments make their contribution, for example, to *T*-sentences for sentences containing indexical elements, such as "Das ist schnee" and "Das ist weiss." Thus requiring that "the totality of T-sentences ... optimally fit", the evidence available to an interpreter will exclude θ_2 and its theorem (*S*).[18]

Secondly, in knowing that a true theory θ_1 logically implies (*T*),[19] we know much more than that (*T*) is true. In knowing that θ_1 logically implies (*T*) we know that (*T*) is true in *every possible world* in which θ_1 is true: anytime and anywhere θ_1 is true, (*T*) *must* be true. Thus, even if *L*-speakers lived in a world *W* in which snow were blue, it would still be the case that "Schnee ist weiss" is true_L if and only if snow is white. (Both sides of the biconditional (*T*) would be false.) Or, to take a different counterfactual circumstance, suppose that *L*-speakers lived in a world *W′* in which snow were white but grass were blue. Again, (*T*) would be true, but since in *W′* snow is white and grass is *not* green we cannot infer (*S*) from (*T*) by way of (2), since by hypothesis (2) is false.[20] Therefore, θ_1 and θ_2 are not logically equivalent; there are circumstances in which (*T*) is true but (*S*) is false. These are not, certainly, circumstances that *L*-speakers could encounter in the actual world of green grass, but circumstances they could be asked about by an interpreter who poses counterfactual questions to her subjects. ("Suppose grass were blue; would "Schnee ist weiss" be true_L if and only if grass is green?")[21]

A collection of *T*-theorems, however, is only as good as the theory that entails them; they are interpretive if the axioms of the theory are true. But what guarantee have we that the axioms *are* true? A theory of interpretation is an empirical theory, hence there is no *guarantee* that they are true. But if the theory meets the formal constraints described in Chapter 2, and it has been fashioned in accordance with the principles of charity outlined in Chapter 3, and the theory "optimally fit[s]" the evidence; then we ought to accept the theory as true, pending disconfirming evidence.

Our confidence in a particular *T*-sentence rises and falls, therefore, not only with its being true or false but also with its being entailed by a true theory of interpretation for the language. In turn, our confidence that a given theory of interpretation is true is a matter of how well that theory fulfils the desiderata set out by the principles of charity: roughly, how well the theory does at making speakers come out to be reasonable people. Finally, our confidence in the principles of charity depends on how well those principles express what it is to be a rational agent. For if those principles capture what we mean by calling a creature's doings rational – if they capture what it is for his behaviour to *make sense* and thus be interpretable – then a theory that is fashioned in accordance with and optimally satisfies those conditions will be a theory of interpretation for agent's actions and attitudes, and its theorems will show what an interpreter knows when she understands his utterances.

Chapter 6

Events and causes

In Chapters 1–5 we examined the theory of radical interpretation, which Davidson presents as a rational reconstruction of the exchange between speakers and their auditors. His purpose, we have seen, is to answer the Socratic-style question "What is meaning?" by setting it aside and answering the different, but related, query "What knowledge would suffice for an interpreter's understanding a speaker's words?" Davidson's idealized sketch of an interpreter's enterprise offers no insight into cognitive or social psychology, but it does lay bare the connections between the concept of linguistic meaning and a network of closely related notions, especially the concepts of knowledge or understanding, belief and desire, and action. It turns out, then, that Davidson's philosophy of language is part of a more general enterprise, and this confirms our observation in §1.2 that Davidson seeks, in effect, a unified theory of mind, language and action. Indeed, because Davidson characterizes meaning in terms of the reasons for which a speaker makes her utterance, the philosophy of language is properly a chapter in the theory of action and mind.

We turn our attention in Chapters 7 and 8 to Davidson's writings on action theory and the philosophy of mind, and in so doing we shall see their close connection to his philosophy of language. Before we can explore that work, however, we need to do some preliminary spadework and set out Davidson's theory of events and the logic of causal relations.

6.1 The logic of event sentences

In §3.2 and §3.3 we looked at the project of taming the idioms of natural language, which is a prerequisite to using a Tarski-style theory of truth as a model for interpreting a natural language. Our goal in those sections was to discern the structure of sentences containing demonstratives and indirect discourse, and to model these logical forms using only those resources available in standard first-order logic. In this section we focus on the occurrence in sentences of certain types of adverbial modifiers, to see how these may be accommodated in a Tarski-style semantic framework, and this will lead us to a discussion of the notion of an *event* and the role it plays in Davidson's philosophy.

Here is the basic semantic datum for which we need to account. The sentence,

(1) Brutus killed Caesar.

contains a simple transitive verb, "killed", and two proper names, "Brutus" and "Caesar", in the roles of subject and direct object. Prima facie, then, the logical form of (1) is that of a two-place relation. To bring this out we formalize (1) as:

(2) K^2(Brutus, Caesar),

where $K^2(x, y)$ = "x killed y", and the superscript indicates the number of argument-places in the predicate (i.e. the verb). Now the deed described in (1) was done somewhere, namely,

(1′) Brutus killed Caesar in Pompey's theatre,

and this sentence contains the same verb and singular terms, now supplemented by a locative prepositional phrase ("in Pompey's theatre"). As every undergraduate logic student knows, we represent the logical form of (1′) by inserting an extra argument-place into the predicate:

(2′) K^3(Brutus, Caesar, Pompey's theatre),

where $K^3(x, y, z)$ = "x killed y in z". But we may be interested to know not only the agent, patient and location of the deed, but also that

(1″) Brutus killed Caesar in Pompey's theatre with a knife on the Ides of March,

and to capture the logical form of *this* we need to locate in the simple transitive verb five argument places:

(2″) K^5(Brutus, Caesar, Pompey's theatre, knife, Ides of March).

Besides being rather inelegant, a problem with formalizing (1), (1′) and (1″) as (2), (2′) and (2″) is that they hide significant logical structure in the three sentences, for intuitively we recognize that the inference "*if* Brutus killed Caesar in Pompey's theatre with a knife on the Ides of March *then* Brutus killed Caesar" is deductively valid. However, in first-order logic any inference of the form,

$K^5(v, w, x, y, z)$,
Therefore, $K^2(x, y)$,

is *in*valid, and the reason is simple. As Lepore explains, the occurrences of the letter "K" in the predicates "K^2", "K^3", and "K^5" are "irrelevant, no less an orthographic accident than the occurrences of the first three letters 'cat' in the word 'cattle'" (Lepore 2000: 285). From the point of view of first-order logic, the open sentences "$K^2(x, y)$" and "$K^5(v, w, x, y, z)$" bear no logical relation to one another, even though it is easy to see that if x kills someone somewhere with something at some time, then x kills someone. The standard formalization, however, fails to capture that logical structure.[1]

Consider, then, this alternative. Let us represent Brutus' killing Caesar as a *three*-place relational sentence,

$\exists x\, K^3(x$, Brutus, Caesar),

or, less obscurely, as:

(3) $\exists x$ Killing(x, Brutus, Caesar),

where the extra argument position in the verb is reserved for a variable indicating an *event*, and we gloss (1′) as:

(4) $\exists x$ [Killing(x, Brutus, Caesar) & In(x, Pompey's theatre)].

Then (3) says, roughly, that there exists an event x, which is a killing by Brutus of Caesar, while (4) says that there exists an event x, which is a killing by Brutus of Caesar and x occurred in Pompey's theatre. We shall see in the next section that this move carries a price, but for now observe that by breaking out the prepositional phrase as an open sentence (satisfied by the event x) conjoined to the original open sentence, where both fall within the scope of the same existential quantifier, we preserve both the relation between the event and its location – through the mechanism of the quantifier – as well as the possibility of tacking on new clauses by conjoining additional open sentences (which, again, will lie within the scope of the quantifier). Thus we catch within the net of our formalization the inference that Brutus killed Caesar from his having killed him in Pompey's theatre, and we can also infer from (4) that *something* happened in Pompey's theatre, that is, from (4) we can infer

$\exists x$ [In(x, Pompey's theatre)].

To take a less violent example, if we represent

(5) Jane climbed,

and

(5′) Jane climbed up the hill

as, respectively,

(6) $\exists x$ [Climbing(x, Jane)]

and

(6′) $\exists x$ [Climbing(x, Jane) & Up(x, the hill)],

then the deductive relation between (5) and (5′) goes over into predicate logic as a series of inferences from (6′) to (6) by the rules of assumption, &-elimination, existential generalization and existential quantifier elimination.[2]

6.2 The existence and identity of events

Obtaining this *logical* dividend, however, entails an *ontological* cost, since (6) and (6′) quantify over events in addition to familiar objects like Jane and the hill. If we follow Davidson in translating (1) as (3) and (5) as (6), and, if moreover, we localize ontological commitment in the quantifiers and variables of first-order logic – and most analytic philosophers, including Davidson, follow Quine in this regard – then asserting (5′) is equivalent to saying that there exists an event, *a climbing*, alongside a climber and the hill she climbs. Accepting Davidson's gloss and Quine's criterion of ontological commitment, in other words, commits us to a universe that includes actions such as climbings and other events, for example, earthquakes and match-strikings.

Investigating what there is lies at the heart of metaphysics, and philosophers have pursued this study at least since Thales speculated that water is the first principle of existing things. Traditionally, the locus of ontological dispute was between *nominalists*, who assert that particular objects (e.g. Jane, the hill, the black hole lying at the centre of the Perseus A galaxy, etc.) are all there is, and *realists*, who believe there are universals (such as the forms or essences of humanity and redness) alongside the particulars that instantiate or participate in them. A contemporary version of this controversy centres on the existence of numbers and other mathematical objects;[3] here, as in the traditional debate, the question partly turns on our attitude to so called abstract objects, which, if they do exist, are unlike concrete objects (girls and hills, black holes and star clusters) in not being located anywhere in space and time.

In the 1950s, Quine gave ontology (in the analytic tradition, at least) a new direction when he argued that we should replace old speculations about what there is, with their often confusing debates and doubtful conclusions, with a more hard-headed set of questions and techniques. The business of the metaphysician, rather than asking what exists *simpliciter*, is to discern what entities a particular theory or way of speaking is committed to. In this respect Quine makes existence relative to a theory, much in the same way that Tarski makes truth relative to a specified language.[4]

This new job description for the ontologist transforms metaphysical enquiry into logical investigation. To identify the ontological commitments of a certain theory, we examine the natural language pronouns and quantity words (e.g. "some", "all", "most") that its statements use; we examine these by regimenting its statements in first-order predicate logic and looking at the bound variables and quantifiers (which correspond to the pronouns and quantity words of natural language). Consider, for example, the truths of number theory, which include the statement that some number is both even and prime. Regimenting this in first-order logic we obtain the generalization "$\exists x$ (x is even & x is prime)", which prima facie says that there *exists* an x such that x is even and (that same) x prime. When we assert that some number is both even and prime, therefore, we say that that number, the number two, exists; and thus number theory commits us to the existence of the natural numbers. Because, further, we use this and other mathematical theories, such as Euclidean geometry, analysis, probability theory and elementary set theory in our ordinary and scientific reasoning, and these theories mention numbers, sets, spaces and so on, we are committed (by Quine's criterion) to a vast menagerie of mathematical objects.[5]

Approaching ontology this way implies laying aside (at least temporarily) worries about numbers being non-spatiotemporal and attending to the truth of theories and the sentences those theories contain. The result is that Quine makes sentences and their truth and falsity central to ontology, as Davidson does to semantics. It has the consequence, too, that ontology is folded into the more general scientific enterprise, because saying what exists becomes a matter of determining what sentences are true, since what exists will be what *those* sentences, the true ones, say exists.

Therefore, if our best theory of the world says that there is an even prime number, and if we interpret the logical form of arithmetical statements at face value, then the number two exists. Similarly, if Jane climbed up the hill, and we gloss this truth as (6′), then this event exists. Numbers and events exist, then, but there remain metaphysical puzzles attending the existence of each. Philosophers of mathematics wonder what sorts of entities numbers are and how we cognize them, and it is reasonable, too, to want to characterize more closely the nature of events.

One question to ask about any kind of thing regards the identity criteria for things of that kind. The intuition here is that if a thing of a certain sort *is*, we should be able to determine when another thing of that same sort is, and when it is not, that very same individual thing at another time or place. In general, for each sort of thing, there is or ought to be a principle that individuates or identifies members of that sort and distinguishes each from other members of that same sort. Quine expresses this idea in the metaphysical slogan "no entity without identity", but the point goes back at least to Frege's concern that there be a criterion of identity associated with each new expression introduced into a language (Frege 1953: §62). The identity criterion of sets, for example, is the axiom of extension, which states that two sets are identical if and only if they share exactly the members; hence the set of creatures with a heart is the same as the set of creatures with kidneys, since the first has exactly the same members as the second. In contrast, the identity of the New York Rangers hockey team, unlike a set, is *not* given by its members, who usually change each year, but rather by a franchise agreement between the National Hockey League and a collection of investors. Note that sometimes the correct identity criterion for a species is controversial; the criterion for *personal* identity is notoriously difficult to decide upon, and it is one of the long-standing problems in modern philosophy.

In an early article (Davidson 1969d), Davidson surveys several proposals for individuating events, and in the end he tentatively affirms that events are identified by their causal relations. Thus two events are identical if and only if they cause and are caused by the same events. For example, Brutus' stabbing Caesar and his betraying Caesar are one and the same event, since both are caused, say, by his concern for the prerogatives of the Roman Senate and both cause, in turn, civil war.

This criterion leads to a number of complications, however, and several critics worry that it is circular, since causes and effects themselves are events.[6] To see this, consider that two events e and e' are identical (according to this criterion) only if they are caused by the same event(s). So suppose that some event e_0 causes e and another event e_0' causes e'; then e and e' are identical (again, according to Davidson's early criterion) only if e_0 and e_0' are identical, which they are only if the events that caused *them* are identical and so on. This sort of circularity may not be vicious, but it does make Davidson's criterion useless as a method of individuating particular events.

In a later exchange with Quine, Davidson disavows his earlier criterion and accepts Quine's proposal that two events are identical when they occupy the "same portion of space time" (Davidson 1985b; Quine 1985). This principle has its own drawbacks: notably, it appears to assimilate events to physical objects. Davidson thinks that we can get around this inconvenience, noting that while a criterion worded in terms of spatiotemporal areas does not serve to distinguish events from objects, "our predicates, our basic grammar, our ways of sorting do" supply the distinction: we speak of objects *occupying* some portion of space-time, while events are said to *occur* somewhere and at some time (Davidson 1985b: 176).[7]

As Davidson and Quine present the issue, however, the matter is misleading, for identity criteria properly attach to *sorts* or *species* of entities, not to metaphysical *genera*. We may indeed ask when two sets are identical, and we may also ask when two earthquakes are really just one earthquake. But there are no identity criteria that attach to sets merely in virtue of their objecthood, as opposed to their being a certain *sort* of object; and there are no identity criteria that attach to earthquakes merely in virtue of their being events, as opposed to their being a certain *sort* of event. The point (which Frege makes) is that it makes no sense to ask how many objects are in a room without indicating what sort of object is being counted, and it is equally senseless to try to count events *per se*, as opposed to numbering geological catastrophes or hill-climbings (where each of these is a species or kind of event). Davidson comes close to recognizing this when he concludes that perhaps the most one can say about individuating events *per se* is that it "poses no problems worse in principle than the problems posed by individuation of material objects" (Davidson 1980a: 180). In the end, the question of when two wars are identical is interesting – for example, whether the Spanish Civil War and the Second World War were a single war or distinct wars – but it is not a question that we should expect a general criterion for event identity to settle.[8]

6.3 Causal relations and causal explanation

It is well known that Jack accompanied Jane up the hill, and he fell down and broke his crown. To speak more precisely, these two individual occurrences – Jack's falling down and the breaking of his crown – are connected by the relation of causation:

(7) Jack's falling down caused the breaking of his crown.

Sentence (7) typifies what philosophers of science call a *singular causal statement*: a sentence that contains two singular terms referring to events ("Jack's falling down", "the breaking of his crown") flanking the predicate "caused" or its equivalent ("produced", "resulted in", etc.). Davidson represents the causal relation in (7) itself with a simple two-place predicate "Causes(x, y)" between the individuals denoted by the singular terms:

(8) $\exists x, y$ [Falling(x, Jack) & Breaking(y, Jack's crown) & Causes(x, y)].

That is, there are two events x and y such that x is a falling by Jack, y is a breaking of Jack's crown, and x caused y.

But suppose that it was not just Jack's falling down that broke his crown; he had fallen before, with no damage thereto. What distinguished *this* fall was that he fell down and struck his crown with great force, say, with a force of 800 newtons. In accordance with his scheme for treating the logic of causal statements, Davidson glosses the prepositional phrase "with a force of 800 newtons" as an extra conjunct appended to (8),

(9) $\exists x, y$ [Falling(x, Jack) & With(x, 800 newtons) & Breaking(y, Jack's crown) & Causes(x, y)],

but one may wonder whether this adequately captures the structure of the causal situation. By hypothesis, it is not *merely* the occurrence of Jack's fall that caused his crown to break, but rather the fact *that his fall had this particular quality*. Hence we might want to say that while (9) is true, (8) is false: *that Jack fell with 800 newtons of force*, and not *that he fell*, was sufficient to cause the breaking of Jack's crown. As Mill argues, the cause of an event "is the sum total of the conditions, positive and negative taken together ... which, being realized, the consequent invariably follows" (Mill 1950: 197–8, quoted in Davidson 1967b: 150). The sum total of conditions that suffice for Jack's breaking his crown include the fact *that he fell with 800 newtons of force*, and because this aspect is lost in the inference from (9) to (8), that inference (so this objection runs) is unsound. Hence far from its being a virtue of Davidson's analysis that (9) implies (8), this shows that there is something amiss with that analysis.

This objection suggests a rethinking of the logical form of event sentences. Roderick Chisholm recommends that events are a species of proposition or states of affairs rather than individuals; thus for Chisholm, events are items referred to by *sentences*, not *singular terms*. In other words, the *entire sentence*

(5′) Jill climbed up the hill,

refers to the event it describes, not a (hidden) singular term, that is, the "x" in

(6′) $\exists x$ [Climbing(x, Jane) & Up(x, the hill)],

as in Davidson's theory.

One attraction of this idea (for Chisholm) is that if we represent the logical form of (5′) as

(10) $\exists x$ (x consists in the fact that Jane climbed up the hill),

then we can "reduce the concept of the *truth* of a proposition to that of the occurrence of a state of affairs" (Chisholm 1970: 20–21):

> Jane climbed up the hill is $\text{true}_{English}$ if and only if
> $\exists x$ (x = the fact *that Jane climbed up the hill*).

In other words, the existence of the (Chisholm-style) event, the fact *that Jane climbed up the hill*, makes (10) and (5′) true. This contrasts with Davidson, for whom the (Davidson-style) event, *the climbing of the hill by Jane*, is not the sort of thing that makes (10) and (5′) true (in fact, for Davidson there is no *thing* that makes any sentence true). Davidson's *the climbing of the hill by Jane* does, however, satisfy the open sentence "Climbing(x, Jane) & Up(x, the hill)'.

A consequence of Chisholm's analysis is that the predicate expression "x caused y" that occurs in (7) or, better, that occurs in:

(11) That Jack fell down with a force of 800 newtons caused the fact that he broke his crown,[9]

generates an *intensional context*.[10] This has the effect of raising the bar for permitting substitutions into places that name a cause. We may lay it down as a rule, for example, that only those substitutions are permitted that include reference to all the causal aspects that are jointly necessary to produce the effect. Hence even though the sentences "Jack fell down with a force of 800 newtons" and "Jack fell down" are materially equivalent – it is true both that he fell down with that much force, and that he fell down – the fact *that Jack fell down with a force of 800 newtons* is not identical to the fact *that Jack fell down*, since the latter fails to mention a causally relevant condition.

Chisholm's proposal carries several liabilities, however. First, if we follow Chisholm and say that sentences refer to facts, and, further, we say that causation is a relation between such facts, then we can run a version of the slingshot to arrive at the conclusion that some event causes any other event.[11]

A second, more localized worry is this. If we find a fault with the inference from (9) to (8), Davidson argues, it is because we fail to distinguish

> between causes and the features we hit on for describing them, and hence between the question whether a statement says truly that one event caused another and the further question whether the events are characterized in such a way that we can deduce, or otherwise infer, from laws or other causal lore, that the relation was causal.
>
> (Davidson 1980a: 155)

This objection makes a point that is crucial for an understanding of Davidson's account of action and mind, which we shall be discussing in subsequent chapters, and therefore we consider it in a somewhat broader setting.

Let us begin by observing that, in general, an object preserves its identity and retains its properties under whatever linguistic guise we may clothe it in. If we want to assert of a certain object that it is the planet whose orbit is closest to the earth's, it is indifferent whether I say that the morning star has that property or that the evening star has that property, since the morning star = the evening star, and my statement is true either way. To take another example, it does not matter whether I say that

> A parent of Chelsea Clinton is the husband of a US senator,

or that

> A president of the United States is the husband of a US senator.

As long as at least one man is both a parent of Chelsea Clinton and a president of the United States, the two sentences are materially equivalent: if one is true then the other is, too.

Recall the point I made in §5.1: that the meanings of the words and sentences of a language are all interconnected. This is the case, we saw, because the meaning of a term is its contribution to the interpretations of all the sentences in which it occurs. There is another way, too, in which the expressions of a language are intertwined. Thus consider the predicate "is a president of the United States". This expression is embedded within the "theory" that describes the American political system, which is composed of the US Constitution, statutes passed by Congress, judicial decisions by federal courts and the traditions that have developed over the course of two centuries of American political life. Now among the written and unwritten directives that define this system, there is the rule that someone who satisfies the predicate "is a president of the United States" has a responsibility to give the State of the Union speech; and, in turn, past experience shows that whoever gives the State of the Union speech is subject to partisan attack by members of the opposition party. Similarly, the predicate, "is a parent of Chelsea Clinton" has its place in the system of concepts we use to talk about parents and their children. These concepts, too, are related in many ways; for example, whoever has the property of being a parent of Chelsea Clinton also satisfies the predicates, "has the right to prevent her from marrying if she is a minor" and "is responsible for paying her Stanford University tuition bills".

Here, then, is the point. Bill Clinton was a president of the United States for two terms of office, and he gave the State of the Union speech on eight occasions. These two truths about him are not unrelated facts: they are connected (as we have noted) by the directives of the American political system. In particular, we may say that Bill Clinton gave the State of the Union speech *because* he was a president of the United States. We can, further, infer that he was subject to partisan attack by members of the opposition party, again, *because* he was a president of the United States, since someone who is a president of the United States gives the State of the Union speech, and whoever gives the State of the Union speech is usually subject to partisan attack. We make these inferences and construct these explanations based on our knowledge of the lore of American political life.

Now, since Bill Clinton is a parent of Chelsea Clinton, it is true, too, that the father of Chelsea Clinton gave the State of the Union speech, and it is true, too, that he was subject to partisan attack by the opposition. But as long as we describe him *as* a parent of Chelsea Clinton, these are unrelated bits of information, for there is no rule obliging a parent of Chelsea Clinton to give the speech nor any generalization from which we can infer that if her parent gives a speech then that parent will be a target of partisan sniping. In other words, although the *truth* of the statements "Bill Clinton gave the State of the Union speech" and "He was subject to partisan attack by Republicans" are insensitive to how we pick out the man – whether we describe him as a president of the United States or as a parent of Chelsea Clinton – the availability of an *explanation* for those truths *is* sensitive to our choice of words. We can account for his making the speech or give reasons why Republicans criticized him only if we employ the language of American political discourse to bring him within the range of the covering generalizations "whoever is the current president of the United States is responsible for giving the State of the Union speech" and "whoever gives the State of the Union speech is subject to partisan attack by members of the opposition party".

To return, then, to Jack and his broken crown. Whether we describe an event as Jack's falling at t, or as his falling at t with a force of 800 newtons, or even as what happened to Jack at t after he saw what Jill was doing on top of the hill, we pick out one and the same event, just as we refer to one and the same man whether we mention his being a president of the United States or his being the father of Chelsea Clinton. Whether an event has the property that it causes the breaking of his crown is *intrinsic* to the event, because the relation expressed by the open sentence "x caused y" *holds between events howsoever we describe them*.

As far as *our understanding* goes of the connection between Jack's falling at t and the subsequent breaking of his crown, though, it may make all the difference whether we describe the event as his falling or as his falling with 800 newtons of force. It may make all the difference, because if the event is presented to us *as* his falling with 800 newtons of force, then we see that it satisfies the antecedent in the generalization,

(12) $\forall x, y, t$ [(Falling(x, y) & With$(x$, 800 newtons of force) & At$(x, t)) \rightarrow \exists! z$ (Breaking$(z, y$'s crown) & At$(z, t + \varepsilon)$ & Causes$(x, z))$][12]

Given the medical knowledge about the frailty of the human skull expressed by (12), we could have predicted that his falling with 800 newtons of force would break his crown; or, if we already know that his crown is broken and that he fell with a force of 800 newtons, we can explain *why* his crown is broken by citing this covering generalization; namely, that whoever falls down on the top of his head with a force of 800 newtons will, everything else being equal (e.g. that he is not wearing a crash helmet), break his crown. The event at *t* involving Jack is what broke his crown, irrespective of how we describe it, but unless we include the detail about the quantity of force we may be at a loss to explain *why* his crown broke. The reason, as Davidson observes, is that causal explanations

> require classifying concepts, a vocabulary that has the resources for sorting objects and events in ways that allow the formulation of useful generalizations. Suppose we want an explanation of the collapse of the Tacoma–Seattle Bridge. Although I have just used a complex system of classification – geographical, political, and structural – to pick out the event to be explained, the description is nearly useless for explanatory purposes: there are no general laws governing collapses of bridges in certain areas. If we want an explanation, we need to describe the collapse in quite different terms, perhaps (as a start) as the collapse of a structure with a certain strength and design that occurred with a wind of a certain strength blowing from a certain direction.
>
> (Davidson 1990b: 18)

Unlike the causal relation ("*x* caused *y*"), which (again) remains true under substitution of co-referring terms for either the cause or the effect, explanation ("Jack broke his crown at *t* because he fell on his head with a force of 800 newtons") is a relation among linguistic expressions. In light of the true generalization expressed by (12), we can explain why Jack's crown broke yesterday afternoon if we know that he suffered a happening that satisfies the description "is a falling with 800 newtons of force"; similarly, we can explain why Venus appears in the evening sky, if we know that the orbits of Earth and Venus satisfy a certain description, given some general truths about *inter alia* the intensity of light reflected by the surface of Venus and the capacity of the human eye to discern objects at low levels of illumination. Explanation, therefore, unlike causal relatedness, is sensitive to the terms we employ or concepts we invoke to classify the occurrences we want to explain. The bridge collapse and State of the Union examples are more complicated than the crown-breaking case, since each involves two entirely different schemes for sorting objects, while the crown-breaking case relies only on the fact that one description, but not the other, contains information without which we cannot see that the falling satisfies the antecedent clause of (12). But the point is the same; the existence of a causal relation between two events depends only on intrinsic properties of the events themselves, while the possibility of our accounting for that relation or fitting it into a general pattern of explanation turns on our describing the case in terms that permit us to cite a generalization they instance.

Chapter 7

Action theory and explanation in the social sciences

All sorts of events occur – bridges collapse, planets appear in the evening sky, people give speeches – and some of these events are special in being *actions* persons perform. Classical Chinese marks the distinction between actions and other events graphically, by adding to the term “*wei*”, meaning “to do”, the radical for “human being”, thus yielding a character that literally means “a person’s doing”.[1] Not everything a person does can be counted among his actions, however; witness Jack’s falling down the hill, about which we say that *it happens to him*, rather than that *he performs it*. Or, to take another illustration, if I raise my arm, then my arm rises; but my arm may rise without my raising it, for example, if my neighbour lifts it. Wittgenstein problematizes this contrast between a doing in which one passively takes part (Jack’s falling down the hill, my neighbour’s lifting my arm) and a doing of which one is the author (Jack’s accompanying Jane up the hill, my intentionally raising my arm) by asking “what is left over if I subtract the fact that my arm goes up from the fact that I raise my arm?” (Wittgenstein 1958: §621). What distinguishes actions from other events, and how are these differences mirrored in the explanations we offer of actions, as compared to other events?

7.1 Volition and reasons

Serious action theory begins with Aristotle, who explains this contrast between an action someone performs and an occurrence he suffers by positing that the "moving principle (*archē*) [of an action] is in the agent himself, [who is] aware of the particular circumstances of the action" (Aristotle 1984: 1111a20–21).[2] Thus two events, one which a person performs as the agent and the other which he suffers as a patient, are distinguished by a psychological difference; in the former, but not the latter, an agent's own desires and thoughts (*dianoia*) comprise or cause his deliberate choice (*proairesis*) to pursue some end, and that choice, Aristotle says, is the efficient cause (*archē*) of the action (*ibid.*: 1139a32).

When we get to the moderns, this picture of the difference between actions and other events is refracted through the ontological lens of dualist philosophies of mind. The thesis that an agent's deliberate choice causes his action metamorphoses into the view that a distinct act of mind, specifically, an act of will or volition, causes movement of the agent's body; my arm's rising and Jack's legs carrying him up the hill are each preceded by a volition that necessitates it. A faculty of volition is needed, on this view, not because matter is inert – after Newton matter is recognized to possess inertia, and in any case other *mental* acts presuppose a volition, too – but because the intellect is conceived as impotent, it being limited to the task of "putting forward [ideas] for affirmation or denial" (Descartes 1984: 40; AT VII 57).[3] Desire is ineffectual, too, and unless a subject who desires an end wills herself to pursue it, she remains unmoved. I may desire that some painful sensation cease, for example, but as long as I fail to will an act that relieves me of the pain I do not move (cf. Locke 1975: II.xxi §30). This is where volitions come in, for they play the role of an executive process that translates a person's beliefs and values into action; an act of will *causes* Jack's striding forwards and upwards and my hand's moving away from an open flame.

Numerous difficulties attend theories of action that distinguish actions from other events by citing their causal histories, especially causal theories that posit volitions as the causes of actions. These difficulties include the fact that if we treat volitions as mental events, then we confront the circumstance that while I am (perhaps) conscious of some acts of will that I perform, there are many others of which I have no awareness. I intentionally and consciously type this sentence, for example, but the movements that make up that typing, for example, my shaping my fingers a certain way and my striking the individual keys, involve no separate mental efforts, if I am a good typist; in this sense they are automatic once I have formed the intention to type a word. And if we concede that somehow I perform *these* acts without individually willing them, then why should any action require a prior volition? Similarly, if a volition is *itself* an action (namely, an act of will), then according to the volitional theory it occurs only if there is a prior act of will that causes it; otherwise, it is an action that does not require a prior volition. If the former, however, we are led to an infinite regress; but if the latter, then, again, we may ask why *any* action presupposes a prior volition, if actions of this type do not.

It may be objected, too, that most appeals to volitions are empty. If we explain that *Jack's climbing the hill* was caused by *his willing himself to climb the hill*, then our account has the same form as that offered by the foolish doctor in Molière's *The Imaginary Invalid*, who cites opium's "dormitive virtue" to explain the drug's putting someone to sleep: we explain Jack's action (his climbing the hill) by citing an event we identify as the mental occurrence that caused just *that* action (his willing his climbing the hill), just as we explain opium's effect upon a user by referring to a property of the drug (its dormitive virtue) that we describe as its capacity for having just *that* effect (its putting one to sleep). In this sense, both "volition" and a substance's "dormitive virtue" are what Davidson calls *causal terms* or *concepts*, in that they are both defined in terms of events they typically cause or are caused by (e.g. one's willing oneself to climb the hill causes one to climb the hill). Since both explanations rely on causal concepts, neither identifies the cause in terms that are *independent* of the effects we want to explain by citing them; in effect, we have explained *x*'s doing *A* by saying that *x* exercised his capacity to do *A*. And since agents are unaware of most of their acts of will (e.g. my shaping my fingers a certain way as I type), volitional explanations usually have no other choice than to cite a causal concept to explain an action.[4]

Setting these worries aside for the moment, it seems to be a *virtue* of causal theories of action that they follow the model of explanation in the natural sciences. We begin to understand the collapse of the bridge when we learn that there were unusually strong winds on the day of the catastrophe, and we begin to understand, too, Antony's ordering the death of Cicero when we learn that Antony knew that Cicero had denounced him as a public enemy. We say that the bridge collapsed *because* strong winds were blowing, and that Antony ordered the murder of Cicero *because* he knew the orator was speaking ill of him. In both cases the "because" reflects a causal relation: the wind's blowing caused the bridge collapse, and Antony's knowing that Cicero had denounced him resulted in his proscribing the orator.

There are those, however, who see this apparent virtue as a vice. Continental thinkers going back to Wilhelm Dilthey have argued that the subject matters of the natural sciences and the human sciences (*Geisteswissenschaften*) differ radically – one is concerned with the natural world, and the other with the human mind and history, and the products of human culture – and this means they have radically different methodologies and patterns of explanation.[5] When we identify an event as an action we establish it as our goal to *understand* (*verstehen*) the occurrence, in the sense of seeing it as reasonable in light of the agent's values and beliefs, and thus her purposes. More generally, our objective in the human or social sciences is to understand human behaviour in terms of the reasons people act as they do, given the situations that condition that behaviour, and the cultural or social structures that surround it; and this stands opposed to explaining (*erklären*) an occurrence in terms of its causal precedents. It is, in effect, the difference between describing an event as an action performed by a rational, moral agent and treating it as molecules in motion. Peter Winch, a leading proponent of the *Verstehen* approach among Anglo-American thinkers, writes that

> "Understanding" … is grasping the *point* or *meaning* of what is being done or said. This notion is far removed from the world of statistics and causal laws: it is closer to the realm of discourse and to the internal relations that link parts of a realm of discourse. (1958: 115)

Understanding a person's actions resembles understanding her words in so far as both achievements display a normative character. We saw the role that norms play in our interpretive practices in Chapters 4 and 5; in action theory, norms enter the picture through our efforts to rationalize a person's behaviour, that is, to explain it in terms of her reasons.[6] We see *x* do *A*, and we understand this doing by attributing to her a desire that *p* and a belief that by doing *A* she will probably bring it about that *p*. These attributions are governed by the same injunctions that played a role in the theory of interpretation: treat *x*'s attitudes as being logically coherent, by and large, and as corresponding to how *we* would see the world, were we to occupy her perspective and share her personal history. In light of this and on the assumption that she is rational, we understand her doing *A* as a moment in the coherent life of a rational animal.

Thus, according to *teleological theories of action*,[7] a necessary condition for an occurrence's being an action is that it can be rationalized, in the sense of its fitting into an intelligible pattern that includes the agent's attitudes as well as her action, and that is governed or constituted by normative principles. When we explain that Jack had his reasons for going up the hill, namely, that he wanted to bring it about that he was atop the hill, we imply that a *rational necessity* joins his action and reasons. Switching to an example from Aristotle, when I explain my drinking by citing a pattern of attitudes and action – "I want to drink, says appetite, this is drink, says sense or imagination or thought; straightaway I drink" (Aristotle 1984: 701a32–33) – I express my objective (my drinking), my belief that I can achieve that objective through means within my reach (doing *this* I can drink) and straightaway I act. This "straightaway" carries the suggestion of an analogy with ordinary inference, in which a conclusion follows immediately from a set of premises without any *tertium quid*: if I want to drink and I can drink, then everything else being equal, it is irrational for me *not* to drink.[8]

This picture differs from causal (e.g. volitional) theories of action in hanging its explanatory force on *final* as opposed to *efficient* causality. On a teleological theory, we understand Jack's going up the hill and my drinking in terms of states of affairs that each of us desires, where these states of affairs "cause" the actions despite their – indeed, on account of their – lying in a future as-of-yet unrealized at the time the action is undertaken. If this is right, it undermines Wittgenstein's query by suggesting that nothing (no *thing*, no *event*) is left over once we subtract the rising from the raising; beliefs and desires or, more generally, an agent's reasons, explain her actions in the sense of *justifying* those actions, not by giving their causal histories. (Of course, this is exactly Wittgenstein's point.) And just as there is no third thing connecting the two premises and conclusion of a syllogism,[9] other than their internal logical relations, so, too, no third thing connects an agent's action with her reasons. It also undermines, therefore, the traditional modern thesis that we need to posit the will as a mental force responsible for translating mere intellection into action: it gives way to the idea that we explain an action (and are, indeed, justified in calling it an action) when we identify the action's background in the agent's reasons.

7.2 Primary reasons and the practical syllogism

Davidson is sympathetic to key elements of the teleological theory. He agrees with Dilthey, Winch *et al.* that reason explanations deal with final causes, and that our goal in the *Geisteswissenschaften*, and in explaining human actions generally, is to grasp "the point or meaning of what is being done or said" (Winch 1958: 115), where this project went out of fashion in the *Naturwissenschaften* 400 years ago. I shall return to this idea in §8.6. Further, Davidson concurs with Winch that the philosophy of language is a chapter in action theory; speech acts are just one instance of what Winch (following Max Weber) calls "meaningful behavior".[10]

Davidson agrees, too, that a necessary condition for an event's being an action is that it can be rationalized. He puts the point this way: "anything an agent does intentionally [is] an action" (Davidson 1980a: 5), where the criterion for something's being done intentionally is that it be possible, at least in principle, to construct a primary reason for the action. A *primary reason* is basically a background desire and belief that explains an action, but before looking at this notion in detail I need to make two comments. First, recall from §6.3 that events are like objects in our being able to redescribe them without affecting their identity. Bill Clinton is the man he is, whether we describe him as the forty-second president of the United States or as the husband of the junior senator from New York; similarly, Jack's falling down the hill is the event it is, whether we describe it as his falling, his falling with a force of 800 newtons or what happened to Jack after he lost his footing. The same is true of actions; Jack's trip up the hill is the event it is, whether we describe it as his fetching a pail of water or his striding up the hill. Suppose, however, that in taking a stride Jack stumbles. This complicates the picture, since he took the step intentionally but he did not (we shall assume) stumble intentionally, hence the same event may be intentional under one description, and unintentional under another. But the striding was a stumbling, and therefore either both or neither is an action. The solution is this: to recognize that the context "x is an action" is extensional, but "x is intentional" is intensional, in other words, being an action is an intrinsic feature of an event, while the property of being intentional attaches to events only under a description. An event is an action, therefore, just in case there is at least one description under which it is intentional.[11]

Secondly, and more simply, there may be actions that we recognize *as such*, and yet do not actually know how to construct a primary reason for. This is the case when someone does something, for example, that strikes us as wildly imprudent or injudicious. We say, "I do not know why she married him, although she must have had her reasons", implying that she married him intentionally, that is, she "had her reasons", but what those reasons are is beyond our ken.

To understand Davidson's notion of a primary reason, it is instructive to survey briefly Aristotle's theory of the practical syllogism. Aristotle represents the deliberation that precedes an agent's action by laying out her reasons on analogy with the two premises of an ordinary syllogism, and the action (or judgement that the action is desirable) on analogy with the conclusion we draw from those premises. The first sentence in a practical syllogism, corresponding to the major premise in a logical syllogism, expresses a pro-attitude the agent has towards an objective she values, or, we might also say, a pro-attitude she has towards a type of action that she believes is likely to help her realize that objective. This notion of a *pro-attitude* is a convenient catchall category that covers, in Davidson's listing,

> desires, wantings, urgings, promptings, and a great variety of moral views, aesthetic principles, economic prejudices, social conventions, and public and private goals in so far as these can be interpreted as attitudes of an agent directed toward actions of a certain sort. (1980a: 4)

In our earlier example from Aristotle, the major premise expresses my pro-attitude towards, or my placing a value on, drinking ("I want to drink"), which we reformulate as:

(1) For any action x, if x brings it about that I drink, then I want to do x.

This, again, expresses my pro-attitude toward any action that is a drinking. The second premise expresses the agent's belief (in this example, my belief) that some *particular* action she can now perform is of that sort, in other words, that *this* action ("*This* is drinking", or, "Doing *this* is drinking") will promote or realize the goal she desires or wants or is urged to pursue:

(2) Raising this glass of liquid to my lips and swallowing brings it about that I drink,

Straightaway, then, the conclusion of the practical syllogism is:

(3) I raise this glass of liquid to my lips and swallow,

if the action *itself* is the syllogism's conclusion; or it is:

(3′) I want to raise this glass of liquid to my lips and swallow,

if (on a different reading of Aristotle) a judgement that the particular action in question is desirable is its conclusion. (Whether Aristotle thinks that the conclusion is (3) or (3′) is a long-standing problem in Aristotle scholarship.[12])

Davidson writes at one point that because Aristotle sees "the practical syllogism ... as corresponding to a piece of practical reasoning", he "is bound ... to think of the conclusion as corresponding to a judgement ... that the action is desirable" (1980a: 9n.), which is our (3′), while elsewhere Davidson records that "Aristotle apparently identifies drawing the [conclusion] and acting: he says 'the conclusion is an action'" (*ibid.*: 32), which is our (3). Davidson's own view is closer to (3′), but in any case he prefers to recast our understanding of the practical syllogism; it does not express a fragment of practical reasoning that precedes an agent's action, as Aristotle thinks it does, but rather it is an "analysis of the concept of a reason with which someone acted" (*ibid.*: 9n.). The practical syllogism marks out the logic of an action by articulating the agent's reason for his action; it situates a doing against the background of the doer's mental economy, as governed by the norms of reason and the principles of charity. We witness Jack's going up the hill or his taking a bet offered to him, and in identifying his doing as an *action* we set about to relate it to his other actions and to his attitudes, calling into play the concepts of truth and probability (as given by a theory of meaning and the probability calculus), and value and the virtues (as governed by decision theory and our favourite moral philosophy). We resolve Jack's taking the bet in the given choice situation into his preference that he selects an option that maximizes his monetary pay-off, and his belief that in the current situation taking a certain bet maximizes his pay-off, that is, his believing – given the parameters of the situation and probabilities that attach to the options – there is no other option open to him that yields a higher pay-off. Moreover, we posit that Jack has no other desires and no moral objections that override his accepting the bet. Given, then, that we attribute to him these attitudes and values, we interpret his action. Indeed, anatomizing and situating his behaviour this way, seeing it as a moment in the rationally ordered life plan of a person, is *what we mean by calling that behaviour an action*.

A primary reason, then, roughly corresponds to the premises of a practical syllogism. According to Davidson, to understand an agent's intentionally performing some action *A*, it is necessary that we see that it is possible, at least in outline, to cite

> [a] a pro attitude of the agent towards actions with a certain property, and [b] a belief of the agent that *A*, under the description *d*, has that property. (Davidson 1980a: 5)

Because the sentence "*x* believes that *p*" is intensional – that is, because *x* can believe that *p* and *not* believe that *q*, even if *p* and *q* are equivalent – we need the complication in (b) that the belief component of an agent's primary reason is a belief that an action *under a description* has a certain property. To see this point, consider Davidson's example of Oedipus' marrying his mother Jocasta (*ibid.*: 194–5). We may suppose that Oedipus marries Jocasta because he wants to do whatever promotes the welfare of Thebes, and he believes that marrying Jocasta has this property; hence he wants to marry Jocasta, and he does. It matters a great deal to our explanation, though, that Oedipus think of and we refer to Jocasta as the widowed queen of the city, as in:

(4) Oedipus believes that marrying the widowed queen of the city will promote the welfare of Thebes.

For although (4) is true and

the widowed queen of the city = Oedipus' mother,

it is false that

(5) Oedipus believes that marrying his mother will promote the welfare of Thebes.

Sentences (4) and (5) differ only in containing co-referring terms, but one is true and the other false. It is not that the act of marrying Jocasta both does *and* does not have the property of promoting the welfare of Thebes; rather, it is that (4) and (5) each expresses a relation that holds between Oedipus, Jocasta and *a description of* Jocasta. In citing an agent's belief that doing *A* will realize some goal of his, therefore, in order to explain his doing *A*, we need to pay attention to the way we specify *A*.

There is a further difference between Aristotle's account of the practical syllogism, and Davidson's notion of a primary reason, and this brings us back to the conclusion of a practical syllogism. Recall that for Aristotle that conclusion is an action or judgement that an action is desirable. I want to drink, doing *this* is drinking, and so straightaway I *do this* or judge that doing *this* is something I desire. It often happens, though, that although I want to drink and have an opportunity to drink I do *not* drink; nor do I see that opportunity as a chance I do not want to miss. For example, an act of drinking may be identical to an act of drinking vodka, and all things considered I may prefer not to drink vodka, although I do want to drink. In general, an action *x* may have the property of being *F* and also have the property of being *G*, and I may want to do something that is *F*, but not do anything that is *G*. The deliberation that justifies an action *A* that I really do perform therefore involves more than my having a reason to do *A*. It involves, too, my weighing reasons that may direct me to undertake *conflicting* courses of action – doing *A* and *not* doing *A* – and my concluding that, all things considered, I ought to do *A*.

To capture this weighing of conflicting desires and hence the weighing of conflicting courses of action (to do, or not to do, *A*), we need to add to the premises of the practical syllogism something about *the description under which* an agent desires to do something. We need to add an indication that an agent desires an action *in so far as* that action has a certain characteristic or property, thus leaving open the possibility that – as often happens –

one and the same action may be desirable under one description and undesirable under another. Davidson thus rewrites the practical syllogism,

(i) For any action *x*, if doing *x* is drinking, then doing *x* is desirable
(ii) Raising this glass of liquid to my lips and swallowing is drinking
(iii) Therefore, raising this glass of liquid to my lips and swallowing is desirable

as:

(i) For any action *x*, if doing *x* is drinking, then doing *x* is desirable *in so far as* doing it is drinking
(ii) Raising this glass of liquid to my lips and swallowing is drinking
(iii) Therefore, raising this glass of liquid to my lips and swallowing is desirable *in so far as* doing it is drinking.

And the following syllogism expresses a reason I have for *refraining from* the same action:

(i) For any action *x*, if doing *x* will make me drunk, then doing *x* is undesirable *in so far as* doing it will make me drunk
(ii) Raising this glass of liquid to my lips and swallowing will make me drunk
(iii) Therefore, raising this glass of liquid to my lips and swallowing is undesirable *in so far as* doing it will make me drunk.

If I have an opportunity to drink, but that opportunity is an opportunity to drink vodka, then I have a dilemma: performing that action is desirable *qua* its being drinking and undesirable *qua* its being drinking vodka. Davidson calls these emended syllogisms prima facie or conditional judgements of value, since each represents a judgement of value (doing *A* is desirable, doing *A* is not desirable) as being governed by a condition on that evaluation (*A* is drinking, which is something I want to do; doing *A* is consuming vodka, which is something I do not want to do).[13]

The difference between an action that is desirable *simpliciter*, which I perform or intend to perform, and one that is merely conditionally desirable, is that my reasons for an action I (intend to) perform are all the relevant reasons there are: *A* is desirable, not only in its being an act of drinking, but *all things considered*. The actions of a rational person are "all-out" in this sense, and thus in accordance with what Davidson calls the *principle of continence*: one ought to "perform the action judged best on the basis of all available relevant reasons" (Davidson 1980a: 41). (In our example, I do not drink the vodka since, taking into consideration all my current goals, I value staying sober more than I value drinking, and I am rational.) The principle of continence takes its place alongside the charity principles discussed in Chapter 4 as partly defining what we mean by calling someone rational.

Which reasons are relevant to an agent's decision-making, and hence which reasons fall within the scope of an "all things considered" judgement, is no easier to figure out than is deciding what evidence is relevant to making any (non-evaluative) judgement. And local irrationalities, such as self-deception, incontinence and so on, will intrude just as they do in non-evaluative cases. Such breakdowns are necessarily local, however, just as breakdowns of logical coherence in interpreting and having beliefs are necessarily local, as we saw in §4.4 and for the same reason: too much incoherence undermines the possibility of interpreting another's actions, and calls into question the very claim that she acts intentionally, that is, that her doings *are* actions. That there are local breakdowns is nothing mysterious, however; nor does it present an objection to Davidson's action theory. The point is that in interpreting what someone does, we sometimes make the best *overall* sense of his doings by identifying some particular behaviour as an instance of incontinence, or so-called "weakness of the will".

7.3 Reasons and causes

Davidson's goal in the theory of action is to chart a third way between volitional theories and their critics. Like Winch *et al.* he believes that reason explanations of human behaviour are special in adverting to final causes, but he asserts that reason explanations are *also* causal explanations, in the sense of efficient causality. But while he presents a causal theory of action, he rejects the concept of volition and returns to a form of Aristotelianism in which an agent's desires and beliefs cause her actions.[14]

By shunning volitions Davidson skirts many of the criticisms associated with causal theories. If my actions are caused by my pro-attitudes and beliefs, then because these attitudes are dispositions, and I am not consciously aware of all my dispositions, it is no wonder that many of my actions are caused without my being aware of their causal antecedents.[15] That Iran is not the second largest Muslim nation is not a thought that had ever occurred to me, but having learned recently that India has that distinction I tacitly believe that Iran does not. Were someone, then, to ask me whether Iran ranks second to Indonesia in the number of its Muslim citizens I would immediately reply that it does not, and my belief that it does not would belong to the primary reason for my speech act. But, again, that belief is not a thought of which I was consciously aware.

A second objection we encountered in §7.1 states that we should not explain an agent's doing *A* by citing her volition to perform *A*, if all we can say about that volition is that it is her willing herself to do *A*. Such an "explanation" is empty, and resembles "explaining" opium's putting a user to sleep by citing the drug's "dormitive virtue". This objection does not strictly apply to Davidson's account, although we may reformulate it and protest that to the extent that desires and beliefs are causal dispositions (i.e. dispositions to cause some effect), explanations that cite an agent's primary reason to explain her actions are empty, too. To take one of Davidson's examples, "we learn little about why someone crushed a snail by being told he wanted to crush a snail and believed … and so on – we learn little more than that the action was intentional under the given description" (Davidson 1987b: 41–2). We have, in effect, explained *x*'s doing *A* by citing her desire to do *A*, where desire is a dispositional concept, as opium's dormitive virtue is its tendency to put users to sleep.

Davidson's response to this objection comes to the defence of Molière's much abused doctor. Contrary to what generations of philosophers of science have said, Davidson argues that there *is* some explanatory force to saying that a drug put someone to sleep on account of its dormitive virtue. Citing a pill's causal powers (i.e. its power to produce a certain effect) to explain an occurrence – such as explaining that it caused someone to fall asleep because it was a *sleeping* pill – says at least this much: it was not some *other* causal power of the pill that produced the user's sleep. A pill may be a sleeping pill, and it may put someone to sleep, and yet its putting her to sleep may not have been produced by the pill's dormitive power; perhaps there were

> special circumstances that obtained [in virtue of which] it acted as a placebo. Similarly, if we explain why someone ate by pointing out that he was hungry we do explain the eating by adverting to a state that is partly understood as a causal disposition to eat; but the explanation is not empty, since eating can easily have other causes. (Davidson 1990b: 22)

Someone may be hungry, and he may eat; but he eats to please his mother, not because he is hungry. (For example, he may have eaten even if he were not hungry.) We generally have many reasons for acting; sometimes these reasons never terminate in an action, as we saw in the preceding section. And when we do act, we may (and usually do) have more than one reason for doing so; I may want to crush a snail, *and* I may not want to step on the geraniums. Either reason may suffice for my stepping down with my left foot, but only one of these reasons genuinely produces my stepping; citing my desire to crush a snail, then, does explain my crushing a snail, at least in so far as it implies that I did not crush a snail to avoid stepping on the geraniums.

This points the way to Davidson's strongest argument that reasons are causes. Teleological accounts explain an action by citing desire–belief pairs that rationalize the action, but they lack the resources for singling out *the* pair that actually explains the action, in the sense of being *the* reason for the agent's doing what he does: "a person can have a reason for an action, and perform the action, and yet this reason not be the reason why he did it" (Davidson 1980a: 9). Oedipus has a reason for killing his father and does kill his father; but his reason is not *the* reason he killed him. It may turn out, too, that a man has a reason for performing an action, and he performs the action, yet he does not perform the action for *any* reason. Fred, we may suppose, wants to shoot Barney, since he believes that Barney and Wilma are cuckolding him, and he may believe that by pulling the trigger of the gun he holds in his hand he will shoot Barney, and he pulls the trigger and shoots Barney. But his desire to shoot Barney, combined with its belief partner, is not effective in producing the shooting; his anger at being cuckolded, we may suppose, involuntarily causes him to clench his fist and shoot his friend, and thus making the act *involuntary*. "When we offer the fact of the desire and belief in explanation, we imply not only that the agent had the desire and belief, but that they were *efficacious* in producing the action [and] here we must say, I think, that causality is involved" (Davidson 1980a: 232). Citing Fred's belief and desire does *not* explain his shooting Barney since his reason did not cause the shooting, his anger did.

7.4 Laws and causes

My desire to crush a snail genuinely explains my crushing a snail, but that explanation is not "high science", as Davidson puts it (1980a: 274). A reason explanation,

> Oedipus married Jocasta because he wanted to promote the welfare of Thebes, and he believed that marrying Jocasta would, under the circumstances, promote the welfare of Thebes,

or, more generally,

(6) A person x performs action A because she has reason R,

suits our purposes when our interest is limited to identifying an event as intentionally caused and hence as an action; or when we want to identify one reason rather than another as *the* reason x did A, for example, that I crushed a snail because I wanted to crush a snail and not because I wanted to avoid stepping on the geraniums (although I wanted to avoid stepping on the geraniums, too.) In the same way, explaining a sugar cube's dissolving in water,

(7) The sugar cube dissolved because it is water-soluble and was placed in water,

suits our purposes, too, when our interests are narrow, for example, if we want to explain informally why sugar works better as a sweetener for water-based beverages than some non-water-soluble substance.

Explanations of physical phenomena that mention causal concepts (a sugar cube's dissolving in water because it is *water-soluble*, an accident's occurring because of the *slipperiness* of a wet road, etc.) are adequate for most common purposes, but we can always, at least in principle, construct more discerning explanations. We move beyond superficial, common-sense explanations when, first, we replace the causal concepts they mention with detailed, non-dispositional descriptions of the physical properties of the objects and events they mention; in the sugar example, we replace the concept of solubility with an exact description of the chemical properties of sugar, namely, the covalent bonds that join the sugar molecules together.[16] In thus moving from causal to non-causal (i.e. non-dispositional) concepts, we describe causes in terms that are independent of their effects, and effects in terms that are independent of their causes; and in this way we avoid the charge of vacuity that dogs Molière's doctor. We identify the pill that caused the patient's falling asleep not as a sleeping pill (i.e. something that usually causes one to fall asleep), but as an opiate, and hence as a substance with such-and-such chemical properties. Then, having identified the cause in terms of its microstructural properties (rather than *as* the cause of its effect), we call upon our general scientific knowledge and subsume a singular causal statement under a general causal regularity:

(8) Whenever an event of type E_1 occurs it causes the subsequent occurrence of an event of type E_2,

In our sugar example, placing the sugar cube (described as a substance with such-and-such physical microstructure) in water is an E_1-type event, and its dissolving is an E_2-type event:

(9) Whenever a non-ionic compound, the molecules of which are linked by polar covalent bonds, is placed in water it dissolves.[17]

More precisely, what we really have in practice are generalizations like (9) supplemented by a *ceteris paribus* ("everything else being equal") clause:

(10) Everything else being equal, whenever a non-ionic compound, the molecules of which are linked by polar covalent bonds, is placed in water it dissolves.

A *ceteris paribus* clause specifies that the generalization holds under normal conditions, where what counts as "normal" is presupposed as part of the background to the generalization. *Ceteris paribus* clauses are a standard part of scientific theorizing, for they provide an "escape clause" for conditions that could go wrong but that lie beyond the scope of generalization's subject matter.[18]

Again, a key feature of (10) is that it identifies the antecedent condition or event ("placing a non-ionic compound, the molecules of which are linked by polar covalent bonds, in water") independently of its usual consequence. This has the salutary effect that when an instance of the antecedent occurs – for example, a sugar cube's being placed in water – but no instance of the consequent occurs (the cube fails to dissolve), it does not necessarily mean that our generalization comes a cropper. It may signal, rather, that we should look for other necessary conditions for the production of the effect, such as that the water is at least a certain temperature and that the solution is not already saturated; and these conditions are then, in turn, incorporated into an improved generalization:

(10′) Everything else being equal, whenever a non-ionic compound, the molecules of which are linked by polar covalent bonds, is placed in water at a temperature of at least 5 °C, and the solution at no time becomes saturated, it dissolves.

Sentence (10′) still contains a generous escape clause – there remain many other things that could go wrong – but we have made progress: the very sort of progress one looks for in scientific work.

Contrast this with the common-sense generalization that has the causal term "water-soluble" in place of the exact description of sugar's chemical structure:

(11) Everything else being equal, whenever a water-soluble compound is placed in water, it dissolves.

We cannot improve on (11) in the way that (10′) improves on (10), since our whittling away at the *ceteris paribus* clause assumes we can identify an occurrence of the antecedent condition (namely, that a *water-soluble* substance is placed in water) in the absence of an occurrence of the consequent. But we cannot identify a substance as water-soluble if it does not dissolve in water.

Reason explanations, like superficial physical explanations such as (11), cannot be perfected unless we switch to a different set of terms or language. Unlike common-sense physical explanations, however, this switch – from talking about an agent's reasons and desires to talking about, for example, the physical microstructure of her neural system – undermines the character of reason explanations: in making this switch we have *changed the subject*, and while we may have an explanation that can be sharpened indefinitely, we do *not* have a reason explanation. *A* is an action performed by *x*, however we describe it, since *A* is an action just in case there is *some* description under which it is intentional; but having switched from psychological to physical (neurological) language, we now describe the occurrence *A* as molecules in motion, and not as an action performed by a rational, moral agent. So while we may have an explanation that subsumes the action under a physical scientific generalization, the language of that generalization, and hence the language of our explanation, is the language of physics. And thus we do not have a reason explanation any more.[19]

To see why reason explanations cannot aspire to "high science" while being true to their teleological character, we need to be clear on exactly what is being denied. Davidson does *not* claim that there are no true generalizations in psychology or the human sciences, nor does he deny that those generalizations chart causal relations, as we have seen, or even that those generalizations are appropriately titled "laws". The basic logic of the human and the physical sciences is the same. What he asserts is that those generalizations fail to measure up to a high standard that is met only by an idealized natural science. The claim that the human sciences are not "high science", therefore, is not an "attack" on psychology and the human sciences, as it may seem to be at first. Nevertheless, it does have some significant consequences, as we shall see in Chapter 8.

For now, let us say more clearly what Davidson is denying. We say that a generalization such as (10) is a *covering law* for the statement that a certain sugar cube dissolves in water, in the sense that from (10) and a statement that a sugar cube (described as a substance satisfying the description "*x* is a non-ionic compound, the molecules of which are linked by polar covalent bonds"[20]) is placed in water, we can infer that it dissolves. We can infer that the sugar cube dissolves, and that it dissolves *because* it is placed in water. When, in this way, we bring a pair of occurrences (placing the sugar in water and its dissolving) under an appropriate covering law, we explain their relation by showing it to be an instance of a pattern or nomological regularity. We show that the dissolving is just what we would have expected, given that the sugar cube has the specified microstructure and was placed in water, on the one hand, and our understanding of the natural world, on the other.

Davidson believes that for every true singular causal statement there is some covering law. Hume is the author most closely associated with this principle,[21] but Davidson's attachment to it owes as much to Kant as to Hume. For Hume, believing that one event causes another is constituted by our mental habit of pairing every impression of *one general sort* with an idea of *another general sort*, and the former's sharing of its "vivacity" of the former with the latter. In this way, the concept of one event's causing another has generality built into it.

Kant gives the cause–law thesis a deep foundation, too, but for him it is anchored in the concept of an object or objective experience. The principle that "everything that happens is determined by a cause according to constant laws" (Kant 1977: §15) is the second analogy of experience and is a condition on the possibility of experiencing the raw perceptual data as composed of objects. Davidson "put off writing for many years" the article in which he most clearly sets out his reasons for endorsing the cause–law thesis,[22] and those reasons are still more than a little obscure; but his point seems to be this. When we identify something as a physical object of a particular sort we attribute to it certain causal properties; in other words, when we identify something as *sugar* or *opium* or *an elm tree* we already sketch out a certain natural history for it, for example, that it was derived from sugar cane or opium poppies, or that it is a hardwood tree. Hence "the ground floor connection of causality with regularity is ... built into the idea of objects whose changes are causally tied to other changes", and changes being events, they, too, are "caught up in this highly general net of concepts" (Davidson 1985a: 227). This being the case, Davidson remarks that "it is not surprising, then, that singular causal statements imply the existence of covering laws: events are changes that explain and require such explanations" (Davidson 1995d: 273). It is "not surprising", since the kinds into which we classify objects and their changes (i.e. events) correspond to our practical interests in seeing patterns in the world. As Ramberg puts it,

> our identification of objects and the changes they undergo implements and is given point by the explanatory generalizations to which they yield and by which we manage our dealings with them ... We couldn't fail to discover general relations by which we understand the changes we perceive in the physical objects about us, because we are by nature disposed to count as changes and as persistent subjects of such changes whatever will yield general patterns allowing us to predict our environment. (1999: 611).

Davidson dispenses with Kant's distinction between raw data and conceptualized appearances, but he retains the idea that in our commerce with the environment we necessarily see individual objects and events as particularizing general causal regularities. Finally, in a vein closer to Hume (and Quine) than Kant, Davidson grounds these patterns in natural selection.

> We are born, as Quine has emphasized, treating some pairs of things as more similar than others. We react differentially to sudden loud noises, and since we do not like such sounds, we soon learn to cringe from what has frequently preceded them. Thus long prior to ... anything that can properly be considered concept formation, we act as if we had learned crude laws. We are inducers from birth; if we were not, infant mortality would be the rule, if there were any infants. Concepts, conceptualized laws, the idea of causal relations between events, build on these foundations.
> (Davidson 1995d: 275)

As we acquire more experience we change and improve our classifications to accommodate more profitable inductions, where the strict and exceptionless laws of a theory of everything provide the theoretical limit of such improvements; but these improvements are possible because from the start we see objects and events as incarnating general causal relations.

We have been talking about laws and generalizations, and it is important to note that while a law is a universal generalization ("All *F*s are *G*s"), not every universal generalization is a law; to meet this higher standard, a generalization has to support counterfactual and subjunctive conditionals, and it has to be supported by its instances. A generalization, "All *F*s are *G*s", supports subjunctive and counterfactual conditionals if we can infer from it not only that if x is F then it is G, but *were* x F, then it *would be* G.[23] And, further, to say that a generalization, for example, "All emeralds are green", is supported by its instances is to say that its degree of confirmation increases each time we observe a new green emerald.[24]

From these two conditions on laws it follows that laws – or what Davidson calls *strict laws* – dispense with causal concepts and *ceteris paribus* clauses. The problem with causal concepts, as we saw earlier in this section, is precisely that they thwart our efforts to improve our generalizations by paring down the control conditions we roll into a *ceteris paribus* clause. And the problem with these escape clauses is that their function is precisely to hold the place of the conditions that lie beyond the scope of our theory and its laws. An idealized or *strict science*, however, treats the world as a closed system, no part of which lies beyond its scope.[25] This is precisely why only physics, which treats the entire cosmos as its domain, can aspire to being a strict science and its laws aspire to being strict laws.

The generalizations of the human sciences, however, cannot do without their causal concepts, and hence without their *ceteris paribus* clauses. We improve upon (7) when we describe sugar in physico-chemical terms, but as Davidson writes,

> the same cannot be said of intentional actions and the propositional states and events that describe them. An intentional action is an action caused by states and events that rationalize it; it is a basic aspect of a belief or desire that it will cause certain sorts of action under appropriate conditions. These are, I think, irreducible aspects of reason-explanations; a science that tries to eliminate the causal element from these concepts will succeed only by changing the subject, for here causality is connected with … rationality.
>
> (Davidson 1985a: 246)

Our concept of the attitudes has their causal or dispositional character written into them. For example, Fred's wanting to shoot Barney just *is* his being disposed to pursue any course of action that would bring it about that he shoots Barney, were his beliefs (such as that it is Barney standing before him, that the gun he holds in his hand is loaded, etc.) true and everything else being equal (e.g. his not having any other, overriding desires);[26] and the concept of an action just is "the concept of something that is caused in certain ways", namely, by an agent's having a reason for performing the action (Davidson 1993d: 302). Reasons cause the actions they rationalize, and reason explanations are superficial, causal explanations; but we can bring a reason and the action it causes under a covering law only at the expense of our explanation's surrendering its teleological character.

7.5 Causes and epiphenomena

Why should we mourn, though, if an explanation loses its teleological character? Fred's having a reason to shoot his old friend is identical to a physical state of his body, hence there is some physical event e_P that causes his action, and there *are* strict laws connecting physical events. Appealing to this strict law we can say that he shoots his old friend *because* e_P occurred, where the "because" indicates that we have embedded the causal relation between e_P and the shooting in a comprehensive picture of the way the world works. There are no strict laws connecting events described as mental events to other events, hence there is no way to bring the causal relation between Fred's having a reason and the shooting into a comprehensive picture of the world; there is no comparable "because" forthcoming. Why, then, should we bother talking about his reasons, or indeed any mental event, causing actions? If we can always (at least in principle) subsume a causal relation under a strict law when we look at the world through the lens of physical theory, why should we invoke mental concepts at all? And if we can get along with physical laws, what prevents mental events from being *irrelevant* to the business of causal explanation?

One reason, which we shall look at in more detail in §8.6, is that subsuming Fred's reasons and actions under strict physical laws undermines the picture we have of him as a moral agent. If mental concepts are an idly turning wheel with which we can dispense – if, that is, the mental merely accompanies or is an "epiphenomenon" of the physical, just as a steam-whistle accompanies the workings of a locomotive engine but has no causal influence on the engine's operations[27] – then our reasons never cause our actions; and if our reasons never cause our actions, then the concept of autonomy, which occupies a central role in moral theory, has no application to human beings.

To the charge of epiphenomenalism, that on Davidson's theory mental events are causally inert, a first defence is that the objection does not apply to his theory. Fred's having a reason to shoot Barney is a mental event e_M and, as we have said and as we shall see in more detail in Chapter 8, there is some physical event e_P such that $e_M = e_P$; hence if e_P causes Fred's shooting Barney then, by the substitution principle, e_M causes Fred's shooting Barney.

This response, though, misses the point of the objection. To see this, we need to introduce a distinction between token-epiphenomenalism and type-epiphenomenalism. Following Brian McLaughlin (who, in turn, follows C. D. Broad's earlier discussion[28]) we introduce *token-epiphenomenalism* as the thesis that mental events cannot cause any events, and *type-epiphenomenalism* as the thesis that no event causes any other in virtue of its falling under a mental type. McLaughlin then goes on to observe that

> When [his critics] charge that [Davidson] is committed to epiphenomenalism, they do not mean that he is committed to denying that mental events cause physical events [= token-epiphenomenalism]. They mean, rather, that he is committed to the view that when mental events cause physical events, they do so in virtue of falling under physical types, and not in virtue of falling under mental types [= type-epiphenomenalism].
>
> (1993: 27)

There is an event that is Fred's having a reason to shoot Barney, and that event does cause him to shoot Barney, but the *causally relevant properties* of that event are its physical properties, such as its having certain neurophysiological characteristics, and not its psychological properties. That the event (with its physical properties) is *also* his having what he takes to be a good reason to shoot his neighbour is irrelevant. Compare, for example, a copy of Shakespeare's plays' being placed on a shelf, and that event's causing the shelf to collapse. The property of that event, in virtue of which the shelf collapses, is the book's being placed on the shelf with a certain force, and not that the book is a book of Shakespeare's plays; the book placed with that force could have been Marlowe's plays, and the shelf would still have collapsed. The placing the book, *as* or *qua* the placing of a physical object and not *as* the placing of a volume of England's greatest poet, caused the collapse.

Davidson typically defends himself against this criticism by charging, in turn, that his critics misunderstand his account of the causal relation.

> Given my concept of events and causality, it makes no sense to speak of an event being a cause "as" anything at all. [My account] is formulated on the assumption that events are ... particulars, and that causal relations are extensional relations between such events. ... But then there is no room for a concept of "cause as" which would make causality a relation among three or four entities, rather than between two. ... If causality is a relation between events, it holds between them no matter how they are described. (Davidson 1993b: 6)

Davidson's complaint is that his critics confuse causation with explanation, and they subvert his picture of causation as a two-place extensional (i.e. subject to the substitution principle) relation. The president of the United States gives the State of the Union speech, and this information is important as long as we want to understand why Bill Clinton was a target of partisan attack, for there is no reason why a speech by Chelsea's father would prompt an attack by Congressional Republicans. But whether we describe him *as* a president or *as* Chelsea's father, one and the same man was attacked by the opposition. Like *v*'s being attacked by *u*, *y*'s being caused by *x* is a two-place relation between particulars, and the terms we use to name those particulars are subject to the substitution principle. We may be able to fit an occurrence of that relation into our understanding of the world, only if we describe *x* as *F*; but regardless of that fact about us, their causal relatedness is insensitive to how we characterize *F*.

This response, however, cannot sustain a defence against the charge of type-epiphenomenalism. Jaegwon Kim observes that

> to talk about the role of properties in causation we don't need to introduce the "*qua*" locution or any other multi-termed causal relation ... all that is necessary is the recognition that it makes sense to ask a question of the form "What is it about events *c* and *e* that makes it the case that *c* is the cause of *e*?" and be able to answer them, intelligibly and informatively, by

> saying something like "Because c is an event of kind F and e is one of kind G" ... This is only to acknowledge that the causal relation obtains between pairs of events because they are events of certain kinds, or have certain properties.
>
> (1993: 21–2)

If x bears R to y, then it is, indeed, because there is something about x and something about y such that they stand in R. Sam is Jack's elder brother because Sam was born of parents P at time t, Jack was born of parents P' at t', and $P = P'$ and t is earlier than t'. Nevertheless, someone's being the elder brother of another is a two-place extensional relation, and likewise that x causes y in virtue of their belonging to certain kinds or types has no bearing on the logical form or extensionality of the causal relation. And, further, it is reasonable to expect that if two events e_1 and e_2 are causally related, but other events e_3 and e_4 are not, then there is some difference between the pair e_1 and e_2, on the one hand, and the pair e_3 and e_4, on the other, in virtue of which the first are causally related and the second are not. What Kim and other critics are looking for is some account of the way that the existence of the causal relation between e_M and Fred's shooting Barney depends on the mental properties of e_M, in effect, some account that gives content to the "because" in "x performs action A *because* he has reason R". This calls for a fuller account of the nature of causation, not a revision of the logical form of causal relations.

Davidson's response is that the mental is causally relevant through its relationship with the physical. To see how this works, let us say:

> A predicate F *supervenes* on a set of predicates $S = \{G_1, \ldots, G_n\}$ if and only for any two objects x and y, if x is F and y is not F then there is at least one predicate G_i in S such that x is G_i and y is not G_i.

Supervenience thus defines a weak dependence between the property we express with the predicate F and the properties represented by the Gs. For example, we might say that a certain landscape painting is autumnal, and, obviously, its being so depends on the way the artist arranges the pigments on the surface of the canvas. Its being autumnal, however, is not *identical* to those physical properties of its surface; for example, some other painting may be autumnal, too, and yet have a quite different physical structure. We thus say that the property of being autumnal *supervenes* on the physical properties of the surface of the canvas, and this captures the fact that, for example, were something to happen to the painting (e.g. if it were inexpertly cleaned) such that we would no longer describe it as autumnal, this would imply that something about the physical properties of its surface would have changed, too.[29]

Davidson's idea, then, is that the mental supervenes on the physical, and in this way an event's mental properties are relevant to its causal relations.

> If two events differ in their psychological properties, they differ in their physical properties (which we assume to be causally efficacious). If supervenience holds, psychological properties *make a difference* to the causal relations of an event, for they matter to the physical properties, and the physical properties matter to causal relations.
>
> (Davidson 1993b: 14, emphasis added)

Were Fred *not* to have a reason to shoot Barney, he would also, therefore, differ in some of his physical properties, since the mental supervenes on the physical. And since physical events can be subsumed under strict laws, we therefore have a full picture of why some, but not other, events are causally related, namely, through those strict laws.

Again, were Fred not to have a reason to shoot Barney, he would differ in some of his physical properties, but the way Davidson defines supervenience does not guarantee that those physical properties are the *right* properties, that is, the physical properties responsible for the shooting. At one point Davidson says, rather unhelpfully, that a person's mental states supervene on *all* the physical predicates true of that person (Davidson 1993b: 17n.). But this leaves open the possibility, however, that Fred's twin could differ in some irrelevant detail – for example, his twin could have a single eyelash slightly longer than Fred's – and that would be sufficient to underwrite their differing in their mental predicates, since all the definition of supervenience requires is that he differ in *some* G_i (Evnine 1991: 69–70).

This objection, though, betrays a failure to appreciate the unity of Davidson's work. Fred's psychological state supervenes on all his physical properties, and the same goes for his twin Ned; but if we are going to say that Fred has a certain reason and Ned does not then that difference will not depend on something hidden or obscure, like the lengths of their eyelashes or events buried in their brains. Rather, if we believe that Fred has a reason to shoot Barney (in the sense of his having beliefs and desires that, everything else being equal, would cause him to shoot his best friend), but that Ned does not have a reason to shoot Barnaby (in the sense of his not having beliefs and desires that would cause him to shoot *his* best friend), then we have interpreted their mental states differently based on something *relevant* we have observed in their situated behaviours or life histories. And it is this – whatever we have seen in their current behaviour or history – that is the physical difference that makes a difference to their respective psychological states. We will, in particular, have seen Fred, but not Ned, do something that leads us to believe that he has homicidal intentions. Certainly, we can hypothesize whatever irrelevant details we like about Fred and Ned, and there is nothing in the way Davidson defines "supervenience" to preclude this irrelevant difference from being the physical difference that makes the psychological difference, as required by the definition. If we combine that definition with Davidson's account of how we interpret an agent's actions, attitudes and meanings, however, then we see that our attributions of reasons *will* be sensitive to the *right* differences in their total physical state. An important point to bear in mind, therefore, is that the base of physical properties upon which a mental property supervenes includes facts that range beyond the surface of an agent's skin and especially includes his situated behaviour. Indeed, what goes on "inside" a person plays little or no role in our interpreting his mental life. We return to this point in §9.2.[30]

Chapter 8

The matter of mind

In this chapter we turn from reason explanation to the nature of human actors themselves. This move takes us, one might say, from the logic of the social sciences to their ontology, except that Davidson's premier achievement in the philosophy of mind has been to reconceptualize and thereby recast the traditional problems. Fodor writes that when he "was a boy in graduate school, the philosophy of mind had two main division: the mind/body problem and the problem of other minds" (1995: 292). Davidson rewrites the mind–body problem by arguing that "there are no such things as minds, but people have mental properties" (1995b: 231). That is, philosophers have erred in looking at the mental through the lens of ontology: "the mental", he says, "is not an ontological ... category" standing opposed to the category of the physical (1987b: 46). And in his recent writings, Davidson has refashioned the issues that underlie and seem to generate the problem of other minds.

We shall return in Chapter 9 to the problem of other minds, which has a bearing upon the basis of modern scepticism and the deep issue of the relation between subjectivity and objectivity. In this chapter we examine Davidson's account of the mind or, better, what John McDowell calls "minded beings". It is worthwhile to remind ourselves that while our discussion will centre on the deep differences between, on the one hand, the natural sciences, especially physics as the paradigm of a strict science, and, on the other, common-sense or "folk" psychology, Davidson's conclusions apply equally to the rest of the social sciences – sociology, economics, anthropology, history, legal studies and so on – since the norms of reason are implicated in these investigations, too.

8.1 Cartesian dualism

Descartes's grand philosophical goal was a comprehensive theory of what he identified as the two spheres of created nature: the physical world and the mental world. As every beginning philosophy student knows, Descartes sees these spheres as distinct *substances*, which is a notion he inherits and reworks from his Scholastic teachers. For the Scholastics, as for Aristotle, a substance is an individual thing: a certain "this" one can point to. Socrates, Aristotle's favourite example of a substance, is just this sort of thing, as are the rose bush outside my window and the fountain pen I grasp in my right hand. For Aristotelians, the propriety of calling these objects "substances" is based on their being able to exist on their own, as opposed to properties (such as *being red* or *human*) and relations (*being taller than*), which always exist *in* or are predicated *of* something else.[1]

Descartes verbally agrees with Aristotle that a substance "exists in such a way as to depend on no other thing for its existence" (Descartes 1985: 210; AT VIIIA 24), but he gives the notion of independence a new meaning. His leading idea is that two entities or types of entities *x* and *y* are mutually independent if there are kinds or families of concepts that apply to *x* but not to *y*, and vice versa. Thus the rose bush and my pen are a single (type of) substance, since spatial concepts (the rose bush *is located outside* my window, the pen *is in* my right hand) apply to both; but Socrates' mind and his body are distinct substances, for although we can say that Socrates' body sits in an Athenian prison, *it makes no sense* to say that his mind is there. Minds are neither here nor there; as *res cogitans*, minds are not anywhere. Similarly, Socrates, as a thing that thinks, believes that fleeing Athens would be unjust, but to his body we can attribute no beliefs or mental attitudes; as *res extensa*, bodies entertain no thoughts.[2]

Descartes is a conceptual dualist, therefore, and his conceptual dualism drives his ontological dualism. *Ontological dualism* is the familiar idea that matter and mind are different sorts of things, respectively, *res extensa* and *res cogitans*, while *conceptual dualism* is the thesis that psychology and physics are conceptually disparate theories of, respectively, mental phenomena and physical phenomena. Psychology is couched in the familiar language of common-sense mental concepts, for example, belief, desire, intention and so on, which, according to Descartes, are united by their all being states of conscious awareness; in contrast, the fundamental or constitutive principle of physics is that physical concepts all reduce to mathematical descriptions of spatial properties and relations. Since Socrates is physically imprisoned and is aware of his imprisonment, he comprises two substances, an idea that would have perplexed Aristotle.

Descartes supports the mutual independence of matter and mind with several well-known arguments. His strongest takes conceptual dualism as its premise, and infers that mind and body belong to different ontological spheres. The argument, as it becomes clear from Descartes's response to Arnauld's criticism in the *Fourth Objections*, is that we possess "complete and adequate" theories of body, on the one hand, and of mind, on the other, and that the constitutive principles of these theories define *res extensa* and *res cogitans* in distinct terms. "The concept of body includes nothing at all which belongs to the mind, and the concept of mind includes nothing at all which belongs to the body"; and "from the mere fact that I can clearly and distinctly understand one substance apart from another", that is, that I possess complete, adequate and non-overlapping theories of each substance, Descartes infers that it "is enough to make me certain that one excludes the other" (Descartes 1984: 158–9; AT VII 225–6).[3]

Descartes's most famous argument, but also his most problematic, is that while I can doubt that my body exists I cannot, without contradiction, doubt that my mind exists, and therefore my body is not my mind. The premises of this argument are drawn from the narrative of the first and second *Meditations*. Here, Descartes draws us into his famously overheated cell, where we meditate along with him and see that the only knowledge that can withstand increasingly powerful sceptical considerations is my knowing the contents of my own thoughts; my mind, I conclude with Descartes's meditator, can exist and perform all its functions independently of my body.

In his early work, *Treatise on Man*,[4] Descartes presents a mirror image to this reasoning. He presents a thought experiment to persuade us that the operations of bodies are independent of mental entities and concepts. He proposes we imagine that God creates a body that is "nothing but a statue or machine made of [the element] earth ... with the explicit intention of making it as much as possible like us" (Descartes 1985: 99). Descartes adopts this tactical conceit in his battle against the Scholastic theory that natural bodies combine formless matter and an intelligible form, and to demonstrate the possibility of a "complete and adequate" theory of the physical world. Despite having most of the details wrong, Descartes's theory represents a major step in the development of modern natural science.

8.2 *L'homme machine*

Davidson has his own version of Descartes's second thought experiment. He observes that a human being "is a physical object which ... functions according to physical laws. So there can be no reason why an object indistinguishable from a natural person should not be ... built by people" (Davidson 1990b: 13), and he imagines that such a research project has been realized:

> Suppose that we understand what goes on in the brain perfectly, in the sense that we can describe each detail in purely physical terms – that even the electrical and chemical processes, and certainly the neurological ones, have been reduced to physics. ... While we are dreaming let us also dream that ... we can build a machine that, when exposed to the lights and sounds of the world, mimics the motions of a man. ... Finally ... let us imagine *l'homme machine* has actually been built, in the shape of a man, and out of the very stuff of a man ... everything we can learn about the physical structure and workings of actual human brains and bodies has been replicated ... [and] Art (as I shall call him or it) has acted in all observable ways like a man. (1973d: 245)

Coming, as we are, from Descartes in the previous section, we expect Davidson to use Art to argue for mind–body dualism and, while this is partly true, his project is more complicated and more interesting. Cartesian dualism, which combines ontological and conceptual dualism, is one of the traditional options in the philosophy of mind, the other being versions of materialism, according to which persons and their states are *tokenwise* identical to physical objects and states of physical objects. Materialists often combine ontological monism with conceptual monism, that is, they posit that persons and their mental states are *typewise* identical to physical objects and states, too.[5] In one of the classic works of philosophy of mind in the twentieth century, J. J. C. Smart argues that mental processes are identical to neurological processes (Smart 1971), and other philosophers have tried to show how we can translate our talk about mental states into talk about the observable behaviour of physical systems (Ryle 1949), or about the sensory inputs and behavioural outputs and the internal "programming" that mediates between them (Putnam 1960). Davidson splits the difference between Cartesian dualism and strong versions of materialism: he combines *ontological monism* (= tokenwise identity) with *conceptual dualism* (= denial of typewise identity) in a theory he describes, for reasons we shall explore in this and the following sections, as *anomalous monism*.

Let us return to Art and assume that we observe him making the sounds represented by the sentence "Das ist ein Kaninchen". Were we ignorant of his provenance, and were we, at the same time, to see Art confronted by a rabbit in good light and without anything blocking his view, we should, without hesitation, say that he believes a rabbit is present, wants to communicate this belief and intends that we should interpret his utterance as meaning that a rabbit is present. However, knowing what we know, should we describe Art's behaviour in these terms?

It is clear that Descartes would say that we should not. By hypothesis, Art is made exclusively from *physical* materials, and believing, desiring and meaning that a rabbit is present are *mental* properties. Contrary to appearances, Art does *not* mean that a rabbit is present, because Art does not mean, believe or desire anything at all. In light of the conception of meaning developed over the course of the preceding chapters, however, this verdict is deeply suspect. To say that Art means that a rabbit is present by his utterance "Das ist ein Kaninchen" is to see that utterance as part of a coherent pattern of linguistic behaviour, and as situated in a context in which it makes good sense to attribute to his words that meaning, as part of the larger project of interpreting Art's other utterances and explaining his other actions. Indeed, as we saw in §4.2, when an interpreter hears Art's utterance she already perceives that action as saturated with meaning, although she may not know what that meaning is.

Certainly, Descartes would reject this model of linguistic understanding, but the difference on which a Cartesian dualist insists – that Art lacks an inner mental space wherein he represents to himself a rabbit's presence – is a difference that makes no difference to meaning and communication. Taking this position, Davidson agrees with Wittgenstein:

> Suppose everyone had a box with something in it: we call it a "beetle". No one can look into anyone else's box, and everyone says he knows what a beetle is only by looking at *his* beetle. – Here it would be quite possible for everyone to have something different in his box. One might even imagine such a thing constantly changing. – But suppose the word "beetle" had a use in these people's language? – If so it would not be used as the name of a thing. The thing in the box has no place in the language-game at all; not even as a *something*: for the box might even be empty. – No, one can "divide through" by the thing in the box; it cancels out, whatever it is.
>
> (Wittgenstein 1958: §293)

On the assumption that "Art ... has acted in all observable ways like a man" we may "divide through" the existence of whatever may or may not occur in an inner mental space as irrelevant to whether Art means anything by his words. As we shall see in Chapter 9, there are "compelling *psychological* and *epistemological* reasons we should deny that there are" (Davidson 1973d: 250) special objects located in an inner mental space when we think, mean, desire and so on; and the failure to renounce this stubbornly persistent thesis vitiates both Cartesian and contemporary theories of language and mind. We shall see these arguments in Chapter 9, and Davidson's argument for ontological monism in §8.3, so for now let us set aside Descartes's negative verdict and suppose that mental and physical properties do not lie within the provinces of distinct and exclusive substances.

Materialists come in a variety of stripes, but many endorse some form of reductionism. *Reductionism* is a common move in scientific theorizing, in which one theory is absorbed into a second, usually more comprehensive, explanatory framework. Reducing a theory θ_1 to a second theory θ_2 may take a relatively unproblematic form if θ_1 and θ_2 differ only in their applying similar concepts to (what are originally taken as) heterogeneous domains. Incorporating Galileo's account of free-falling terrestrial bodies into Newtonian mechanics and gravitational theory, which applies to both terrestrial *and* celestial phenomena, is a straightforward and uncontroversial reduction in this manner. Alternatively, the reduction may be more complicated and contentious if, prior to subsuming θ_1 within the framework of θ_2, the theories draw upon substantially different concepts. The obvious example here is the project of reducing folk psychology to the natural sciences.[6]

In its general form, the thesis that we can reduce θ_1 to θ_2 comprises two claims. First, θ_1 reduces to θ_2 only if we can define the terms and predicates of θ_1 in the vocabulary of θ_2. For example, we can use the general term "H_2O" from the language of chemistry to define the word "water" of colloquial English, since being H_2O is a necessary and sufficient condition for anything's being water: for any sample x, x is water if and only if x is H_2O. Secondly, we can reduce θ_1 to θ_2 only if we can explain the general principles of θ_1 by deducing them from statements in θ_2, perhaps with some additional assumptions. For example, it is possible to derive the laws of thermodynamics, such as the Boyle–Charles law for ideal gases, from the principles of classical mechanics. To carry off the reduction, one first defines the special vocabulary of thermodynamics in terms of concepts drawn from mechanics, for example, we define the temperature of a gas as the mean kinetic energy of the molecules that constitute the gas. This definition serves as a first *bridge principle* between the two theories, and it allows us to begin to connect statements in thermodynamics with statements in mechanics: replacing occurrences of the special thermodynamic expression "temperature of *x*" with the classical mechanical expression "mean kinetic energy of the molecules that constitute *x*", we can infer statements of thermodynamics from truths of mechanics. Sometimes a definitional equivalence is all we need to complete the reduction, such as in the reduction of number theory to set theory, but at other times something more is needed. In the thermodynamics example, we first have to assume that a gas *is* a collection of spherical molecules of equal but negligible masses and volumes, and we also have to make certain statistical assumptions concerning the positions and momenta of the molecules. With these bridge principles in place, then, physicists can derive from Newtonian mechanics the thermodynamic law that the product of the pressure and volume of an ideal gas is directly proportional to the absolute temperature of the gas, and thus reduce thermodynamics to mechanics.

To return to the mind–body problem, the possibility of reducing the mental to the physical depends on finding psychophysical bridge laws relating Art's mental states to the physical states of his body. If we knew such principles, we could resolve the question of whether Art means that a rabbit is present by identifying the corresponding physical state and checking to see whether Art is in that physical state. A behaviourist, for example, looks for bridge laws that relate mental states to dispositions to engage in characteristic patterns of behaviour (described in a way that makes no mentions of mental concepts). On this view, Art means or believes that a rabbit is present just in case he behaves in those ways we would expect him to, were he to believe that a rabbit is present and want to communicate that belief to his audience.

It is easy to see that the prospects for this style of reduction are dim. No behaviour can be lined up with a mental state taken in isolation, for unless a person has other complementary beliefs and desires, that mental state will not suffice to cause the behaviour. For example, we can identify Art's walking away from a place with his desire to stay away from rabbits *only if* we think he believes, say, that there is a rabbit in that place and he believes, too, that he is allergic to rabbits. Moreover, a person's having a certain belief (that a rabbit is present) at two different times in his life may correspond to quite different ways of behaving (walking or not walking away from a place), depending on what desires (to avoid an allergic reaction, to test the allergist's claim that it is all in his head) that belief combines with to produce that behaviour.

An alternative to behaviourism, which has especially gained currency recently, is the thesis that psychology is reducible to neurophysiology or, more generally, to the neurosciences (which are themselves, so the argument goes, ultimately reducible to physics). The increasing sophistication of medical imaging devices, especially positron-emission tomography (PET) scans, permits scientists to image neural activity by monitoring patterns of energy consumption in the brain, and this nourishes the hope that we can identify types of mental states and events with types of physical states and events. According to this version of materialism, then, Art's meaning that a rabbit is present is typewise identical to a state of his nervous system. If this is right, then we should be able to formulate psychophysical bridge principles that define the special vocabulary of psychology in neurophysiological or even physico-chemical terms, and explain psychological principles by absorbing them into a natural scientific framework. Thus it may be possible one day to derive the psychoanalytic principle that a person will, everything else being equal, displace aggression when her fear of retaliation bars the normal direction of emotional release, from a detailed understanding of the micro-structure of the human brain, via bridge principles connecting psychoanalysis with neuroscience. And it may be possible, too, to embed in a comprehensive framework of the natural sciences the folk-psychological generalization that if someone believes that a rabbit is present and wants to communicate that belief to an audience then, *ceteris paribus*, he intends that his audience should interpret his utterance "Das ist ein Kaninchen" as meaning that a rabbit is present.

8.3 The argument for monism

The leading idea of Davidson's philosophy of mind is that despite the ever more remarkable achievements that scientists announce daily, these hopes are unfounded. There can be no psychophysical bridge laws, and therefore reductive materialism is false. Davidson acknowledges that this assertion sounds like "a form of *hubris* against which philosophers are often warned" (1980a: 216), but are sometimes guilty of; he is persuaded, though, that the claim is warranted. We examine his reasons in the remainder of this chapter.

Davidson thus departs from Smart, Ryle and the neuro-philosopers[7] in denying conceptual monism, and in this respect he agrees with Descartes *vis-à-vis* conceptual dualism. Interestingly, though, while Descartes and Davidson agree that the difference between psychology and physics is a *deep* difference, they draw contrary inferences from that difference. This stems partly from Descartes's making a quick inference from conceptual to ontological dualism, facilitated by his definition of substance and the principle that "each substance has one principle property which constitutes its nature and essence, and to which all its other properties are referred" (Descartes 1985: 210; AT VIIIA 25). As we saw in Chapter 6, Davidson insists upon the distinction between entities and their descriptions; hence where "there is a single ontology" there may, nevertheless, be "more than one way of describing and explaining the items in that ontology" (Davidson 1995a: 4). In fact, Davidson exploits the difference between the mental and the physical as a premise in the argument for ontological monism, and he observes that if there is anything surprising about his argument, it is this appeal to conceptual *dualism* "to help establish the identity of the mental with ... the physical", that is, ontological *monism* (1980a: 223).

Let us see how this works. The argument for ontological monism rests on three premises:

(i) For every mental event there is some physical event with which it causally interacts.
(ii) Any two events related as cause and effect can be brought under a covering law.
(iii) There are no (a) psychological laws nor (b) psychophysical laws.

And here is the argument:

1. Select a mental event e_m; by premise (i), it causally interacts with some physical event e_p.
2. By premise (ii), there is a law that connects e_m and e_p.
3. By premise (iiia), however, that law cannot be a psychological law.
4. By premise (iiib), there are no psychophysical laws. Therefore, we look to physics for the law connecting e_m and e_p.
5. If, however, e_m instantiates a physical law, then it must have a physical description, and hence e_m is a physical as well as a mental event.

This last inference, that if e_m has a physical description then it is a physical event, follows from the way Davidson defines *being a mental event* and *being a physical event*. To identify an event as either mental or physical, a Cartesian looks to the type of object (i.e. the kind of substance) that performs the action or suffers the happening, whereas Davidson eschews the mental and physical as ontological categories. "There are no such *things* as minds," he writes, "but people have mental properties, which is to say that certain psychological predicates are true of them" (1995b: 231, emphasis added). Something is a mental event or state just in case it satisfies a description (i.e. a psychological predicate is true of it) that contains at least one psychological term essentially, in the sense that there is no logically equivalent description not containing some psychological term; and similarly for physical events and states. Jack's seeing Jill at the top of the hill is a mental event (if we read "seeing" as synonymous with "perceiving"), and it is, let us suppose, identical to a pattern of neural activity caused by an inverted Jill-shaped image's falling on the back of his retinas, which are physical events (since "pattern of neural activity" and "an inverted Jill-shaped image's falling on the back of his retinas" describes physical states of Jack's brain and eyes). It is the same event, alternatively in psychological and physical guise, but this duality is no more mysterious than one man's being *both* a parent of Chelsea Clinton *and* a president of the United States. The identity of an event, to the extent that it resembles an ordinary, extensional object, is indifferent to the terms we use to characterize it, as we saw in §6.3.

Note that since the argument is valid, if the premises are all true then the conclusion – that any arbitrarily selected mental event is *also* a physical event – is true. Our examination of the argument, therefore, will focus on the premises. In the remainder of this section we discuss premises (i) and (ii), with a brief word about (iiia), and in §8.4–§8.6 we focus on premises (iiia) and (iiib).

Premise (i) of the argument, that mental events causally interact with physical events, is certainly right. Light rays emitted from the sun bounce off the surface of Jill (a physical event); some of that light travels through the transparent corneas and lenses in Jack's eyes, striking the back of the retinas and initiating a series of impulses along the optic nerve, leading to a pattern of activity in Jack's visual cortex (all physical events); then Jack recognizes Jill and recalls the memory of their trip up the hill (both mental events); and these thoughts, in turn, cause him to walk towards her (which a behaviourist would characterize as certain motions in his body, and hence, let us say, is a physical event). Short of adopting occasionalism, it is hard to see how this commonplace chain of events could come about unless mental and physical events are causally related. Indeed, Descartes allows that they causally interact, despite his claim that the mind and body are complete and separate entities. He submits that the nature of the soul "is such that it receives as many ... different perceptions as there occur different movements in" the centre of the brain; and, conversely, the soul can move the body "in various different ways" (Descartes 1985: 341; AT XI 355) Notoriously, though, the precise mechanism whereby the body and soul causally affect one another is more than a little mysterious.[8]

Certainly, these observations show only that *some* mental events causally interact with physical events, not that *every* mental event fits somewhere into a causal sequence leading from or to physical events. From this weaker thesis, it follows only (if the rest of the argument is sound) that some mental events are identical to physical events. This may be enough to persuade us that ontological monism is true, since it would be odd if some mental events were physical events, but others were not. Moreover, given that at least some mental events causally interact with physical events, and the fact (examined in §7.3) that there are causal relations among mental events themselves, it is doubtful there could be a proper subset of mental events that were causally isolated from physical events. For one thing, if there were such a set, it would represent a singular break in the causal chain and render those events unknowable, if the Kantian idea that we understand the world by discovering causal connections among the diverse events and objects we come across is right.

We saw Davidson's argument for the premise (ii) back in Chapter 7, where we examined his argument for the cause–law thesis. Recall from the discussion in §7.4 that a law is a true universal generalization that *covers* a singular causal statement, in the sense that from the law and a statement that one event of a type mentioned in the law occurs, we can infer that a second event of a sort described by the law will occur, too, and that this second event was caused by the occurrence of the first event. The idea, again, is that when we subsume a singular causal statement under a covering law, we explain the facts it expresses by showing they are an instance of a pattern or nomological regularity; we show that those facts are just what we would expect, given the particulars of the situation and our understanding of the natural world. Recall, too, that not every true universal generalization is a law: a universal generalization counts as a law only if it supports counterfactual and subjunctive conditionals.

Premise (iiia) denies to psychology the status of a strict science. (This is intended to cover both folk psychology and scientific psychology.) Something is an exact science just in case its generalizations are (or can be reformulated as) strict laws, and psychology fails this test on account of the presence of causal terms and *ceteris paribus* clauses in its generalizations. We shall have more to say about (iiia) below, in §8.5.

8.4 Intentionality

In this section we turn to the reasons Davidson cites for the anomalism of the mental – which is the thesis that psychophysical generalizations fail to qualify as laws – and this takes us to the heart of his philosophy of mind. The background to premise (iiib) lies in our discussion in §6.3, where we saw that whether we can explain why an event occurred may depend on how we describe that event. To explain Bill Clinton's writing a cheque to Stanford University, we mention his relation to a Stanford student; and, appealing to the principle that whoever is a parent of a college student bears financial responsibility for her tuition, we explain that he wrote a cheque to the university *because* he is a parent of a Stanford student. Similarly, to explain Bill Clinton's speaking to a joint session of the US Congress, we observe that he satisfies the open sentence, "*x* is a president of the United States"; and, given the directive that a president gives the State of the Union speech, we explain that he spoke *because* he is a president of the United States. Bill Clinton is Chelsea Clinton's father, hence a parent of a Stanford student gave a speech to a joint session of Congress; put in these terms, though, his speaking resists our efforts to fit the occurrence into any pattern. There are no generalizations that bridge the classificatory schemes of the rights and duties of parents, on the one hand, and the American political system, on the other. Hence while it is true that Chelsea Clinton's father spoke to a joint session of Congress, we cannot explain why he did so, unless we change the subject and describe him as a president of the United States.

The claim that there can be no psychophysical laws is analogous to the idea that there are no bridge principles connecting US politics with the system of parental rights and duties, only stronger; it is the thesis that there *could be* no law-like generalizations linking psychology and the natural sciences. In this respect a psychophysical generalization resembles "All emeralds are grue", which has one foot in each of two disparate families of concepts.[9] Psychophysical and grue-emerald statements are *heteronomic*, unlike "All emeralds are green", "All emerires are grue" or "The pressure of an ideal gas in a closed container is directly proportional to its temperature", which are *homonomic* generalizations, that is, they draw together concepts or predicates "that we know *a priori* are made for each other" (Davidson 1980a: 218). That there are no psychophysical laws follows from the fact that heteronomic statements fail to satisfy the criteria for being law-like set out in §7.4, hence while there may be true psychophysical generalizations, there are no such laws.

We need, therefore, to examine Davidson's reasons for calling psychophysical generalizations heteronomic, and to this end we ought to fix the scope of Davidson's conception of the mental. He restricts the term "mental" or "psychological" to verbs

> that express propositional attitudes like believing, intending, desiring, hoping, knowing, perceiving, noticing, remembering, and so on. Such verbs are characterized by the fact that they sometimes feature in sentences with subjects that refer to persons, and are completed by embedded sentences in which the usual rules of substitution appear to break down.
> (*Ibid*.: 210)

Hence, unlike Descartes, Davidson avoids the notions of privacy and conscious awareness when he determines the measure of the mental; its "distinguishing feature", rather, is "that it exhibits what Brentano called intentionality" (*ibid*.: 211).[10]

Intentionality is the property shared by *inter alia* maps, portraits, and blueprints, and also mental states and linguistic expressions, of being directed at objects or states of affairs that are external to themselves. Thus, on the one hand, the sentence

(1) Antony ordered the death of Cicero,

is a physical object like any other – one can imagine, for example, weighing it or analysing the chemical composition of the ink in which it is written – but, on the other, it is (as Wittgenstein would say) a *queer* sort of thing; unlike the fountain pen I grasp in my hand or the rose bush outside my window, (1) is *about* things (Antony and Cicero) and events (the death of Cicero) that exist outside and independently of it. In this sense (1), but neither my pen nor the rose bush, exhibits the property of intentionality.

Similarly, the report that

(2) Livia believes that Antony ordered the death of Cicero,

attributes to a human subject (Livia) a mental state that, if ontological monism is true, is identical to a state of a person's body, just as the property having a temperature of 37°C is a state of a person. Having a temperature of 37°C and having a belief are localized in the subject in the sense of being modifications of the subject's body; to have a belief is to sustain some pattern of neural activity (again, assuming the truth of ontological monism), while having a temperature of 37°C consists in the molecules of one's body having a certain mean kinetic energy. At the same time, though, Livia's mental state has the queer property of being about something, and this is reflected in the fact that her mental state has a truth-condition: her belief is true if and only if Antony ordered the death of Cicero.

The status of psychophysical generalizations, therefore, turns on the relation between descriptions of persons couched in intentional terms and descriptions in the language of exact physics, which employs no intentional language. The reductive materialist believes she can fill out bridge principles such as:

> Livia believes that Antony ordered the death of Cicero if and only if she satisfies physical predicate φ,

or

(3) (Art holds "Das ist ein Kaninchen" true_{German} at *t* just in case there is a rabbit present at *t*) if he satisfies physical predicate φ.

These schemata are each of the form,

(4) *x* satisfies mental predicate ψ if [or: if and only if] *x* satisfies physical predicate φ,

where the language of ψ includes our familiar talk of beliefs, desires and so on, which as *propositional* attitudes we partly identify by their contents (represented by a subordinate clause in the report of an attitude), and the language of φ mentions only non-intentional physical properties, states and events.

Let us focus on (3). An interpreter's drawing this inference about the relation between Art's mental state and local situation (i.e. that Art holds the sentence true just in case that situation includes the presence of a rabbit) is a single moment in a larger story she tells about him, including that he is a competent German speaker. Speaking a language is a complex disposition to intend that one's words be interpreted a certain way, and the bulk of this disposition will remain unrealized; in the course of his life Art will verbalize only a finite subset of all the possible German sentences. Hence most of this mental state exists, so to speak, in the subjunctive mood, that is, Art speaks *German* just in case he *would* be inclined to hold certain sentences true, *should* specified conditions obtain.

If the reductive physicalism is true, then there exists a physical correlate to this complex mental state. Once the physicists, neuro-anatomists, biochemists and so on, finish their work, we shall be able to insert a description of this state into the right-hand side of a psychophysical generalization,

(5) Art speaks German if he is in physical state φ.

Unlike the mental state of knowing German, the physical state φ is not a disposition, but rather a fully realized state of Art's nervous system. This, indeed, is why some researchers pursue such a reduction. If being in physical state φ were a mark based on which we could identify Art's mental state, it would be a first step in replacing the qualified generalizations of folk psychology (e.g. "If Art scores well on the exam then he speaks German, unless someone passed him the answers") with exact and exceptionless laws, which we could use to describe and predict his mental states and actions based on our knowledge of his neurophysical state. It would parallel the advance made when chemists and physicists discovered that

(6) A non-ionic compound is water-soluble if the molecules are linked by polar covalent bonds,

and thereby gained a criterion in the language of exact physics that avoids the caveats present in the generalizations of common-sense physical explanations (if a sample dissolves in liquid identified as water, then it is water-soluble, unless the liquid is not really water).

That there exists such a predicate φ may seem doubtful. But consider that, as it stands, (4) is a material conditional and hence states a *de facto* relation between two classes, namely, that *as a matter of contingent fact* the set of creatures that satisfy the psychological predicate ψ contains the set of creatures that satisfy the physical predicate φ. Since both sets are finite we can form a (potentially very long, but still finite) disjunction of open sentences that mentions for every thing with ψ some physical property it has, for example, where each thing with ψ is located on the surface of the earth at 12:00 noon GMT on 1 January 2001; trivially, this complex open sentence in the language of physics will be satisfied by all and only those things that are ψ. Obviously, though, this is not the sort of property that reductive physicalists hope to substitute for φ, for they make the much stronger claim that φ will nomologically correspond to ψ. The physical predicate φ *nomologically corresponds* to the psychological predicate ψ if they are bound together by something stronger than a *de facto* regularity. How exactly we should understand this stronger connection is debated among philosophers of science, and Davidson has not committed himself on the matter. As we noted in Chapter 7, though, causal laws state something stronger than true generalizations, and one consequence of this stronger relation is that the properties expressed by nomologically corresponding predicates continue their side-by-side march into the subjunctive and counterfactual. While every man in a certain room may have a black beard, this fact (i.e. if something satisfies the open sentence "*x* is a man in the room" then as a matter of contingent fact it satisfies "*x* wears a black beard") does not support the inference that *were* another man to enter the room, he *would have* a black beard, too. This *de facto* correspondence differs from the nomological regularity that every ball dropped from the top of a 10-foot tower reaches a terminal velocity of approximately 18 feet per second. Thus, while it is trivially true that we can rig a connection between psychological and physical predicates, it is far from trivial and rather more interesting to claim that *were* we to observe some creature *x* with the physical property φ, he *would* speak German.

8.5 Anomalism of the mental

Over the years, Davidson has defended the anomalism of the mental (premise (iii)) with arguments based on the indeterminacy of interpretation, the dispositional character of mental concepts and the normativity of the mental.[11]

"I once thought that the indeterminacy of translation supplied a reason for supposing … that mental concepts are … not nomologically reducible to physical concepts" (Davidson 2001a: 215), Davidson writes, but now he concedes that he was mistaken: indeterminacy also afflicts explanations in the natural sciences. A healthy human body has a temperature of around 99°F, and it has a temperature of approximately 37°C, too; here we have two measurements, each of which does equally well at tracking a person's temperature, since our real interest is the pattern in the relationship between people's temperatures and other factors, for example, the presence of an infection. This exactly parallels the situation in psychology, where the pattern of a person's mental economy and situated behaviour embodies the same structure, whether we interpret him as having beliefs about rabbits or undetached rabbit parts.

Let us turn, then, to the dispositional character of mental concepts or, as Davidson puts it, the fact that mental concepts are causal concepts (in the sense defined in §7.1):

> An action, for example, must be intentional under some description, but an action is intentional only if it is caused by mental factors such as beliefs and desires. Beliefs and desires are identified in part by the sorts of action they are prone to cause, given the right conditions. (Davidson 1991: 216)

The concept of an action, therefore, cannot be understood apart from its causal history, and, conversely, the concepts of belief and desire cannot be understood apart from their typical causal consequences. But strict scientific laws employ no causal concepts, hence psychological generalizations neither fit with the laws of physics (premise (iiib)) nor can they themselves be refined into strict laws (premise (iiia)).

However, the generalizations of the special sciences, as well as common-sense explanations of physical phenomena, are anomalous in this sense, too, since they also employ causal concepts. When I explain that the accident occurred because the road was slippery, or that an aeroplane's wing does not break when it bends because it is elastic, I employ the causal concepts of slipperiness and elasticity. Now in some cases these explanations merely finesse details we fill in when we replace, for example, the notion of a substance's elasticity with an exact description of its atomic structure; and hence the generalizations of some of the special sciences (e.g. metallurgy), with their causal concepts, can be translated into the language of exact physics as science marches on. But there are other cases, such as the theory of natural selection in biology, where the concepts of the special science do *not* line up in an orderly fashion with physical concepts; in such cases a translation, therefore, means surrendering much of the explanatory content of the generalizations of the special science.

It turns out, then, that psychology is not unique in being anomalous; so are biology, geology and a good deal else. "Much of what I have said about what distinguishes mental concepts from the concepts of a developed science could also be said to [distinguish] the concepts of many of the special sciences such as biology, geology, and meteorology" (Davidson 2001a: 217). Thus psychology shares its anomalousness with those natural sciences that fall short of the exact and exceptionless generalizations of physics. Indeed, it is interesting that we could run Davidson's argument for ontological monism for, for example, biology (substituting "biological" and "biophysical" for "mental" and "psychophysical") to undermine vitalism: the thesis that animate beings are distinguished from the inanimate by their possession of a "vital force" that controls their development and directs their activities. Certainly, vitalism has even fewer defenders today than dualism, but the point is that an argument against one exactly parallels an argument against the other.

This result reminds us of the structure of Davidson's argument and how he departs from Descartes and the tradition. That psychology is neither a strict science (premise (iiia)) nor reducible to a strict science (premise (iiib)) are *premises* in an argument for ontological monism. Neither of these characteristics, however, distinguishes psychology from biology, geology and so on; rather, the fact that psychology (and biology, etc.) possesses them belongs to a general line of reasoning that demonstrates that *the anomalism of psychology has no bearing on its ontology*, or whether psychological phenomena are "as real" as physical phenomena. Indeed, psychological (and biological, etc.) phenomena *are* physical phenomena. The import of the argument, rather, is that "we should feel no pressure to bring about the reduction of the terms by which we typically characterize what is going on in people's minds" to validate our standing as naturalists (Ramberg 1999: 602), nor should we feel pressure to posit mental substance to preserve the autonomy of minded beings.

good pt

confirms

Naturalism in *this* sense is an *ontological thesis* and stands opposed to Cartesian ontological dualism and forms of supernaturalism, and it differs from naturalism as the *conceptual thesis* that equates the natural with the domain of (natural) law. On a conceptual reading, naturalism is the view that something is real only if it can be captured within the explanatory net of physical science; properly speaking, then, naturalism in this sense is a thesis about properties rather than objects. Consider, for example, Fodor's remark that

> sooner or later the physicists will complete the catalogue they've been compiling of the ultimate and irreducible properties of things. When they do, the likes of *spin*, *charm*, and *charge* will perhaps appear upon their list. But *aboutness* surely won't; intentionality simply doesn't go that deep. ... If the semantic and intentional are real properties of things, it must be in virtue of their identity with ... properties that are themselves *neither* intentional *nor* semantic. If aboutness is real, it must really be something else. (1987: 98)

If intentional properties are irreducible to non-intentional and non-semantic ones, that is, if they are irreducible to physical properties, then either intentionality is not a real property of physical things, or it is a real property, but is a property of something non-physical. Fodor denies the antecedent of the hypothesis – that is, he believes that intentional properties are *not* irreducible to non-intentional and non-semantic ones – hence he avoids the dilemma. Unlike Fodor, Davidson and Descartes both affirm the antecedent, but like Fodor they are also intentional realists, so they reject the first horn of the dilemma in the consequent (i.e. they *deny* that intentionality is not a real property of things). Descartes, of course, is an ontological dualist, and thus he grasps the second horn, but Davidson denies that, too!

Davidson's way out is to treat *the natural* as an ontological rather than a conceptual category, and thus to condemn the inference from conceptual dualism (the antecedent, that intentional properties are irreducible to physical properties) to the choice in the consequent between anti-realism (the first horn) and ontological dualism (the second horn) as a *non sequitir*. The natural cuts across the mental and the physical, which *are* conceptual (and not ontological) categories. As naturalists, therefore, we should equate the real with the natural and affirm that everything that exists (with the exception, perhaps, of numbers and other abstract objects) is empirically accessible and lies within the domain of physical theory; as it happens, though, some configurations of real things can be understood (i.e. explained) through reason explanations, too. Conceptual dualism, however, is consistent with our naturalism (= ontological monism), and indeed complements it.

8.6 Norms of the mental and the physical

Davidson does see a fundamental difference between our understanding of human beings and of physical phenomena, and he locates this difference in the normativity of the mental. One sense in which the mental is normative is that to say that someone believes, desires and so on, that *p* rules out certain patterns of thought. If I believe that *p* then I cannot, on pain of contradiction, believe that not-*p*, nor ought I to deny statements on which *p* confers a high degree of probability; and if I believe that *p* and want that *q*, and I believe, too, that doing *x* will probably cause it to be the case that *q* given that *p*, then everything else being equal, I ought not, on pain of incontinence, to not do *x*. The mental is normative, therefore, in so far as the basic principles of logic and inductive reasoning, and the principle of continence, define the structure of a person's attitudes and actions, and therewith what it is to have a thought or perform an action.

In this sense, then, logical and other rational norms are *constitutive principles of the mental*. The rule that one cannot believe that not-*p* if he believes that *p* is not merely an empirical constraint, but makes that belief *that* attitude with *that* content.[12] I cannot defeat Gary Kasparov at chess, and I cannot check the queen in chess, but the "cannot" carries a different modal force in the two cases; in one it describes an empirical limitation owing to my lack of skill at chess, while not even a grandmaster can place his opponent's queen in check. This difference signals that the second statement, in describing a pattern of activity, prescribes a property the queen cannot lose without ceasing to *be* a queen and thereby identifies both the piece and the game one plays with it. Similarly, there are logical and other rational

> relations amongst beliefs; amongst beliefs, desires and intentions; [and] between beliefs and the world, [and these

> relations] make beliefs the beliefs they are; therefore they cannot in general lose these relations and remain the same beliefs. Such relations are *constitutive* of the propositional attitudes. (Davidson 1985c: 351–2)

Jack's intention to mean that he saw Jill standing by the well at the top of the hill when he says, "I saw Jill standing by the well at the top of the hill", is precisely *that* intention in virtue of its relation to his beliefs about women named "Jill" and the local geography. Without this normative background of other attitudes, we cannot interpret him to have had that intention, since someone could sincerely mean that he saw Jill standing at the top of the hill only if he believes he can recognize a certain woman named "Jill" and a location as the well at the top of the hill.

We can express the same idea in terms of radical interpretation. An interpreter's first step is to apply the principles of charity to her subject's situated behaviour, thereby preparing that behaviour for a reason explanation. This move is crucial, since it allows her to constrain her evolving interpretation by her observations and by her knowledge of her subject's personal history; she reasons that his actions and thoughts are what they ought to be, given his beliefs and other attitudes, and that he is a rational agent. Failing this, the thin evidence afforded by her observations would not support her attributing to the subject or his words a given intentional content.

Consider, for example, my pronouncing the words, "Please bring me the fish and tofu soup" as I sit down to eat in my favourite Chinese restaurant. My waiter understands this action as my expressing a request that he bring me the fish and tofu soup, based on his observations and on his knowledge of my beliefs (that I believe that the restaurant serves this dish) and my past actions (that I always order the fish and tofu soup whenever I eat there). This information singles out that interpretation as correct, however, only if he presumes that I act reasonably: given (as he believes) that I prefer this selection over their other soups, and that (reasonably) I believe that he will serve it, if I ask him, it *makes sense* that my utterance would be that request.

We can strengthen the point, for he does not *interpret* my behaviour (as opposed to explaining it via physics, say), unless he locates in that behaviour a pattern that conforms to the norms of theoretical and practical reason. This point is exactly parallel to the chess case, where we cannot say that someone plays chess unless she moves the pieces in compliance with the rules of chess. Seeing someone as *rational* is a *sine qua non* for finding him and his behaviour *intelligible*, and "to the extent that we fail to discover a coherent and plausible pattern in the attitudes and actions of others we simply forego the chance of treating them as persons" (Davidson 1980a: 222).

Some authors see a threat to the objectivity of mental states and theories of interpretation in this appeal to constitutive norms and the charity principles. Louise Antony writes that, for Davidson,

> psychology is not fully empirical because its domain is not "objective," in the sense that psychological attributions are human constructions ... this alleged non-objectivity is ... due to ... an essential methodological feature of psychological theorizing ... it's the holistic nature of psychological ascription taken together with its normativity that makes the difference. (Antony 1998: 177–8)

The key premise, Antony says, is the normativity of the mental; holism alone, since this property is shared by the natural sciences, is not enough to weaken psychology's claim to objectivity. Normativity, though, because it forces attitude ascriptions to answer to an "ideal of rationality" – for example, we say that Art believes a rabbit is present because that is what he *ought* to believe, given his situation and what (we think) he knows about the appearance of rabbits – renders those attributions non-empirical. Therefore, she concludes, "one should look upon psychological hypotheses not ... as our best guesses about the nature of an objective phenomenon, but rather as artifacts that reflect our interpretive practices"; "Dennett's ... is the theory of mind Davidson should really have" (Antony 1998: 179, 185n.).

The reference to Dennett is instructive. We may summarize Dennett's position as a species of instrumentalism: the thesis that folk psychology is a method interpreters employ to describe systems "whose behavior can be predicted by the method of attributing beliefs, desires, and rational acumen". In adopting this method, which Dennett calls the "intentional stance", one ascribes to the system "those acts that it *would be* rational for an agent with those beliefs and desires to perform" (Dennett 1987: 49, emphasis added). In adopting an *as if* posture, however, an interpreter does not credit her subject with individual, discernible mental states; mental states, rather, are functionally defined intermediaries that an interpreter uses to rationalize her subject's behaviour. The intentional stance is a heuristic, and attributions made from within that stance are artifacts of the process of interpretation.[13]

Davidson rejects the comparison with Dennett and the claim that invoking charity undermines the objectivity of mental states.

> Anomalous monism does not suggest that mental events and states are merely projected by the attributor onto an agent; on the contrary, it holds that mental events are as real as physical events, being identical with them, and attributions of states are as objective. (Davidson 1997b: 112)

The conclusion of the argument we have been examining is that mental events are tokenwise identical to physical events, hence, unless he is guilty of gross inconsistency, Davidson cannot have denied existence to mental events but not physical events. The methods that govern our psychological attributions have no bearing on whether the subjects of those attributions exist, as we saw at the end of the preceding section, therefore their normative character cannot undermine the objectivity of mental events. As for mental *states*, as opposed to events, Davidson finds a confusion in Dennett (and hence Antony, too). What exists (or does not exist) are persons, who have as properties mental states like belief; but beliefs are not "things" or objects that exist (or do not). (In this respect Davidson follows Aristotle.) Finally, as for the question of whether there is an objective basis for saying that someone has a certain belief (as opposed to whether that belief is objective, or exists), Davidson follows Kant in tracing the objectivity of judgement back to intersubjectivity. But another person is a subject (in this sense) only if he has propositional attitudes; therefore, the objectivity of judgement *presupposes* that others have attitudes. We shall return to this point in Chapter 9.

It turns out, ~~though~~, that the fact that reasoning about mental properties answers to strong constitutive principles does not distinguish it from reasoning about physical properties, since it is governed by normative considerations, too. I cannot consistently describe objects drawn from some collection as having this or that temperature, or, more simply, cannot rank those objects in the order of their temperature, unless my attributions satisfy the principle of transitivity, that if x is warmer than y and y is warmer than z, then x is warmer than z. Measurements of temperature are normative, therefore, in the sense that the principle of transitivity partly defines a structure or theory that constitutes our notion of temperature. Were we to come across an intransitive triad, we could say either that our thermometer is defective, in which case we would be unable to apply the theory, or that the principle of transitivity or some other constraint imposed by the theory is false. Taking this latter route, however, would call into question whether our saying that something has a temperature of 37°C, or that one object is warmer than another, means anything at all. In this sense, then, the principle of transitivity is among the constitutive principles of the concept of temperature.

Both the mental and physical are governed by norms, but Davidson finds in the disparate character of those norms "the ultimate springs of the difference between understanding minds and understanding the world as physical" (Davidson 1991: 164). The precise contrast between these norms that makes the difference between folk psychology and the social sciences, on the one hand, and physics, on the other, a *deep* difference – deeper than the difference between physics and biology – is hard to make clear but, in response to prodding from Richard Rorty, Davidson says:

> Interpreting others is not like comparing one insect with another *only in this respect*: interpreting others is a matter of using … my values and thoughts, my norms and rationality, to understand someone else's. I do not expect to find propositional attitudes, or the kinds of norms and rationality they entail, in a beetle. I cannot see the harm in pointing out this difference, nor point in arguing about its magnitude.
>
> (Davidson 1999a: 600, emphasis added)

The distinctive feature of interpretation and, more generally, reason explanation, is that I employ *my* thoughts and values to construct a picture of another *person's* thoughts and values, and do this with the aim of explaining certain occurrences as the intentional doings of a being whose actions and attitudes are, by and large, logically coherent, mostly true and conform to decision-theoretic principles; "psychology is different", Davidson writes elsewhere, "due to our special interest in interpreting human agents as rational agents" (Davidson 1993d: 303). The norms of physical theory partly constitute what we mean by "physical object", and the norms of the mental partly constitute what we mean by "rational agent"; the difference, and hence the significance of the double use of mental concepts in reason explanations – including especially interpretations of speech acts – is that in reason explanations (as opposed to those in the *Naturwissenschaften*) the object of my description is itself a rational subject.

We shall return to this point in Chapter 9, where we shall see Davidson's claim that my subjectivity (as a thinker) has its source in my interactions with other subjects. It is also true and important that my seeing others as bearers of mental states underwrites my explaining their behaviour as subject to final as well as efficient causes. In the physical sciences this mode of explanation went out with Descartes's *The World* and Galileo's *Dialogue Concerning Two Chief World Systems*, but it remains essential to our understanding of persons as autonomous actors in a world otherwise governed by physical necessity. In this connection Davidson quotes Kant:

> We think of man in a different sense and relation when we call him free, and when we regard him as subject to the laws of nature. ... [Speculative philosophy] must therefore show that not only can both of these very well co-exist, but that both must be thought *as necessarily united* in the same subject. (Kant 1990: 76, quoted in Davidson 1980: 225)

In Kant's view, the presuppositions of moral experience – what Kant calls *the metaphysics of morals* – require that agents are autonomous and hence morally praiseworthy and blameworthy for their actions. If we fail to recognize that persons are self-governing beings, then we miss the fact that not only is a human being, as a physical object, subject to causal laws, but she is also, as a free moral agent, the *author* of *moral* laws, to the extent that she acts (according to Kant) for the sake of her moral duties. People are physical objects, but we are also moral beings.

Davidson is hesitant, even diffident, about the impact of his work on ethics,[14] but "the anomalism of the mental is", he writes, "a necessary condition for viewing action as autonomous" (Davidson 1980a: 225). We cannot sacrifice our understanding of persons as the bearers of mental states without sacrificing our conception of persons as *autonomous agents*, as this notion, too, is part of the web of mental concepts; thus Davidson denies, in effect, that the mental is nomologically reducible to the physical in order to make room for freedom. He has no argument that we *should* view people as autonomous beings, but seeing our fellows this way is, in turn, a necessary condition for seeing them as moral beings, and were we to cease to do this we would have to ask ourselves whether we were seeing them (and ourselves) as persons in anything like the sense we currently use that term.

Finally, it remains to be seen how this deep difference implies the anomalism of the mental. To begin to see this, consider the apparent discovery that at least some advanced specimens of *Homo erectus* exhibit a cranial morphology similar to modern human beings; based on casts of the interiors of several skulls, anthropologists have shown that in these individuals the specialized region of the brain known as Broca's Area is enlarged, as it is in modern humans. Neuro-anatomists and psychologists have shown, too, that Broca's Area is associated with language functions in modern humans; according to their studies, it contains subregions that control *inter alia* facial muscles involved in speech, sequential ordering of behaviour and associations between words.[15] From these two sets of facts, some anthropologists have inferred that these early hominids, who died out perhaps 1.6 million years ago, were verbal.

This inference derives from a statement to the effect that:

(7) If x exhibits a certain cranial morphology, then x is verbal,

which, we may assume, was originally formulated to describe an observed relationship between certain (modern human) patients' having suffered damage to Broca's Area and linguistic disability. (Advances in neuro-anatomy often start this way.) Further investigation of willing human subjects, using sophisticated imaging techniques, strongly supports this correlation. Taking the next step, then, and assuming that the correlation is the product of an underlying mechanism, psychologists and others have promoted (7) from a well-confirmed empirical equivalence to a nomological equivalence, that is, a law.

Here is where the trouble arises. Claiming that (7) is a law engenders a conflict between, on the one hand, the modal force that links the antecedent and consequent of the (putative) law and, on the other, the allegiance each clause ("x exhibits a certain cranial morphology", "*x* is verbal") owes to the constitutive principles of its home theory. Focusing on the latter, this means, as we have seen, that to be verbal is to have a disposition we characterize against the background of the constitutive principles of the mental (since "is verbal" is a mental predicate), and we attribute it to an agent by bringing the methods of interpretation and reason explanation to bear on his behaviour. Similar remarks apply to "*x* exhibits a certain cranial morphology", which is a physical property; we identify it within the theory defined by the constitutive principles of physics, and we determine whether an object satisfies it by bringing the methods of physical theory to bear on it.

If (7) is a law, however, we may reason as follows. Suppose there is some test C_φ formulated in the language of physical theory that governs whether an individual satisfies the open sentence, "*x* has a certain cranial morphology". For example, C_φ may be something like:

> If a cast of *x*'s skull shows such-and-such characteristics, then *x* has a certain cranial morphology

or

> If a CAT scan of *x*'s brain shows characteristics *y* and *z*, then *x* has a certain cranial morphology.

Thus we have a rule,

> If $C_\varphi(x)$, then *x* has a certain cranial morphology.

As Kim observes, though, to say that the C_φ "is an attribution condition for [a physical property] must be more than to affirm a mere de facto coincidence of" C_φ and the property of having a certain cranial morphology; "it is to commit oneself to a statement with modal force" (Kim 1985: 378), that is:

(8) Necessarily, if $C_\varphi(x)$, then *x* has a certain cranial morphology.

In other words, the presence of C_φ is *decisive* for *x*'s having a certain cranial morphology. (Kim's point is parallel to the Wittgenstein's distinction between some phenomenon's being a *symptom* of a certain property and that phenomenon's being a *criterion* for the presence of that property.[16]) But if this is right, and we further assume that (7) has the status of a law, that is,

(9) Necessarily, if x has a certain cranial morphology, then x is verbal

then we may combine (8) and (9) to obtain the relation that

(10) Necessarily, if $C_{\varphi}(x)$, then x is verbal.

But (10) makes our attributing the mental property of being verbal – which is defined within the background *theory of intentional psychology* – conditional on criteria formulated in the language of *physical theory*, and this subverts the allegiance it owes to the constitutive principles of the mental.[17]

Suppose that field researchers turn up no direct evidence supporting the claim that *Homo erectus* was verbal, for example, no artifacts beyond simple tools. Contrast this with the case of other archaic human species, such as the Neanderthals, who, we know, had a sophisticated and varied tool culture, buried their dead and practised cultic rituals centered on animals they hunted. These facts about Neanderthals strongly suggest that their lives followed patterns ordered by something more than merely physical necessity, and if we are to understand them we are obliged to explain their remains using the methods of interpretation and reason explanation. In contrast, the only evidence that (putatively) supports the view that *Homo erectus* had language is anatomical evidence, since from the point of view of intentional psychology, *Homo erectus* was a cipher. (That is, there is no evidence of cultural artifacts, intentional funerary practices, religious beliefs, etc.) In absence of evidence of a mental life, however, it is not clear what it *means* to attribute language to *Homo erectus*. Saying that *Homo erectus* was verbal because members of *Homo erectus* had the right cranial morphology is at best a bold hypothesis calling for further study of the archaeological remains, and at worst a *non sequitir*.

In promoting (7) to (9), we thus dump the interpretative character of anthropology and the principles of charity as so much detritus, and validate attributions of propositional attitudes based on non-intentional criteria. But this is like saying that we can identify an artifact as a chess queen based *solely* on its physical appearance, regardless of the manner in which the piece is used. Clearly, having a certain shape is well correlated with being a queen in chess; the sentence,

> An artifact *x* is a chess queen if *x* has a certain shape,

states an empirical relationship upon which we rely. But were anthropologists to discover a queen-shaped object among the artifacts left by a people who did not possess the game, the piece would *not* be a queen. Or, to vary the example, were we to use the queen-shaped object to play draughts then, again, it would not be a queen. Were someone to insist that it is, then unless she means that the piece is *usually* employed as a queen in chess games – that is, unless the correlation between shape and use is good, but imperfect – then it is not clear what she claims, since the concept of being a queen makes sense only against the background of the game of chess, and this is defined by the rules of chess.

Similarly, having substituted conceptually alien criteria for its defining criteria, it is no longer clear that the predicate "is verbal" designates a mental property, which, we can recall, is constituted by its role in a comprehensive system of mental events and states. It is probably true that there is an empirical correlation between possessing certain psychological and physical characteristics; but treating instances of (7) and, more generally, (4), as laws posits something very different. Moreover, making that stronger tie undermines our concept of the mental and with it our conception of what it is to be a person. "There cannot be tight connections between the" mental and physical, Davidson concludes,

> if each is to retain allegiance to its proper source of evidence. ... The point is ... that when we use the concepts of belief, desire, and the rest, we must stand prepared, as the evidence accumulates, to adjust our theory in light of considerations of overall cogency: the constitutive ideal of rationality partly controls each phase in the evolution of what must be an evolving theory. An arbitrary choice of translation scheme would preclude such opportunistic tempering of theory. ... We must conclude, I think, that nomological slack between the mental and the physical is essential as long as we conceive man as a rational animal. (Davidson 1980a: 222–3)

From the point of view of intentional psychology, attributing language to *Homo erectus* is an "arbitrary choice". Should evidence of a mental life present itself, we would be warranted in projecting our rational standards and linguistic abilities on to these archaic cousins, but that move should be governed by "considerations of overall cogency" in our interpretation of their lives, for example, our deciding that it would make the most sense to interpret the placement of certain artifacts as evidence of their intentionally burying their dead. But such a decision cannot, on pain of incoherence, be forced by neuro-anatomical evidence.

Chapter 9

Conclusion: scepticism and subjectivity

In his presidential address to the American Philosophical Association in 1973 and in subsequent writings,[1] Davidson turns his attention to the "philosophical fallout from the approach to truth and interpretation" that he recommends and which we have been surveying over the course of the preceding chapters (Davidson 1984a: xviii). This fallout casts doubt on central threads of the weave that defines European philosophy since the seventeenth century.

The early modern philosophers are linked to one another and to their twentieth-century heirs by their efforts to answer the sceptic's challenge to validate the objectivity of human knowledge. Russell, for example, writes that Descartes

> invented a method which may still be used with profit – the method of systematic doubt. ... By inventing the method of doubt, and by showing subjective things are the most certain, Descartes performed a great service to philosophy, and one which makes him still useful to all students of philosophy.
> (Russell 1912: 18)

And Moritz Schlick, one of the founders of logical positivism in the early-twentieth century, observes that "all important attempts at establishing a theory of knowledge grow out of the problem concerning the certainty of human knowledge. ... This problem in turn originates in the wish for absolute certainty" (Schlick 1959: 209). This "wish for absolute certainty" is heir to the Cartesian drive to meet the sceptical challenge. Finally, Quine identifies experience – naturalized, in the form of patterns of nerve stimulations – as a subjective intermediary between our beliefs, on the one hand, and the objects our beliefs are about; in doing so he produces an epistemology that is "essentially first person and Cartesian" (Davidson 2001a: 194), despite its treating mental phenomena as part of the natural order.

9.1 Concepts and causes

The relation between our beliefs and the external world becomes a problem when Descartes, in introducing the concept of *res extensa* to underwrite a science of efficient causes, rejects the intelligible forms that for Aristotle and the Scholastics unite minds and their objects; and it becomes grist for the sceptic's mill when Galileo observes that some phenomenal qualities of objects, "so far as their objective existence is concerned, are nothing but mere names for something which resides exclusively in our sensitive body" (Galileo 1960: 28).[2] The problem of their relation, then, takes on its distinctive shape when the moderns adopt a theory of mind according to which, in Hume's famous image, consciousness is "a kind of theatre" wherein representations of external objects make their appearance (Hume 1978: 253). On this picture, the contents of a thinker's perceptual beliefs are "in" the subject in some fashion and hence are, in that fashion, subjective; and their correspondence to the situations of external objects is the point on which their reliability and the epistemic standing of all our empirical beliefs turn. Finally, Kant bestrides the empiricist and rationalist streams within the tradition and divides the representations that populate the mind-as-theatre into concepts and intuitions (i.e. sensations). The manifold of data presented to the mind in sense experience comes unconceptualized and therefore unorganized; to become the content of a possible judgement (or the content of a belief, in contemporary jargon) requires the mind to synthesize the raw data of sense according to its own categories.

This move finds among the mind's own resources the answer to Hume's sceptical doubts about *inter alia* the objectivity of our causal beliefs, but as often happens this solution engenders a new problem. If the objectivity of my empirical beliefs is grounded in my mind's own activity, then the objective world *I* construct may differ from the world *you* construct, especially if we live in very different eras or belong to cultures remote from one another. Kant's Copernican Revolution answers Humean scepticism, in other words, at the price of enabling conceptual relativism: the thesis that the truth of a set of beliefs can be evaluated only relative to the framework of concepts within which those beliefs are stated, where these frameworks may differ radically from person to person. On this view "reality itself is relative to a scheme [of concepts]: what counts as real in one system may not in another" (Davidson 1984a: 183). Of course, Kant would reject the inference from the mind's spontaneity to the possibility that people may differ in their conceptual schemes; for Kant, our common humanity partly rests on our minds' sharing their cognitive structures. As Rorty observes, though, once Kant's picture of the mind's activity is in place,

> it occurs to us, as it did to Hegel, that those all-important a priori concepts, those which determine what our experience or our morals will be, might have been different. We cannot, of course, imagine what an experience or a practice *that* different would be like, but we can abstractly suggest that the men of the Golden Age, or the inhabitants of the Fortunate Isles, or the mad, might shape the intuitions that are our common property in different molds, and might thus be conscious of a different "world." (Rorty 1982: 3)

Conceptual relativism, like the sceptic's doubts, rests on the picture of mind current in the tradition from Descartes through Kant and beyond. Davidson's reconceiving the notions of meaning and mind subverts the pair of related dichotomies (scheme versus content, subjective versus objective) that comprise what he calls the "third dogma" of empiricism: that stream within the tradition that most strongly influences twentieth-century Anglo-American philosophy. In the remainder of this chapter, we explore Davidson's challenge to these dichotomies.

The notion that different people may conceive different worlds "is a heady and exotic doctrine", or at least it would be "if we could make good sense of it" (Davidson 1984a: 183). Davidson argues that we cannot, and his most compelling argument against conceptual schemes and the scepticism they carry in their wake also appears to be his shortest. To have a concept entails having some ability or set of abilities; to have the concept of a bivalve is to have beliefs about what bivalves are, for example, and this entails being able to classify selectively some animals as satisfying the open sentence "*x* is a bivalve" and others as not.[3] Now someone may be able to pick a bivalve out in a crowd and yet not know what one is, in as much as she may be trained to utter "There goes a bivalve" when and only when she sees a bivalve, without her knowing that bivalves are a species of mollusc. (To take another example, someone may be able to recognize a carburettor without knowing its role in the operation of an internal combustion engine, and in that case we ought not to say that he knows what a carburettor *is*.) But whatever else there is to knowing what bivalves are is manifested in being able to do what fishermen and marine biologists do when they describe bivalves' anatomy and natural history, and place them alongside snails, squid and their other cousins. Thus possessing a sortal concept entails understanding and being able to use a corresponding expression and some fragment of the theory in which it occurs; and the scheme of concepts through which a person conceives some portion of the world is expressed by her actions and in the language she speaks. Since, though, a French marine biologist and her German counterpart will use superficially different languages to express their common concepts – superficial, since French mollusc theory can easily be translated into German mollusc theory – a single conceptual scheme is expressed by any one member of a set of *intertranslatable* languages.

If this is right – and most conceptual relativists assume it is – then the question of whether we can sensibly speak of people's possessing radically different conceptual schemes, such that what is *true* for the one is *false* or even *inexpressible* or *unthinkable* for the other, becomes the question of whether there *are* languages that are not intertranslatable.[4]

Davidson's short argument against the very idea of conceptual schemes and the scepticism that attends them is that there can be no language that I cannot translate into my home idiom.

> Nothing, it may be said, could count as evidence that some form of activity could not be interpreted in our language that was not at the same time evidence that that form of activity was not speech behaviour. If this [is] right, we probably ought to hold that a form of activity that cannot be interpreted as language in our language is not speech behaviour.
>
> (Davidson 1984a: 185–6)

If, to paraphrase Wittgenstein, I were to come across a people for whom I could describe no regular connection between their utterances and their actions, such that I could not interpret their (putative) speech behaviour using the methods that we outlined in Chapters 2–4, then there would "not be enough regularity for us to call it 'language'" (Wittgenstein 1958: §207). Putnam makes the same point: if it were really true that the "terms used in another culture" could not "be equated in meaning or reference with any terms or expressions we possess ... if [it] were really true that we could not ... interpret [other] organisms' noises at all, then we have no grounds for regarding them as ... speakers" (Putnam 1981: 114). In short, if there is sufficient regularity among the actions and local environment of a people such that we *can* interpret their utterances, then their language does not express a radically different conceptual scheme, given our premise that intertranslatable languages express a common scheme of concepts; while if we *cannot* interpret their utterances, then we have no grounds to attribute meaning to the sounds they produce nor evidence to support our saying that they possess concepts. We ought, therefore, to reject conceptual relativism; and having disposed of the idea of *different* conceptual schemes, the scheme idea loses much of its attraction.

Rorty characterizes the argument as verificationist, and although it is not clear whether he intends that description as a criticism it could easily be turned into one.[5] An argument is *verificationist*, in this sense, if it infers that something does not exist based on our inability to confirm or verify that it exists. Here, the inference is from our never having adequate grounds to ascribe a radically different conceptual scheme to someone – since that radical difference blocks our efforts to interpret his utterances and attribute concepts to him – to there being no such thing as a radically different conceptual scheme. The obvious objection to this style of argument is that it confuses *what we can know* with *what there is*: our inability to discriminate or identify radically different conceptual frameworks is not necessarily a mark against their existence. For all we know, they may be out there.

A first, fast reply to this objection is that it is very nearly, if not completely, empty. It is not enough *to claim* that there may be alternative schemes; to take conceptual relativism seriously we need to be presented with *some reason* to believe that alternative schemes exist. Unless a persuasive example can be cited – and, as

by Davidson

Rorty observes, we "cannot, of course, imagine what an experience or a practice *that* different would be like" (1982: 3) – the dialogue degenerates into an effort to shift the burden of proof to one's adversary.[6]

More fundamentally, though, the effort to drive a wedge between the *ordo cognoscendi* and the *ordo essendi*, between what we know and what there is, misses the deep foundation of Davidson's "short" argument. A similar fault vitiates Colin McGinn's dismissal of the argument. McGinn writes (speaking of Davidson's anti-scepticism, but it all comes to the same thing) that he had once had the idea of using the brevity of the argument "as a *reductio*" of Davidson's position, before he learned that Davidson regarded that inference as "a *virtue* of his account" (McGinn 1986: 359n.). Again, though, Davidson's argument is not *really* all that brief, for its unstated assumptions lie in the deep picture of meaning, mind and action that we have been sketching over the preceding chapters.

The problem with the idea of speech acts we could never interpret or concepts we could never grasp is that it makes a muddle of "what we mean by" language or "a system of concepts" (Davidson 2001a: 40). To simplify, let us say that concepts are the meanings of our words and the contents of our reasons and other mental states; concepts are publicly available, then, in as much as what a speaker means by her words is determined by what she intends them, and what her audience takes them, to mean. If Archie Bunker utters the sentence, "We need a few laughs to break up the monogamy", intending to mean that we need a few laughs to break up the monotony, and his audience understands him to mean that we need a few laughs to break up the monotony, then by his words he *does mean* that we need a few laughs to break up the monotony. "We understand a speaker best when we interpret him as he intended to be interpreted" (Davidson 2001: 199); and he cannot intend to be interpreted to mean that *p* unless he has reason to believe that his audience *can* interpret him to mean that *p*. Meaning, as we have seen, is a cooperative enterprise among interlocutors in a common setting, and it is constituted by their triangular relationship (between speaker, audience and situation) as governed by the principles of charity; there is, therefore, no sense in which there could be concepts available to one partner in a speech situation that were *in principle* unavailable to the other.

Consider, for example, the familiar idea that we learn the meanings of our first words by being conditioned to associate certain sound patterns with salient feature of our immediate surroundings. "The conditioning works best", Davidson notes,

> with objects that interest the learner and are hard to miss by either teacher or pupil. But here is the point: this is not just a story about how we learn to use words: it must also be an essential part of an adequate account of what words refer to, and what they mean. (2001a: 44)

On a traditional, for example, Lockean view, my baby's words mean (incipient) ideas in his head and my words mean ideas in mine, and my teaching him to speak and to understand consists in my manipulating the world in such a way that through its (that is, the world's) agency the private contents of his mind are synchronized with the private contents of mine (and other speakers of English). If something like the familiar picture is right, the private mental entities that Locke and the tradition posit look very much like gears that turn while failing to engage any other part of the mechanism, the real work being done by the common objects and situated interactions between teachers and students, or speakers and audiences. Again, Davidson writes that

> in the simplest and most basic cases, words and sentences derive their meaning from the objects and circumstances in whose presence they were learned. A sentence which one has been conditioned by the learning process to be caused to hold true by the presence of fires will (usually) be true when there is a fire present; a word one has been conditioned to hold applicable by the presence of snakes will refer to snakes. (2001a: 44–5)

When I refer to an animal that falls under the general term "snake", and when my son Sam points out another, our speech behaviours and situations are (typewise) identical; we share a disposition to engage in a certain pattern of situated verbal behaviour, and we mean the same thing; and our respective "snake-ideas" drop out of the picture.

Notice, too, that the same goes for Quine's materialist version of ideas, namely, the firing of sensory neurons, to which he appeals in his efforts to update empiricism. The firing of a speaker's sensory receptors drops out of the picture, in as much as it is the *distal*, not the *proximal*, stimulus – the snake we both see and not the pattern of firings in Sam's visual receptors – that plays a role in the conditioning process and which, therefore, is the object that our words mean or refer to. Our shared disposition to engage in patterns of interpretable, situated behaviour *is* our meaning the same thing by our words, regardless of what goes on, or does not go on, inside our heads; and our shared verbal behaviours are formed in relation to objects and events that lie in the external world, not in relation to what occurs in our respective neural nets. Davidson has urged him to locate meaning in the distal stimulus, but Quine holds fast to his proximal theory of meaning: "I remain unswerved in locating stimulation at the neural input, for my interest is epistemological" (Quine 1990: 41).

Certainly, our sensations are *causal* intermediaries between the world and our beliefs and utterances, but the point is that our sensations play no epistemic or semantic role. They play no *epistemic role*, in particular, they do not play the epistemic role that empiricism assigns to them, as the ultimate foundation for our beliefs about the world. Sensations do not play this role because they *cannot* play it; only attitudes and utterances participate in logical relations, and sensations are neither.[7] This result is benign, though, since there is no ultimate foundation for our beliefs; even our simplest attitudes are open to revision, hence there is no *ultimate* foundation, and the causal relations between our sensations and beliefs are enough to connect our beliefs, in turn, with the external objects that cause our sensations.[8]

And sensations play no *semantic role*, in as much as the grasp and communication of meanings "is determined by the terminal elements in the conditioning process, and is tested only by the end product" (Davidson 2001a: 44). Languages and the concepts they express are causally anchored to the world by a series of steps leading from the distal through the proximal stimuli, but interpreters attribute attitudes and meanings to speakers by observing their (i.e. speakers') responding to distal stimuli: if I observe that, for the most part, Sam holds a sentence *S* true when and only when a snake is present and visible to him, then I can and will infer that his sentence *S* probably means that he sees a snake.

Let us look at this reasoning more closely. Sam holds *S* true when and only when a snake's presence causes him to hold it true, but – as Quine stresses – he holds it true, too, when and only when there are certain patterns of activity in his optic nerve. This neural activity thus has an equal claim to being called a cause of his holding *S* true. Why, then, do we say that the former, rather than the latter – the distal as opposed to the proximal – has a semantic role? The answer is that it is in relation to the former, not the latter, that Sam's verbal behaviour is formed. Sam experiences seeing many things, and he naturally and regularly classes some of those perceptual experiences together; and I reinforce some, and not others, of those classifications based on my observations of his interactions with his local environment. Now on certain occasions that *he* classes together (namely, occasions that resemble one another *vis-à-vis* his seeing a snake) he also observes *my* behaving in a regular way (namely, uttering "snake" on all and only those particular occasions); he follows my lead – he, too, utters "snake" on exactly those particular occasions – and I, in turn, reward him. Or, rather, I reward him just in case he says "snake" *and I* observe *him* observing a snake. I judge, then, that he has learned the meaning of "snake" to the extent that he says "snake" in situations where I observe him observing a snake.

Notice, then, that Sam forms his verbal behaviour in response to two things: the presence of snakes and my behaviour, in particular, my responses to *his* behaviour and the environment. Learning a language, therefore, involves a triangle of teacher, learner and *shared* stimulation. Interpretation, too, involves the same triangle of audience, speaker and shared scene; when I interpret Sam I respond to two things, namely, the presence of snakes and his behaviour. Each is a vertex of the "essential triangle ... which makes communication about shared objects and events possible. But it is also this triangle that determines the content of the learner's words and thoughts" (Davidson 2001a: 203). Again, there *are* causal intermediaries, for example, stimulations of Sam's optic nerve, but these play no role in Sam's acquisition of language or in determining the semantics of his utterances; what do play a role, rather, are the snakes we both see and to which we both respond. I thus attribute meaning to Sam's utterances in virtue of our engagement with a common world of objects that I perceive to condition his verbal behaviour, and his acquisition of language depends on the same trio of elements. The existence of a shared world is indispensable to my knowing what he thinks and means, and *that* he thinks and means.

We can follow Davidson and take this reasoning a step further. All animate creatures and many inanimate objects selectively respond to their environments: photocells generate a voltage when a light source is present, wolves howl at the moon and Sam says "There goes a snake" just in case there goes a snake, to mention a few examples. What separates thinkers from non-thinkers among such creatures and objects, however, is that the former have a capacity for *judgement*, in the sense of recognizing the truth of a sentence or thought. What distinguishes thinkers from non-thinkers, in other words, is that thinkers have at least an implicit grasp of the concept of objective truth: they see that there is a difference between how they take the world to be and how it *is*. We take the next step, then, and observe that our grasp of the concept of objective truth has its source in our interactions with other subjects and in our coordinated responses to the environment we both share. I experience the world around me, but that experience lacks the needed perspective for the question of truth to arise for my internal states until I measure them against what I observe to be Sam's responses to that world and to my behaviour; that extra element gives me an intersubjective norm against which to conceive the difference between what I perceive and how the world is. In more traditional terminology, my subjectivity *as a thinker* has its source in my relation to other subjects, that is, in intersubjectivity.

Meaning, therefore, is located at the distal stimulus. The problem with following Quine, and locating meaning at a speaker's nerve endings, is that "when meaning goes epistemological ... truth and meaning are necessarily divorced" (Davidson 2001a: 145). For Quine, meaning "goes epistemological" in the sense that he identifies meanings with patterns of sensory stimulation, and this in the service of securing empirical content for perceptual beliefs and thereby the other attitudes as well. Making *this* connection, however, leads to "truth relativized to individuals, and skepticism. Proximal theories, no matter how decked out, are Cartesian in spirit and consequence" (Davidson 1990d: 76). Proximal theories lead to relativism and scepticism in as much as once something is interposed between the world, on one side, and our beliefs and our sentences, on the other, nothing can assure us that there is no radical break between how the world *is* and how it *seems to be*: "since we can't swear intermediaries [such as a person's neural firings] to truthfulness ... they could be just as they are and yet the world outside very different. (Remember the brain in the vat)" (Davidson 2001a: 144–5).

Thus the problem with ungraspable concepts and uninterpretable languages is that the very idea severs meaning from truth. It supposes that once I have paired Sam's sentence "There goes a snake" on the left of a *T*-sentence with an interpreting condition expressed in my home language on the right, there is still *something*, some *meaning*, that I have failed to capture. This confidence that there is some such residue underlies not only conceptual relativism, but also the problem of other minds and scepticism of the external world. It supports the problem of other minds by substantiating Descartes's suspicion that the figures he sees from his window, while he judges them to be men, may be automatons, if their "real essences" consist in something hidden from view. They may go through all the motions we associate with people – asking questions, writing poetry, making love and so on – while doing none of these things, in as much as querying, authoring and loving imply mental states with contents that, for all we know, may be missing. And it underwrites scepticism about the external world, since it posits that what I mean and think have no necessary connection with an objective world I share with my fellows; the meanings of my words and contents of my thoughts are, according to this view, independent of contexts in which they were learned or first thought, and in which I presently use and think them. I could be a brain in a vat while meaning and thinking everything I do mean and think.[9]

The connection Davidson forges between meaning and truth, therefore, constitutes a break with the traditional dualism of subjectivity and objectivity, or between inner meaning and the external world. That connection, we have seen, anchors meaning in an objective world available to all; someone's behaviour is a speech act only if we can locate it in a pattern that is reasonable *vis-à-vis* her situation in the world. In thus removing meaning from the subjective sphere, and making it available to both speakers and their interpreters, the possibility of untranslatable languages and ungraspable concepts vanishes. Certainly, nothing guarantees that translating Hopi into English or Spanish is easy; nothing guarantees that we can "understand those with whom we differ on vast tracts of physical and moral opinion … [but] there are no definite limits to how far dialogue can or will take us" (Davidson 2001a: 219). Driving out the bogeyman of scepticism, however, helps us see that our inability to understand the thoughts of people very different from ourselves is not a metaphysical failure, but a moral fault.

9.2 Externalism and the mind's eye

The dependence of meaning on truth, or more generally of intentional mental contents on the properties of a thinker's social and physical environment, has seemed to many philosophers to pose challenges to the concept of subjectivity. One form these challenges take derives from Putnam's famous "twin earth" thought experiment.[10] We are asked to imagine a planet, twin earth (or twearth, for short), that is exactly like earth (almost) down to the last molecule. On twearth there is an identical twin of everything that exists on earth: there is a twin rose bush outside the twin window of my twin office, there is a twin England with a twin for each Englishman and woman, and, in particular, there is a twin of a man Oscar (twin Oscar, or Twoscar). In fact, the *only* difference between earth and twearth is that where, on earth, water – which we know today to be H_2O – falls from rain clouds, fills the seas and quenches thirst, on twearth there is something twerrans *call* "water", which falls from rain clouds and so on, but is XYZ. However, Oscar and Twoscar lived in 1750, before water was discovered to be H_2O on earth and twin water ("twater") was identified as XYZ on twearth; and since water and twater are indistinguishable at normal temperatures and pressures, their difference is unknown to Oscar and Twoscar.

The point of this science-fiction scenario is that the contents of a thinker's psychological states and the meanings of his words supervene or depend on more than what is going on inside the surface of his body; it is also partly constituted by his history of interactions with his physical and social environments. When Oscar expresses his belief by the utterance "Here is a glass of water", he believes and says there is a glass of *water* before him, while when Twoscar expresses his belief by his twin utterance, he believes and says there is a glass of *twater* before him. This seems right, but the difference between their respective intentional states cannot be accounted for by any difference in their internal or physical states, which *ex hypothesi* are typewise identical. That difference, rather, lies in the fact that Oscar's beliefs and meanings were formed through his history of interacting with water, and Twoscar's through his history of interacting with twater. By assumption, these differences left no marks that could be detected by looking within the bodies of Oscar and his twin; yet in Oscar's language the utterance "Here is a glass of water" is true if and only if there is a glass of water before him, and in Twoscar's language the utterance "Here is a glass of water" is true if and only if there is a glass of twater before him. These considerations have led many philosophers to adopt an *externalist theory of intentional content*, according to which a person's natural history partly determines the meanings of his words and the contents of his thoughts.

Davidson agrees with Putnam up to this point, and to support their common conclusion he (somewhat uncharacteristically) presents his own thought experiment. Suppose, Davidson premises, that his exact duplicate, call him "Swampman", materializes at the exact instant, although quite by accident, that Davidson is vaporized by a lightning strike. His doppelgänger moves into his house, teaches courses at the University of California and seems to recognize Davidson's friends; in general, Swampman (so called, since its creation occurs in one of the swamps that dot the Berkeley hills) looks and behaves in ways that are indistinguishable from the ways Davidson looks and behaves. Nevertheless, until Swampman accumulates its *own* store of interactions with Davidson's friends, it cannot be said to *re*cognize those friends, since

> it never cognized anything in the first place. It can't know my friends' names ... it can't remember my house. It can't mean what I do by the word "house", for example, since the sound "house" Swampman makes was not learned in a context that would give it the right meaning – or any meaning at all.
>
> (Davidson 2001a: 19)

Swampman's singular origin is no objection to its eventually meaning or thinking about houses – recall Art from Chapter 8 – rather, it is its lack of a causal history with houses that prevents Swampman's meaning a house by its word "house" and its never having met Quine that subverts its meaning Quine by "Quine".[11] This is the case since, for example, it is precisely Davidson's having been conditioned to hold the term "house" applicable *by the presence of houses* that makes *his* word mean what it does. From this – indeed, from our examination of Davidson's philosophy of language and mind over the preceding chapters – Putnam's conclusion that our meanings and thoughts are individuated in ways that depend on external factors immediately follows.

Putnam formulates his conclusion as the thesis that "'meanings' just ain't in the head" (Putnam 1975: 227). He derives, too, the corollary that speakers do not know the meanings of many of their own words, since if meanings are not in speakers' heads they must lie (at least partly) outside those heads, and hence cannot be immediately "grasped" in the way that Cartesian thoughts and their ilk are. Putting things this way begins to open some daylight between Putnam's externalism and Davidson's; let us, therefore, look at Putnam's thesis and its corollary to see where the positions of the two philosophers begin to come apart.

In his original article, Putnam sets up the twin earth experiment to illustrate that two assumptions that philosophers of language typically make are, in fact, inconsistent. These assumptions are that (i) "knowing the meaning of a term is just a matter of being in a certain psychological state", and (ii) "the meaning of a term ... determines its extension" (Putnam 1975: 219), that is, a word's meaning determines the (sort of) object to which it refers. These conflict in the thought experiment, in as much as Oscar and Twoscar are in typewise identical mental states when they say or think "Here is a glass of water" and hence, by (i) their words have the same meaning or sense, but their words refer to different substances (water versus twater), violating (ii). We are faced with a choice and, based on the twin earth scenario, Putnam sacrifices (i): Oscar and Twoscar refer to different things, and therefore their words differ in their meanings – but then there is more to knowing the meaning of a word than being in a certain psychological or mental state.

Davidson's response is at once more conservative and more radical than Putnam's. It is more conservative, in as much as he follows Frege *et al.* in believing that the reference of a speaker's words is a function of their meaning *and* that understanding is a mental state; but his conservatism is underwritten by his rejecting the traditional conception of mind that underlies the putative incompatibility that Putnam identifies. This conception of mind is a product of the metaphysical and epistemological programme in modern philosophy that is most familiar from Descartes's *Meditations*, and it assumes we can make sense of a mental state's having a certain intentional content without regard to how the person (whose state it is) is situated in her environment.

Rejecting the Cartesian picture can itself take a more or less radical form. Less radically, we can say that Twoscar's believing he sees a glass of twater before him has its intentional content *partly* in virtue of something we can characterize without mentioning his twatery environment – for example, that his brain exhibits a certain pattern of neural activity or is in a certain computational state, either of which may be typewise identical to Oscar's internal state – and *partly* in virtue of Twoscar's relations to his twatery environment, wherein he differs from Oscar. This compromise picture thus incorporates a notion of a *narrow psychological state* (e.g. his neural or computational state), which is then contextualized, yielding a *wide* or *broad psychological state*, to capture the external contribution highlighted in the twin earth thought experiment. Fodor, for example, recommends something along these lines in order to preserve the possibility of a scientific psychology; according to Fodor, there ought to be room in psychology departments for people doing "computational psychology" ("a theory of formal processes defined over mental representations") and "naturalistic psychology" ("a theory of the ... relations between representations and the world which fix the semantic[s]" of mental representations[12]) (Fodor 1981: 233). However, only computational psychology can be scientific – perhaps the naturalistic psychologists can be shuttled off to the humanities division – since only its generalizations hold out the promise of being reduced to something that involves no semantic or intentional terms.

Davidson, who has no interest in a scientific psychology in this sense, rejects Descartes in a more radical fashion. For Davidson, Twoscar's twatery environment "inextricably permeates" his believing there is a glass of twater before him, to borrow a phrase from Pettit and McDowell (1986: 14). As McDowell puts it elsewhere, "talk of minds is talk of subjects of mental life", and "where mental life takes place need not be pinpointed any more precisely than by saying that it takes place where our lives take place"; in other words, our mental states are "no less intrinsically related to our environment than our lives are" (McDowell 19978b: 281). This is not to deny the obvious point that a person's brain or nervous system is an organ, the proper functioning of which is necessary for one to have a mental life; Davidson acknowledges this point in embracing ontological monism. However, it is a mistake to characterize anything "internal" as having any bearing on *psychology* until we expand our view to include a person's cognitive and practical relations with her environment since, after all, what we are talking about is *intentional psychology*. The notion of a narrow mental state is a dodge, "a self-deceptive attempt to conceal the disappearance of the cognitive subject" in, for example, computational psychology (Pettit & McDowell 1986: 14). If there cannot be a scientific psychology – since a (putative) psychology of narrow states is not *psychology*, while a psychology of broad states is not *scientific* – then so much the worse for scientific psychology.

Davidson is equally unsympathetic to Putnam's corollary that speakers do not fully grasp the meanings of many of their own words. Anyone without a theoretical axe to grind assumes that, Freudian anomalies aside, speakers generally know what they mean and thinkers know what they think. This is just the idea, articulated as *the principle of first-person authority*, that people speak with a special authority when they (honestly) declare their contemporaneous mental states. This is not to say that people are not occasionally mistaken; sometimes, though rarely, a first-person avowal, for example, that I enjoy escargot, may be overturned based on evidence available to an observer (such as the expression on my face when presented with a plate of snails).

As we observed earlier, Descartes and the early moderns account for the intuition underlying the principle of first-person authority, with the model of the mind as a kind of theatre wherein a person's thoughts come under the direct gaze of her mind's eye. The lineage of this relational model of the mind is far older, though, and at the same time it is completely current. Aristotle, for example, believes that someone's mental state has a certain content (and thus is the state it is) in virtue of the presence in her mind of an entity that gives it that content; and this conception of the attitudes as relations between thinkers and certain sorts of objects survives in functionalism, which replaces the mind's eye and its ideas with mental representations written on something like the memory tape of a Turing machine.

The twin earth scenario presents relational models of mind with a dilemma.[13] If to have a thought is to have an object before the mind, which a thinker apprehends, intends, grasps, is acquainted with and so on, then either that object is wholly internal in a way that makes each of its properties discernible to a subject's complete and infallible inspection; or it has properties to which a subject has no special access and is, in that sense, at least partly external. Grasping the first horn of this dilemma preserves first-person authority, but our "internalism" founders on the water/twater difficulty; grasping the second horn we escape this danger, but at the price of conceding that Oscar does not know what he means or thinks, and neither do I.

One way to avoid these twin troubles is to appeal to the narrow–wide split we mentioned earlier. Oscar and Twoscar, on this proposal, are in the same narrow state, or share the same narrow concept of water, and to this extent each enjoys first-person authority over his mental states; but Oscar and Twoscar have different wide concepts, which involve factors beyond their respective grasps and over which, therefore, each has no special authority. Thus we explain how it is that Oscar and Twoscar are physically indistinguishable, including their behaviour, in as much as their psychological states have identical narrow contents; and appealing to the notion of wide content, we explain how their beliefs have different satisfaction conditions, since they grew up in watery and twatery environments, respectively.

A problem with the narrow–wide split is the difficulty it poses in explaining the relation between the two. Narrow states have to be construed, in some way, as functions from a thinker's environment to the contents of her wide mental states, but how this works is problematic and subject to counter-examples. A deeper objection, closely allied to Wittgenstein's private language argument, is that as soon as we try to express the contents of a person's narrow mental states, we use words that express contents of wide states.[14] As Davidson observes, the general features that water and twater share, and that one might take to be common to Oscar's and Twoscar's mental states, for example, quenching thirst, falling from rain clouds and so on, "depend as much on the natural history of how the[se] … concepts were acquired as" the wide concepts of water and twater; "there are no … concepts … that are not … [acquired through] causal relations between people and the world" (Davidson 2001: 50–51).

A second way to face the dilemma that confronts relational theories of mind is to reject that theory and its account of how external factors play a role in individuating intentional contents. Certainly, we informally speak as though the propositional attitudes were directed at objects; we speak as though "we … share thoughts, discard and embrace beliefs, entertain, consider, reflect on, contemplate ideas and propositions – one could go on for a long time" (Davidson 2001a: 56). As Wittgenstein observes, though, there is something queer about this relation to an object: I can, he observes, imagine a stag that does not exist, but I cannot shoot it

(Wittgenstein 1974: 137). This should give us pause before leaping to a decision about the structure of the attitudes.

Conceiving the attitudes as relations gains further support, though, by what is undoubtedly the relational structure of sentences that ascribe propositional attitudes to thinkers. When I say that Oscar believes that he sees a glass of water before him, I utter a sentence that relates Oscar to an entity specified by the nominal phrase "that he sees a glass of water", which gives the content of his belief. "Believes", in other words, like other propositional attitude verbs, is a two-place predicate, the first argument place of which is filled by a term for the believer (thinker, desirer, etc., in this case, Oscar) and the second by a subordinate noun clause that describes what is believed (thought, desired, etc.; here, the thought *that Oscar sees a glass of water before him*). It is a quick inference, then, to the conclusion that the entity that that noun clause names is the object of Oscar's belief and to which he has special cognitive access, thus guaranteeing his first-person authority over his mental states. It is a quick inference, in other words, from the relational semantics of propositional attitude reports to a claim about the structure of thinkers' psychological states.

It is an inference we should resist, however. The sentence I employ to track the contents of Oscar's thoughts ("He sees a glass of water before him") belongs to *my* language, and there is no reason to assume that Oscar has access to it or to any "proposition" it names. In §3.3 we saw the details of Davidson's account of indirect discourse, which may be extended to cover the propositional attitudes, too.[15] On that account, when I report that Oscar believes that he sees a glass of water before him, I specify the content of his attitude by referring to an utterance I make, and I posit that we are samesayers, that is, that my utterance means the same as a sentence of Oscar's own language that he holds true. (Applied to the contents of Oscar's thoughts, rather than his utterances, we might say that he and I are samethinkers.) This analysis facilitates seeing Davidson's point, although that point does not rest on the details of that analysis; it is that when anyone reports the attitudes of another she will need an infinity of structured entities to track those attitudes and the relations among them, but those structured entities that do the work have to be available *to the reporter*, not *to the thinker*. We use sentences of our own language or (on Davidson's proposal) our utterances of sentences to track a thinker's attitudes; but when I ascribe to Oscar a belief that there is a glass of twater before him I do not suppose that he distinguishes between water and twater, although I do. When I attribute to Galileo a belief that the earth moves, I do not presume that he understands English, and much less do I attribute English to my cat when I give an intentional explanation of his behaviour (e.g. he went to the kitchen because he believed that I was going to feed him). This latter example shows, too, that were we to posit propositions as the meanings of sentences, and use these (in place of sentences or utterances) to track the structured contents of thinkers' thoughts, we should still resist the idea that the thinker accesses those propositions, in as much as all we need to say is that the reporter has such access.

Rejecting the relational model of mind opens the door to an account of the authority people enjoy over their intentional states. First, the propositional attitudes are subjective in the uninteresting sense that they are identical to a physical state of a person's body, presumably, a state of his brain or nervous system; and they are subjective in this sense, despite the fact that to identify his propositional attitudes *as such* we may need to mention external objects. By analogy, consider that if Oscar spends too much time in the sun his skin will redden, feel warm to the touch and produce in him a slight burning sensation. A dermatologist, then, can diagnose his having a minor burn simply by examining his skin, since that burn lies entirely within the confines of (or on the surface of) his body; in this respect his burn is "in" his skin – it is, in that sense, subjective – since it is identical to a physical state of his skin. To identify that burn *as* sunburn, though, presupposes that Oscar's doctor has information about Oscar's history of interacting with the sun, since to be *sun*burned is to have a burn that was caused by exposure to the sun. Nevertheless, this has no bearing on the subjective character of his burn, which, again, is identical to a physical state of his skin. Oscar's sunburn, like his belief that he sees water, is a physical state of his body, and Twoscar can be in typewise identical states, despite there being no water or sun in his world (there being, instead, twater and the twin sun); but those states can be described *as such* only by referring to objects outside his head and events in his personal history. But the dependence of those *descriptions* on those external entities no more makes his beliefs and meanings lie outside his head than does the reference to me as part of a description of Leon Joseph as Marc Joseph's paternal grandfather make the man's existence dependent on mine.

Secondly, when the dermatologist seeks to discover whether Oscar suffers from sunburn, she has to gather evidence about Oscar's history of interacting with the sun. Oscar, on the other hand, knows that history in as much as it is *his* history. Similarly, to decide whether Oscar means water or twater by his word "water", we rely on whatever information we can gather about the environment in which Oscar learned to speak, and depending on how good our information is our decision will be more or less well supported. If our evidence points to that environment being watery, or twatery, we shall say, respectively, that Oscar's sentence "I see a glass of water before me" is true if and only if he sees a glass of water, or a glass of twater, before him; and our hypothesis will be correct as long as that evidence is, in fact, reliable. In either case, we use our word "water" or "twater" to capture what we take to be the content of Oscar's word "water".

It is precisely here that the asymmetry between first- and third-person reports of meaning comes in. Were *Oscar* to explain his meaning,

(1) My sentence "I see a glass of water before me" is true in my language if and only if I see a glass of water before me,

his *T*-sentence, unlike ours, would be trivially true, whether he means water or twater, by his use of the word "water" on the *right-hand side* of (1). Because he acquired it in a watery (or twatery) environment, his word "water" means water (or twater), and it does not matter whether Oscar knows the difference; his meaning is (partly) fixed by the contexts in which he acquired his word "water", and that connection assures us that what Oscar reports himself to mean by "water" *is* what he means by water. As Davidson observes, whatever objects or events a speaker "regularly does apply them to gives her words the meaning they have and her thoughts the contents they have" (Davidson 2001a: 37). If, unbeknown to Oscar, we transported him to twearth, it would make no difference to his meaning; when he said that the clear liquid before him was water he would be mistaken, but he would know what he meant, although, again, he would not know that what he meant was false. The basis of first-person authority over the meanings of our words, and hence the contents of our mental states, is immediate, but it is also trivial, in as much as "aside from pathological cases, our way of interpreting others has no application to ourselves" (Davidson 2001a: 80).[16]

We noted earlier that relational theories of mind have an ancient and distinguished lineage. Aristotle's version of the theory differs from Cartesian accounts though, since for Aristotle the object of a thinker's psychological state is not a mere representation; it is, rather, the very form or essence of the external object she perceives or thinks about. In as much, then, as a thinker's beliefs about a rose bush and the rose bush itself are informed by the same essence – they are literally identical *vis-à-vis* their forms – there is no gap for the sceptic to challenge us to bridge, nor any question that her concepts are identical to ours (assuming we have experienced the same objects). Thus it is precisely in freeing us from an ontology of substantial forms that Galileo and Descartes make the epistemic status of our perceptual beliefs, and the edifice of empirical knowledge built upon them, doubtful. And it is in their efforts to reclaim the objectivity that Aristotle's account guarantees that the moderns posit knowledge of our own subjective states as an Archimedean point on which to make a stand against the sceptic.

Davidson's philosophy of meaning, mind and action reveals the vanity and uselessness of that effort. Our beliefs about our own subjective states are largely reliable, but that reliability has a trivial basis and for that reason *inter alia* it cannot support our other empirical beliefs. But neither are our empirical beliefs genuinely threatened once we surrender Aristotle's ontological guarantee that we have access to the natures of external things. The mistaken conception that our beliefs *are* threatened rests on the flawed assumption that the contents of our empirical beliefs are logically independent of the truth of those beliefs. Belief and truth, however, along with meaning, action, desire and cause, are bound to one another by our interpretive practices, with the consequence that "the acquisition of knowledge is not based on a progression from the subjective to the objective; it emerges holistically, and is interpersonal from the start" (Davidson 2001a: xvii). Recognizing this, we see the flaw in Descartes's *First Meditation* – it does not follow that all of my beliefs may be false from the fact that any particular one might be – and surmount the subjectivist epistemologies of the moderns. We thus set aside the problem of trying to answer the sceptic and, with it, a tangle of related problems that define modern European philosophy; and we undertake instead to locate the place of minded beings in the world order.

Notes

Chapter 1. Introduction: Davidson's philosophical project

1. There is more to linguistic communication than can be uncovered by investigating theories of meaning, and Davidson does not touch on many topics that philosophers of language have considered important. For example, he has little to say about the nature of modality, other than to follow Quine's lead and express a preference for extensional languages. (On this point, see §2.2.) On the other hand, many of Davidson's writings do evince his sensitivity to what linguists and philosophers of language refer to as "pragmatic elements" in linguistic communication, such as the notion of illocutionary force and the ways that social and other external factors shape a person's speech behaviour. Some of these pragmatic elements are discussed in Chapters 5 and 9.
2. Davidson (1990c: 2). Davidson submitted the dissertation for his degree in 1949, after which he began teaching philosophy at Stanford University.
3. Davidson notes that at the beginning of his career he "had not settled on any particular field in philosophy as the one in which [he] wanted to specialize"; he was, he says, "interested in almost everything" (1999b: 30). The idea to work in decision theory came at the prompting of his colleagues J. J. C. McKinsey and Patrick Suppes.
4. Philosophers of language use the term "theory of meaning" in (at least) two different senses. Some (e.g. Michael Dummett) use it interchangeably with the expression "philosophy of language" to mean the general investigation of linguistic meaning and allied concepts; Davidson, in contrast, always means something narrower; namely, a model of an interpreter's (or speaker's) linguistic competence – the knowledge she has of the grammar and lexicon of a *particular* language. For further discussion of meanings of the phrase, see Heal (1978).
5. See, for example, Searle (1969), Shiffer (1982) and Loar (1981). More

recently, Shiffer has renounced the intention-based approach for what he terms "the no-theory theory of meaning" (see Shiffer 1987).
6. See Grice (1967).
7. For other differences that separate natural from linguistic (or what Grice calls more generally "nonnatural meaning"), see Grice (1967: 377–8).
8. See Carnap: "Traditional empiricism rightly emphasized the contribution of the senses, but did not realize the ... peculiarity of logical and mathematical forms" (1967: vi).
9. Another reason is that a defining feature of Carnap's work, and that of the other logical empiricists, is their vehement rejection of Kant's characterization of these a priori truths as synthetic truths, which Kant considered his greatest innovation.
10. "Two Dogmas of Empiricism", which first appeared in 1951 and *Word and Object* (1960).

Chapter 2. Meaning and Truth I

1. See Plato's *Euthydemus*, 286c2–3.
2. As we shall see later in this chapter, Davidson argues for a close connection between a sentence's having meaning and its possessing a truth-value. The separation Plato enforces touches a different point; namely, that having meaning and being true (as opposed to being *either* true *or* false) are two different matters.
3. The letters "t", "h" and so on have *phonic* value, in the sense that they represent certain sounds, but they have no *semantical* value taken individually.

   Strictly speaking, the word "flies" is not semantically primitive; it is composed of the root "fly" and the conjugation ending "s" (here in an irregular form) that indicates the third person present tense of the verb "to fly". For the sake of simplicity, however, I ignore this complication.
4. For Plato's discussion and solution to the paradox of false propositions, see *Sophist* 259d–261c and *Theaetetus* 187c–189b. For the new questions it raises, see §2.2.
5. Thus a collection (e.g. a collection of sentences) is *compositional* in this sense if its complex members are generated by applying an operation to one or more of its simpler members, drawn from some specified list of operations, that can be carried out in some finite number of steps. Another way this is sometimes put is to say that the members of the collection are defined *inductively* or *recursively*.
6. From a logical point of view, traditional grammar divides into the studies of syntax and semantics. In doing *syntax* we look at the way in which types of words and other linguistic elements (such as prefixes, verb and case endings and so on) may be combined to assemble well-formed expressions of a given language, and we disregard the meaning and reference of expressions. In doing *semantics*, what is at issue is precisely these properties and relations. Semantics studies the relations between linguistic expressions and the (typically) extra-

linguistic world that they mean or to which they refer. *Pragmatics*, about which we will have something to say in Chapter 5, is a third area of linguistic research, and focuses on the relation between languages and language users. Charles Morris, who coined the term, suggests that the traditional study of rhetoric is an early and restricted form of pragmatics (1938: 30).

7. This way of putting the matter is overly restrictive. An adequate theory of meaning should show how speakers and their interpreters construct or discern the meaning of a complex expression given their knowledge of the expression's structure and the meanings of certain semantical primitives; but it is not necessary for the semantics to parallel exactly the syntax in the picturesque manner described in the text.
8. Most, but not all. Shiffer (1987) argues that there can be no systematic theory of meaning for a language, and he rejects the principle of compositionality as a key component of such discarded theories. For different lines of attack against Davidson's commitment to compositionality, see Chihara (1975) and Hintikka (1980).) Shiffer's main argument against compositionality is indirect. The first step is to observe that compositional meaning theories entail *inter alia* compositional analyses of propositional attitude sentences. For example, a compositional meaning theory will treat the sentence "Tanya believes that Gustav is a dog" as composed of three elements: the name "Tanya"; the two-place relational predicate "*x* believes *y*"; and a complex noun phrase, "that Gustav is a dog", that describes what she believes. (The alternative would be to treat the predicate phrase "*x* believes that Tanya is a dog" non-compositionally as a one-place predicate of the form *Fx*. In that case, though, there would be infinitely many substituends for *F* – "*x* believes-that-Gustav-is-a-dog", "*x* believes-that-Jesse-is-a-dog", "*x* believes-that-George-is-a-cat", and so on – and no finite thinker could learn them all. Hence the need to treat the predicate as a complex composed of two elements: a verb "*x* believes *y*" and an object expression taken from an extendable list of noun phrases.) The last link in Shiffer's chain of premises, then, is that compositional analyses of attitude sentences correspond to conceiving propositional attitudes (the *psychological states* themselves, not the *verbs* that refer to them) as relations between thinkers and objects named by the noun phrase in the *y*-place. Shiffer's argument, then, is a series of contrapositions: theories that conceive the propositional attitudes as relations between thinkers and objects are false – this he shows by demonstrating that none of the usual suspects (Fregean *Gedanken*, propositions, mental representations and natural language sentences) meet the desiderata for being the objects of the attitudes – therefore the corresponding compositional analyses of propositional attitude sentences are false, and so, too, are compositional meaning theories generally.

   Davidson rejects the last link in Shiffer's premises. While he believes that propositional attitude sentences have compositional semantics, Davidson rejects the inference to the structure of thinkers' psychological states. We will return to this point in §9.2. This does not immunize Davidson from Shiffer's argument though, unless he can produce an adequate compositional analysis of propositional attitude sentences. We examine Davidson's treatment of such sentences in §3.3.

More generally, Shiffer's argument is unconvincing. Certainly, sometimes the only way to prove a negative ("There is no *x* that is *F*") is to survey and show that each candidate ("*a* is not *F*, *b* is not *F*, and *c* is not *F*") falls short of the mark; and so it is unfair to complain that while Shiffer has (claimed to have) proved that no recursive semantics currently on the market meets all the desiderata, he has not shown that the project is *doomed* to fail. Nevertheless, to reject the principle of compositionality based on the difficulty presented by one apparently anomalous fragment of discourse is overly hasty. A peacock's extravagant plumage resists analysis in terms of natural selection, but rather than rejecting that keystone of biology, scientists have constructed an epicycle (the theory of sexual selection) to that theory, based on a new set of principles. By analogy, a clever addendum to compositional meaning theories is needed, rather than a wholesale rejection of Frege's project of finding an orderly structure in language.

9. See, for example, Chomsky (1972).
10. Any textbook on formal logic contains examples of such constructions. See, for example, Mates (1972: Chs 3 & 4).
11. Blackburn (1984: 3). (I have modified Blackburn's diagram somewhat.) Blackburn's image is probably influenced by Ogden and Richards's triangle of reference; see Ogden & Richards (1946: 11).
12. For the term "correspondence theory of meaning" see Gamut (1991: Ch. 1). Gamut (or rather the group of Dutch logicians for whom "Gamut" is a collective pseudonym) identifies as a *correspondence theory of meaning* any account that "start[s] out from the … principle [that] meaning is a relation between the symbols of a language and certain entities which are independent of that language" (1991: 1). A correspondence theory of *meaning* differs from a correspondence theory of *truth*, which we may define (following Russell) as any account according to which "truth consists in some form of correspondence between belief [statement] and fact" (Russell 1912: 121). A philosopher of language can hold a correspondence theory of meaning without endorsing a correspondence theory of truth, and vice versa. For example, after 1910 Russell argues for a correspondence theory of truth (in, for example, Russell 1984), but by then he rejected the correspondence theory of meaning of his *Principles of Mathematics* (1938). For the conceptual apparatus needed to support simultaneously a correspondence theory of meaning and a correspondence theory of truth, see the next note.
13. False sentences, for example, "Charles I died in his bed", refer to situations, too. The difference between false sentences and true ones lies in Russell's contrast between *being* and *existence.* "Being is that which belongs to [everything] conceivable" including conceivable but nonexistent situations like the death of Charles I on his bed;

"Existence, on the contrary, is the prerogative of some only amongst beings", namely, those beings that are not *merely thinkable* but which, in fact, *exist in the actual world* (Russell 1938: 449). Thus false sentences correspond to situations that merely *are*, that is, that have *being*, whereas true ones correspond to situations that, in fact, *exist*. In other words, false sentences refer to merely possible situations, whereas true sentences refer to facts. Russell soon rejects this early theory, deciding that *inter alia* its ontological extravagance was too high a cost to bear.

14. Or, at least, it was Russell's goal that his theory should have this result. In fact, what Russell called the problem of the unity of a proposition – in effect, how *exactly* it is that the parts of the meaning of a sentence (Charles I, the scaffold, etc.) combine with one another to generate that meaning (the fact that *Charles I died on the scaffold*) – continued to vex him through the 1900s and 1910s, and the inadequacies of his various proposals was a point to which Wittgenstein continually returned (e.g. in Wittgenstein (1933: §5.5422)) when he criticized Russell.
15. To see what the logic of a non-extensional or *intensional* expression would look like, consider the following sentence, which we assume to be true:

    (i) Livia believes that Antony ordered the death of Cicero.

    Suppose that Livia does not know that Tully = Cicero; suppose, for example, that she believes that "Tully" names her gardener and not the Roman orator. Then (i) and

    (ii) Livia believes that Antony ordered the death of Tully

    report two very different situations: (i) says (truly) that Livia believes that Antony ordered the death of Cicero, while (ii) reports (falsely) that she believes that the future emperor ordered her gardener's death. This example shows that

    x believes that p,

    like other *propositional attitude expressions* (such as "x desires that p", "x doubts that p", etc., which are propositional attitude expressions because the second argument place is filled with a sentence or proposition), violates the substitution principle and is therefore logically anomalous. Many philosophers of language, including correspondence theorists, who identify the meanings of sentences with thoughts, assume that "x means y" is an intensional context; on this point, see the discussion of Locke later in this section.

    This distinction between intension and extension corresponds roughly to Frege's contrast between *Sinn* and *Bedeutung*. The intension or *Sinn* of an expression is its sense or cognitive significance (Frege describes it as the expression's "mode of presentation"), while the extension or *Bedeutung* of an expression is the thing to which the expression refers. (Note, though, that Geach and Black confusingly translate *Bedeutung* as "meaning" in their 1980 translation of Frege:

Geach & Black (1980).) In general, whenever one speaks of intensions or intensional contexts, the connection is with Fregean *Sinn*, and whenever one mentions extensions or extensional contexts, the connection is with Fregean *Bedeutung*.

16. A term of the form $\{x: Fx\}$ names a set, and the sentence to the right of the colon (here, Fx) states a condition on any object x such that if that condition is true, then x belongs to the set. For example, the set $\{x: x$ is mortal$\}$ is the set of all mortals. Thus $\{x: x = x\}$ is the set of all self-identical objects, and since everything is identical to itself, this set is the set of everything. The peculiar-looking but formally unobjectionable set $\{x: x = x$ and there is a coffee mug on my desk$\}$ is the set of all objects such that two conditions are satisfied: (i) x is self-identical and (ii) there is a coffee mug on my desk. If (ii) happens to be true, then since everything is self-identical both conditions are satisfied and the set $\{x: x = x$ and there is a coffee mug on my desk$\}$ contains everything; but if (ii) turns out to be false, then despite everything's being self-identical the conjunction of conditions (i) and (ii) is false (since, by assumption, (ii) is false), and hence the set $\{x: x = x$ and there is a coffee mug on my desk$\}$ is empty. If, therefore, (ii) is true, then $\{x: x = x\}$ and $\{x: x = x$ and there is a coffee mug on my desk$\}$ are identical, while if (ii) is false, they are not.
17. Note that the sentences "Antony ordered the death of Cicero" and "Grass is green" are not *logically* equivalent. As a matter of *fact* (and not logic), Antony did order Cicero's death, hence the first happens to be true; and also as a matter of *fact* (and not logic) grass is green, and hence the second happens to be true. The technical term for their logical relationship is that they are *materially* equivalent, that is, they have the same truth-value, but that coincidence is a matter of how things stand in the world and not of necessity.
18. Barwise & Perry (1981: 395). See also Barwise & Perry (1983).
19. Alternatively, we could hold on to the substitution principle and the assumption that logically equivalent expressions have the same reference, but deny that a sentence *refers to* the fact, or complex of objects and properties, that it *means*. (For example, in the *Tractatus*, Wittgenstein says that sentences have only sense (*Sinn*) and not reference (*Bedeutung*), thus effectively denying that sentences refer to the states of affairs to which they correspond.) This would oblige us to revise the standard logical *formalism*, since the assignment functions that model-theorists employ map sentences onto truth-values, considered as objects in the domain of the interpretation; but this would be a modest price compared to revising our *logical practices*, that is, *logical laws*, as Barwise and Perry recommend.

    To oppose this strategy we need a reason to ban outright all appeals to facts. One might argue, for example, that the concept of a fact is just the concept of a certain sort of articulated structure, where our grasp of such an articulation is really just our grasp of logical or semantical concepts and categories. If this is right, then we have no purchase on the notion of a *fact* apart from our knowing what a *sentence* or *language* is. Hence it is idle to hope that we can illuminate language and meaning by talking about facts, since whatever we know about facts (so the argument goes) depends on our already knowing about sentences. (Note that the early Wittgenstein would accept this criticism, if Cora Diamond reads the *Tractatus* rightly; see Diamond 1991.) Presumably, though, this line of argument will be unpersuasive to theorists who *do* think they can give substance to the notion of a fact apart from facts being just like sentences (but with objects and properties where a sentence has singular and general terms). For an overview of the different theories of facts, see Olson (1987).

20. See above, note 15.
21. That is, the meaning of "The morning star is the closest planet to earth" is the set of possible worlds in which Venus is the brightest body in the morning sky, and "The evening star is the closest planet to earth" is the set of possible worlds in which Venus is the brightest body in the evening sky. These two sets are different; it just so happens that the actual world is in their intersection.
22. Intensional concepts *may* figure in a sentence's interpretation if those concepts already appear in the sentence being interpreted; see the discussion of "samesaying" in §3.3.
23. The *metalanguage* is the language in which the theory of meaning is being formulated, while the *object language* is that for which the theory is being given. The metalanguage may contain or be identical to the object language, for example, if we construct a theory of meaning *for* English *in* English; in that case, the theory of meaning is said to be *homophonic*. In example 5, German is the object language and English the metalanguage; thus the theory is *heterophonic*, that is, the metalanguage does not contain the object language.
24. The distinction between use and mention is standard in logical practice but may appear mysterious to the uninitiated. To dispel that mystery, first consider the distinction applied to something non-linguistic. There is a clear difference, for example, between *using* the sword Excaliber and talking about or *mentioning* it. Arthur uses the sword to battle Mordred, while he mentions it (i.e. uses a name for it) in conversation with Gawain. The linguistic case is exactly parallel, although perhaps harder to see. We distinguish between using words to say, for example, that snow is white, and mentioning or talking about them, such as when we say that the sentence, "Snow is white" contains 11 letters. In mentioning words, we use a name of those words to say something about them, just as we use the name "Excaliber" when we say that Excaliber was given to Arthur by the Lady of the Lake. A mentioned sentence, like the name "Excaliber", functions as a noun in the sentence in which it is mentioned.

    The easiest way to name a linguistic expression is to enclose it within quotation marks, thus forming its *quotation-mark name*. (For example, the term to the left of the predicate "means that" in example 5 is the quotation name of a German sentence.) The *locus classicus* for the distinction between use and mention is Quine (1981: §4); see also Mates (1972: 21–2), or, for an informal account, Hofstadter (1979: 431–7).

25. It is a definition of truth for L, again, in the sense that it specifies a predicate ("is true_L") that applies to all and only the true sentences of L. The truth theory achieves this result recursively, as we will see in the next section, and one can turn this recursive definition into an explicit definition, exploiting some set-theoretic apparatus deriving from Frege; but this extra step plays no role in Davidson's use of truth theories.

A theory's being a definition of truth is different from its being a criterion of truth for a language. A theory of truth merely states what *would* have to be the case, were a sentence to be true, whereas a *criterion of truth* can be used to determine whether *in fact* a sentence is true. That extra information, albeit useful, has no part in the theories of truth that Davidson employs.

Chapter 3. Meaning and Truth II

1. Tarski (1983); see also Tarski (1944, 1967).
2. Here is an example of a theory of truth that does *not* satisfy Convention *T*. Consider a theory θ'_L that assigns to the sentences of L one of *three* truth-values: true, false or indeterminate. Suppose, then, that θ'_L assigns to a particular sentence s of L the truth condition

$$s \text{ is true}_L \text{ if and only if } p$$

and suppose, further, that s turns out to be indeterminate. Then the left-hand side of the biconditional is false, while the right-hand side is indeterminate; hence the biconditional is false or, perhaps, indeterminate, depending on the background logic of θ'_L. (I have adapted this example from Haack (1978: 101–2.)

Davidson has in mind a different, rather more technical, sort of failure to conform to Convention *T*, although the details of his objection are difficult to make out. The theorems of a truth theory that satisfies Convention *T* tell us how things stand in the world if the object language sentences mentioned in the theorems are true; contemporary model theorists, however, often find it convenient to work with a different notion, namely, how things stand in a *model* or *possible world* if the object language sentences are true. Thus, unlike instances of Convention *T*, which look like this:

$$s \text{ is true}_L \text{ if and only if } p$$

a *T*-sentence of a theory of truth *relativized to a model* or *possible world* will have the form,

(i) s is true_L-in-M if and only if $M \vDash p$,

that is, s is true_L in the model M just in case p is a logical consequence of M.

One problem with (i), or rather the theory of truth that has instances of (i) as its theorems, is that the extra logical machinery on the right-hand side is surely beyond the ken of most L-speakers. If, therefore, we are trying to model what an L-speaker knows when he utters s, it behoves us not to appeal to conceptual resources he does not possess. Another problem is that the extra machinery includes a semantical notion, namely, logical implication, and therefore raises doubts about the formal adequacy of the theory.

Neither of these complaints, however, bears on the failure of (i) to meet the demands of Convention *T*. Davidson writes at one point that "theories of absolute [i.e. non-relativized] truth necessarily provide an analysis of structure relevant to truth and inference" (Davidson 1984a: 71), that is, they are compositional. The implication, then, seems to be that theories of relativized truth do not provide such an analysis, but it is hard to see why Davidson thinks so. For Davidson's discussion of the matter, see Davidson (1984a: 68–71). (I am indebted to Akeel Bilgrami for help in clarifying this apparent lacuna in Davidson's position.)

3. At this stage we are just describing the syntax of the language, but for the sake of illustration we note that the connectives "~" and "&" may be read, respectively, as "not" and "and". Hence "~(Socrates is Roman)" would be "Socrates is *not* Roman", and "Empedocles is Italian & Socrates is Greek" would be "Empedocles is Italian *and* Socrates is Greek". Further, the existential quantifier "$\exists x$" should be read as "there exists an x such that", thus read "$\exists x$ (x is mortal)" as "there exists an x such that x is mortal".
4. It is a serious question, though, whether this approach is consistent with Davidson's holistic account of language. See Haack (1978: 121).
5. An *idiolect* is a language idiosyncratic to one individual person over a given stretch of time.
6. P. F. Strawson characterizes the concept of an sentence's *logical form* in terms of the idea of its

> formal powers ... meaning by this the range of parts it could play in inferences ... In so far as two different statements may play similar parts in inferences ... we may speak of an analogy between their formal power. ... We say that two statements are of the same logical form when we are interested in an analogy between their formal powers. (1960: 50)

Thus the sentences "Jesse is a black dog" and "George is a happy fellow" are of the same logical form, since similar inferences may be drawn from each (that Jesse is black and that George is happy), but "Mickey is a large rat" is of a different logical form (since one cannot infer from it that Mickey is large). There is more to the logical form or semantical structure of an expression than its inferential properties, but those properties are generally a good indicator of those other features.

7. For further technical discussion of demonstratives from a Davidsonian perspective, see Weinstein (1974).
8. Here is why the inference does not go through. If whatever term replaces t in the sentence "Galileo believed that t moves" refers to its customary *Sinn* or intension, and "the earth" and "the planet on which D.D. was born in 1917" have different intensions, then we are *not* substituting one

co-referring term for another when we move from (9) to "Galileo believes that the planet on which D.D. was born in 1917 moves", and thus the substitution principle does not apply.

9. As Gabriel Segal points out, though, phonology seems to tell a different story, in as much as there are differences in the pronunciation of "that" used as a demonstrative and as a relative pronoun: the "that" in "Galileo said that the earth moves" typically undergoes a stress reduction, which it never does in "Hey, look at that" or "Galileo said that. The earth moves." See Segal (1989: 79).
10. In addition to the articles cited in the preceding and following notes, see also Lepore & Loewer (1989) and Burge (1986).
11. See Higgenbotham (1986: 39–40). Higgenbotham is sympathetic to elements of Davidson's proposal, for example, the role he accords the notion of samesaying, but in place of Davidson's paratactic theory, Higgenbotham analyses indirect discourse using tools borrowed from contemporary linguistics, especially phrase markers, the values of which he relativizes to their contexts.
12. See, for example, Davidson (1989c) and §9.2. Compare this line of objection with Shiffer (1987: 126ff.).
13. The Polish version, *Pohecie prawdy w jezykach nauk dedukcyjnych*, was published in 1933; it was first translated into German, then English and French, two years later.
14. Ramsey (1931a: 142). Ramsey proposes that we gloss contexts where the affirmed sentence is described and not explicitly given, for example, "He is always right", using second-order quantification, as in

    "*p* (if he asserts that *p*, then *p* is true),

    and then eliminate the truth predicate, taking the assertion that *p* is true as equivalent to the assertion that *p*. This proposal does not appear viable, though, at least not in the form in which Ramsey sketches it; see Davidson (1990e: 282–3) and Haack (1978: 127–34).
15. The truth predicates "is $\text{true}_{English}$", "is true_{Urdu}" and so on, are *relativized* in the sense that "is $\text{true}_{English}$" picks out the true sentences of English, "is true_{Urdu}" picks out the true sentences of Urdu and so on. That relativization has nothing to do with metaphysical or epistemological relativism, according to which there are different "facts" for different cognitive agents; the sense in which English speakers and Urdu speakers hold different sentences true is just the mundane sense – the sentences an English speaker holds true are (of course) English sentences, and the sentences an Urdu speaker holds true are (of course) Urdu sentences. Nor does it have anything to do with the logical notion of truth relativized to a possible world, or truth within a model; in this logical sense, Davidson works with an absolute concept of truth. On this point, see note 2, above.
16. Like Ramsey, deflationists hold that our grasp of the truth predicate is grounded in our understanding of something that resembles Tarski's *T*-schema; but they are impressed by the *ineliminability* of the predicate in expressions such as

    (A) Every proposition of the form "*p* or ~*p*" is true,

or

(B) Oscar's claim is true.

Deflationists conclude that truth *is* a genuine property of statements, that is, the truth predicate is not empty; but they hold that its explanatory function is exhausted by its use in generalizations like (A) and (B) (which can be read as "there exists an x such Oscar claims x, and x is true"), and its content by the equivalence schema (P) (given in the text). For a defence of the deflationary theory, see Leeds (1978) and Horwich (1990).

17. Criticisms of the correspondence and coherence theories are well known; see, for example, Haack (1978: 91–7). Davidson discusses both theories in his Dewey lectures (1990e: §2).

Chapter 4. Radical interpretation

1. See especially Ramsey's "Truth and Probability" (1931b), reprinted in Ramsey (1931c). Among the many places Davidson cites Ramsey, see Davidson (1990e: 318; 1984a: 145, 160).
2. An ordinal preference among options is a ranking of those options as first most desirable, second most desirable, third most desirable and so on.
3. For details of Ramsey's construction, see "Truth and Probability" (1931b). Also see Jeffrey (1983: Ch. 3) and Collins (1999: 508–10).
4. There is more than a parallel between Davidson's work and Ramsey's. Recall from Chapter 1 that Davidson's goal is a unified theory that simultaneously interprets a speaker's words and gives an account of his attitudes, without either part of the theory presupposing the other. In some writings Davidson sketches a unified theory of meaning and theory of rational choice, where the former incorporates something akin to Ramsey's notion of partial belief and the latter is "freed from the assumption of independent access to meanings" (Davidson 1990e: 322). This combined theory takes as the basic evidential datum an agent's preferring the truth of one (uninterpreted) sentence to another (in place of, as we will see in §4.3, a speaker's holding sentences true). Which sentences an agent has this attitude toward is a function of the meanings he attaches to the sentences, the values he places on different states of the world and the conditional probabilities he assigns to those states; the interpreter's task, then, is to take advantage of multiple observations of the agent's ordinal preferences among the truth of (uninterpreted) sentences to infer these properties. See Davidson (1990e: 321–8; 1980b). Most of the interesting philosophical issues raised by Davidson's theory of meaning arise in connection with the more streamlined work that abstracts from its connection with decision theory, and hence we focus our attention there.
5. Unlike Dennett, though, Davidson denies that adopting the "intentional stance" is a purely instrumental move. See §8.6, for a discussion of the difference between Davidson's account and Dennett's.

6. While *holding true* it is not an *intensional* relation, it is an *intentional* concept, and hence Davidson's account of the evidential base of linguistic understanding (like Grice's account) violates Jerry Fodor's description of naturalism:

   > I suppose that sooner or later the physicists will complete the catalogue they've been compiling of the ultimate and irreducible properties of things. When they do, the likes of spin, charm, and charge will perhaps appear on that list. But aboutness surely won't ... Here, then are the ground rules. I want a naturalized theory of meaning; a theory that articulates, in nonsemantic and non-intentional terms, sufficient conditions for one bit of the world to be about ... another bit. (Fodor 1987: 98)

   Davidson, therefore, believes that Fodor asks too much. On this point, see §8.5.
7. See Mulhall (1987: 322). For a survey of sense-datum theories, see the essays collected in Swarz (1965).
8. This picture is informed by McDowell's understanding of the Wittgensteinian dictum that the meaning of a linguistic expression is manifest in its use. On this point, see Bilgrami (1986: 119–22).
9. This quotation and the two that precede it are from Davidson (1994b: 3).
10. For a critique of Davidson's theory from a Heideggerian perspective, see Mulhall (1993: Ch. 4). However, as we have seen, Mulhall's discussion of Davidson is vitiated by his misreading Davidson as a behaviourist.
11. Davidson (1995a: 10). This understanding of the project is especially important for Davidson, who (as we have seen) recommends that a theory of interpretation take the form of a Tarski-style truth theory, for it is implausible to credit ordinary speakers and their interlocutors with possessing a mechanism corresponding in detail, rather than output, to such a theory.
12. "Quine is, and has been since I took my first logic course with him some sixty years ago, my teacher and inspiration" (Davidson 1999a: 80).
13. Quine concedes that observationality is vague at the edges. For example, depending upon how one divides the population, the sentence "Hydrogen sulphide is escaping" will be observational for some people and not for others. The same goes for individual speakers, too: "What had passed for an observations sentence, say 'That's a swan', may to the subject's surprise leave him undecided when he encounters a black specimen" (Quine 1990: 3).
14. More precisely, the *affirmative stimulus meaning* of an observation sentence is the set of stimulations that would prompt a speaker's assent to a query (e.g. his experiencing the presence of a rabbit, after being asked, "Gavagai?"), and the *negative stimulus meaning* is the set of stimulations that would prompt his dissent (his experiencing the presence of a squirrel). Taken together as an ordered pair, these constitute the expression's stimulus meaning. Bear in mind that by

the term "stimulus", Quine means the pattern of sensation, literally, the ordered sequence of triggerings of nerve cells on the speaker's bodily surface. Thus the *stimulus* of Quine's "stimulus meaning" is the *proximal stimulus*. Davidson, as we will see in Chapter 9, locates meaning in the distal stimulus, the ordinary external objects lying open to both a speaker's and auditor's view.

Given Quine's definition, then, the translator's mapping of "Gavagai" onto her own "Lo, a rabbit" is justified by the utterances sharing the same stimulus meaning, in the sense that "Lo, a rabbit" has a stimulus meaning Σ for the translator; and she, observing the native assert "Gavagai" when she, in his position, would assert "Lo, a rabbit", that is, when she would have Σ, assigns Σ to "Gavagai". See Quine (1990: 42–3).

15. The Roman deity Janus is the god associated with archways and doorways, and he is traditionally pictured with two faces on opposite sides of his head.
16. Quine writes that after it is cleared of its vitiating dogmas, what remains of empiricism is its commitment to two cardinal tenets, "that whatever evidence there is for science is sensory evidence. The other ... is that all inculcation of meanings must rest ultimately on sensory evidence" (Quine 1969: 75). Davidson concedes the "pallid claim that all knowledge of the world comes through the agency of the senses" but repudiates the stronger claim, embodied in Quine's dicta, that "this fact is of prime epistemological significance" (Davidson 1990d: 68). On Davidson's rejection of the empiricist philosophical problem, see Chapter 9.
17. Translation and interpretation, although different projects, are obviously closely related. We can think of an interpretation of a language as the merger of (i) a translation manual from an unknown, alien language into a familiar one and (ii) a Tarski-style theory of truth for the familiar language. Once the combination has been effected, though, "all reference to the known language [becomes] otiose; when this reference is dropped, what is left is a ... theory of interpretation for the object language – couched, of course, in familiar words" (Davidson 1984a: 130).

Some commentators criticize Davidson for his blanket use of the term "interpretation" to describe a person's understanding of known, as well as unfamiliar, languages. Ian Hacking cites his old *Concise Oxford Dictionary* and defines "interpretation" as the process of "expound[ing] the meaning of (abstruse words, writings &c.)"; if this is what we mean by "interpretation", then when an interlocutor uses words from a common language in circumstances where his meaning is clear, there is no interpretation (in the *Concise Oxford Dictrionary*'s sense) going on (Hacking 1986: 450).

Davidson is unrepentant in the face of such criticism, and he maintains that "interpretation is domestic as well as foreign" (Davidson 1984a: 125). There is, he argues, no essential difference between understanding words spoken in familiar and alien languages because the relative semantic poverty of our experience of linguistic intercourse means that all understanding consists in moving from semantically unrevealing descriptions to revealing ones, and thus it does not matter whether the transition is from:

Kurt holds true$_G$ the uninterpreted sentence "Es schneit"

to:

Kurt says that it snows.

or from:

Sheila holds true$_{English}$ the uninterpreted sentence "It snows"

to:

Sheila says that it snows.

For further discussion, see §4.2.

18. The term "principle of charity" first occurs in Wilson (1959). Davidson has recently taken to calling charity the "principle of rational accommodation", which is more apt to his intention. He explicitly divides the principle into the principles of coherence and correspondence in "Three Varieties of Knowledge", reprinted in *Subjective, Intersubjective and Objective*.
19. Compare Hacking (1975: 149–50).
20. The first quotation is from Bennett (1985b: 601), and the second comes from Heal (1997: 187).
21. For this way of speaking, see, for example, Davidson (1984a: 27, 101, 169, 197).
22. See Grandy (1973: 445).
23. See Quine: "It is precisely this sharing of words, by observation sentences and theoretical sentences, that provides logical connections between the two kinds of sentences and makes observation relevant to scientific theory ... it is the shared vocabulary that links them" (1990: 7–8).
24. For Quine's use of the phrase "fact of the matter" in this context, see Quine (1981c: 23).
25. The contrast between a straight solution and a sceptical one first appears in Hume (1975). For the classic contemporary discussion of the pair, see Kripke (1982) and note 26. One might say that while Quine and Davidson agree that there is no straight solution to the sceptical problem that Quine formulates, Davidson sees room for a sceptical solution. A *straight solution* to a sceptical argument accepts the argument's premises but rejects its conclusion, based on some flaw or oversight in its reasoning. Thus Descartes famously avoids the sceptical conclusion of the *First Meditation* by finding, in the *Second Meditation*, an incorrigible statement ("I think, therefore, I am") that his earlier regimen of doubt cannot touch. In contrast, a *sceptical solution* concedes that a sceptical argument is valid, but avoids its conclusion by finding some principled failure in the argument, such as finding that its key concepts stand in need of reinterpretation. Hume, for example, sceptically solves the

argument that our causal beliefs have no rational basis by reconceiving those beliefs and showing that they do not stand in need of rational justification. For Davidson, the problem with the arguments for indeterminacy lies in the assumption that there are fixed, determinate meanings, which assumption Quine demonstrates to be untenable.

26. The burden of the opening sections of Wittgenstein's *Philosophical Investigations* is the same, and therefore Kripke (1982) is right to see Wittgenstein as engaged in putting forward a sceptical solution to sceptical arguments. In effect, Wittgenstein's point is that meaning cannot be what many philosophers (including not only Augustine but also the author of the *Tractatus*) have taken it to be. As many commentators have argued, though, Kripke misconceives the nature of that sceptical solution. See, for example, McDowell (1992b).

Chapter 5. Interpretation and meaning

1. If, though, the meaning of a term is given by its definition (*logos*) in a fully developed scientific language, and that definition is a statement of the essence of the kind to which the object belongs, and, further, if the statement of a kind's essence partly consists in a statement of that kind's functional role in the cosmos, then Aristotle's theory of language incorporates a holistic element. For a discussion of Aristotle's philosophy of language, see Modrak (2000).
2. For Locke's philosophy of language, see Locke (1975: Bk 3); for a terse statement of Aristotle's, see *De Interpretatione*, 16a3–8.
3. For refinements to the version of Fodor's theory presented here, which is a first approximation of what he calls "the crude causal theory", see Fodor (1987: 99–127). For Fodor's reasons for thinking that mental representations are symbols in a language of thought, see (1987: Appendix).
4. In Akeel Bilgrami's phrase, "holism for Fodor has become something akin to what Carthage must have been for Cato: he lets no opportunity pass for saying that it must be utterly destroyed" (1992: 141).
5. Fodor and Lepore attribute this intuition to Michael Dummett. See Dummett (1981: 597–600).
6. The term "literal meaning", Davidson says, is too protean and "incrusted with philosophical and other extras to do much work" (1986c: 434).
7. On the relation between pragmatics and semantics, and the possibility of doing one in isolation from the other, see Travis (1997).
8. See Putnam (1978: 99) and Higgenbotham (1999: 679–80).
9. This terminology goes back to J. L. Austin (1962).
10. Compare McDowell (1976: 44).
11. Compare Searle (1969: 66).
12. A fuller analysis of metaphor as an illocutionary force would find similarities between it and assertion, otherwise we would deprive metaphor of its "punch". (On this point I am indebted to Jerry Clegg.) The present point is that a feature of assertion that metaphor lacks is the

requirement that if an agent asserts that p then she believes that p. Searle calls this the *sincerity condition* on assertion.

13. See, for example, the language G defined in §3.1, and the remarks at the beginning of Chapter 4.
14. In "A Nice Derangement of Epitaphs" (1986c), Davidson calls the theory an interpreter begins with the "prior theory", and the new and improved theory she constructs *in vivo* the "passing theory"; later, though, he concedes his critics' point that this terminology is unwieldy.
15. Wittgenstein (1958: §201), partly quoted in Kripke (1982: 7).
16. See Kripke (1982: Ch. 3), for the details of the sceptical solution Kripke attributes to Wittgenstein. McDowell (1998d) argues that Kripke's (or Kripke's Wittgenstein's) community-based solution to the sceptical paradox, in fact fails to solve the sceptic's challenge.
17. For an account of Tarski's goals in his work on the concept of truth and its relation to semantics, see §2.4 and the first part of Etchemendy (1988).
18. This may not exclude other types of deviant T-sentences and satisfaction conditions, however. Consider, for example, that there are and have been only finitely many camels in the world; call them c_1, c_2, ..., c_n. Then the satisfaction condition,

    a satisfies "x is a camel" if and only if $a = c_1$ or c_2 or ... or c_n

    will satisfy the constraints that Davidson lays out; in particular, the holistic constraint will not exclude it, since every fact about camels is a fact about c_1 or c_2 or ... or c_n. As Brian Loar argues, this

    > will have a systematically perverse effect on the truth conditions of every sentence which contains "camel". For each such sentence S, ⌈S is true iff ...⌉ would not intuitively "give the meaning" of S; for knowing the equivalence would not be to understand S.
    > (Loar 1976: 141)

    This perversity challenges the adequacy of Davidson's revised Convention T, for to know (for example) that the camel is the ship of the desert is to know more than that c_1 or c_2 or ... or c_n is a ship of the desert. In effect, there is more to knowing what a camel is than being able to pick one out. (For a related point about concepts, see §9.1). This difficulty illustrates the challenge of modelling an *intensional* concept with merely *extensional* resources.

    For a Davidsonian response to the problem of deviant theories of interpretation, see Ramberg (1989: Chs 5 & 6). Ramberg argues that because an interpreter has a never-ending stream of new evidence, the process of theory construction is incompletable. The virtue of this dynamic character of interpretation is that

    > it is only on the assumption there is some one theory or other that definitively captures the meaning of the words of a language that we can imagine a situation where Convention T could not be used to rule out a "counterfeit theory". (Ramberg 1989: 61)

Giving up the view of language as a static entity and interpretation as frozen in time, as Davidson does, means that novel circumstance that would exclude counterfeit theories are forever on the horizon. For the ongoing character of interpretation see §5.3. For another approach to deviant theories, see the reference in note 20.

19. A standard definition of logical consequence is that a sentence *s* is a *logical consequence* of a set of sentences Γ if every interpretation (in the model-theoretic sense) that makes each of the members of Γ true also makes *s* true. A common feature of this and other definitions is that logical consequence comes out as a *modal notion*: if Γ is true (that is, if each of the members of Γ are true), then it is *impossible* that *s* be false.
20. Davidson sometimes expresses the point in this paragraph by saying that "the axioms and theorems [of theories of interpretation] ha[ve] to be viewed as laws" (Davidson 1984a: xiv) and, again, that the sentences of a theory of interpretation "must not only be true but lawlike. (*S*) presumably is not a law, since it does not support appropriate counterfactuals" (1984a: 26n11). On the concept of a law, see §7.4.
21. But consider θ_3, which contains in place of (*T*) the truth-condition:

    (*T**) "Schnee ist weiss" is true_L if and only if snow is white and $7 + 5 = 12$.

    Since it is true in all possible worlds that $7 + 5 = 12$, there is no conceivable counterfactual circumstance that an interpreter could exploit to justify preferring θ_1 over θ_3, even though the latter contains a *T*-sentence that is *not* interpretive (i.e. *T**). See Higginbotham (1991) for the suggestion that we can eliminate θ_3 on the grounds that (*T*), rather than (*T**), expresses the strongest information that speakers can be expected to know about the truth-conditions of "Schnee ist weiss", that is, they can be expected to know that "Schnee ist weiss" is true_L if and only if snow is white, but not that $7 + 5 = 12$.

Chapter 6. Events and causes

1. The inadequacy of the customary symbolization is described by Kenny (1963), who dubs the underlying phenomenon the "variable polyadicity" of action verbs (although it is not restricted to only action verbs.)
2. See, for example, the résumé of rules in Lemmon (1978: 39–40, 145).
3. See, for example, the articles in Benacerraf & Putnam (1983: pt II).
4. In doing so, Quine follows Rudolf Carnap, who argues that existence questions are properly posed relative to an accepted theoretical framework; Carnap calls such questions internal questions. When a natural scientist pursues an *internal question*, she does so within a fixed background taxonomy that specifies the sorts of things there are and how they are related; and she focuses relatively narrowly on whether a new thing or species of thing should be incorporated into that accepted theory. Palaeoanthropologists, for example, when they debate whether *Kenyanthropus platyops* represents a distinct genus of hominids, and cosmologists, when they wonder whether there is

such a thing as dark energy, ask internal questions. As these examples demonstrate, the answer to an internal question may have broad implications, but Carnap wants to hold them separate from questions that concern "the existence or reality of the system of entities as a whole" (1956a: 206), which he calls *external questions*. In practice, according to Carnap, natural scientists can rely upon well-settled and largely extra-linguistic empirical methods, defined by or following from the background theory, to answer their internal questions; while ontologists, because external questions arise when the background theory *itself* comes up for reconsideration, have to compare the efficiency, fruitfulness and simplicity of competing frameworks and thus make a "practical decision" about which theory form to adopt.

Quine, however, rejects Carnap's internal versus external dualism as of a piece with the analytic–synthetic distinction. A natural scientist, too, considers the efficiency, fruitfulness and simplicity of her hypotheses; and, as holism implies, rejecting her theoretical framework, with its "system of entities as a whole", is always open to the scientist if she is willing to tolerate the disruption that rejection causes in order to save some data that conflict with that old theory.

5. Unless, that is, we either deny that endorsing a mathematical theory means accepting that its sentences are true, a path that Hartry Field calls *fictionalism* and which he defends in *Science Without Numbers* (1980); or we accept their truth but gloss them so as to avoid quantifying over any objects peculiar to mathematics. Putnam employs modal logic to take this path in "Mathematics Without Foundations" (1983). Quine himself does place a limit on how far he is willing to go in recognizing some of the more exotic entities conceived by modern mathematics; see Quine (1986: 400).
6. See, for example, Wilson (1974) and Sher (1974).
7. Lemmon (1962) presents a proposal very similar to Quine's, about which Davidson remarks at the time that he is "not at all certain [that Lemmon's suggestion] is wrong" (Davidson 1980a: 124); by the time of Davidson's "Incoherence and Irrationality" (1985c), and through Quine's mediation, Davidson evidently believes that it may be right. For a criticism of the Lemmon–Quine criterion, see Bennett (1985a).
8. Sufficient controversy attends the existence and nature of events, as Tyler Burge quips, to have "supported a modest sector of the publishing industry" (1983: 611). In §6.3 we briefly consider Roderick Chisholm's theory of events as an alternative to Davidson's; here, we observe that Jaegwon Kim also challenges Davidson's account. Kim characterizes events as "exemplifications by substances of properties at a time" (1976: 160); that is, Kim defines an event as an ordered triple $<x, P, t>$, where x is an object that has the property P at time t. This supplies clear identity criteria for events (namely, event $<x_1, P_1, t_1>$ = event $<x_2, P_2, t_2>$ if and only if $x_1 = x_2$, $P_1 = P_2$ and $t_1 = t_2$), and it nicely captures the idea that events are changes, where a change occurs when an object acquires (or loses) a property that it previously (did or) did not

have. However, it also has the effect of closely tying events to properties in a way that Davidson's theory does not. For Davidson, an event is no more closely associated with its properties (e.g. being a killing of Caesar) than is an object (such as Bill Clinton) tied to *its* properties (being a former president of the United States). One consequence is that for Kim it is problematic to take an event (Brutus' killing of Caesar, or <Brutus, being a killing of Caesar, 15 March>) and *re*-describe in terms of a different property (being a betrayal of Caesar), for, given the way he defines events, that re-description would seem to generate a *different* event (<Brutus, being a betrayal of Caesar, 15 March>). As we shall see in the next section, and in Chapters 7 and 8, not losing the distinction between an event and its description – this distinction guaranteeing the possibility of re-describing one and the same event in different terms – is key to Davidson's philosophies of action and mind.

9. If we follow Chisholm's analysis, this formulation is more perspicuous, since the terms that now flank the verb "caused" ("that Jack fell down with a force of 800 newtons" and "the fact that he broke his crown") are more "sentence-like" than the terms in (7), and hence it brings out that causation is a relation between the referents of sentences, rather than singular terms.
10. See Chapter 2, note 15, for the notion of an *intensional context*.
11. Recall from §2.2 that starting with the substitution principle and the principle that logically equivalent sentences have the same reference – both of which are assumed in standard logic – it can be shown that any two sentences (e.g. "Antony ordered the death of Cicero" and "Grass is green") have the same reference. If, further, we identify events with the references of sentences, it is a short step to showing that any one event causes every other event.
12. The term "$t + \varepsilon$" indicates some time soon after time t, and read the quantifier "$\exists!z$" as "there exists exactly one z such that".

Chapter 7. Action theory and explanation in the social sciences

1. Xunzi, for example, writes: "When the mind conceives a thought and the body acts on it, this is called *wei*", where *wei* may be translated as "conscious activity", "deliberate effort" or simply "action" (1963: 139–40). (I have slightly modified Watson's translation of this passage.)
2. More carefully, Aristotle in this passage distinguishes the voluntary from the involuntary; and, indeed, the Greek term *hekousin* has a broader sense than its standard English translation, meaning also "to be willing" (in the sense of "he was willing to throw the cargo overboard to save the ship and its crew"). We should note, too, that describing Aristotle's as the first "serious" treatment of action is not to denigrate Plato's discussion in the *Timaeus* or in the *Laws*; Aristotle, though, does give us the first sustained account of action in the European tradition. In the Chinese tradition, the Confucian philosophers Mencius and Xunzi (fourth and third centuries BC,

respectively) each developed sophisticated theories of moral psychology.

3. This view reaches its culmination, of course, in Hume's assertion that "Reason is, and ought only to be the slave of the passions, and can never pretend to any other office than to serve and obey them" (Hume 1978: II. iii. 3, 415).
4. For this objection see Melden (1961: Ch. 1).
5. The *locus classicus* is Dilthey (1991).
6. It is important to bear in mind that the norms spoken of here – essentially the principles of charity, decision-theoretic principles (e.g. agents act to maximize the satisfaction of their desires, everything else being equal) and logical laws – are an entirely different matter from the norms we spoke of in §5.2 and §5.3. In those sections, we examined Davidson's critique of lexical norms ("the meaning of 'arthritis' determines that it can correctly be used only to describe diseases of the joints") and grammatical norms ("to ask a question use the interrogative form"), but that critique has no bearing on the role of charity, and so on in interpretation.
7. The term "teleological" derives from the Greek word *telos*, which is usually translated as end or goal. Teleological theories of action, therefore, explain actions in terms of an agent's reasons (i.e. her ends), as opposed to causal theories, which explain events in terms of their causal histories.
8. The "logical" relation between actions and their reasons is obscured when we collapse the deliberation that justifies an action. Jack goes up the hill, we say, because he wants to fetch a pail of water, but in these terms we do not see any necessity connecting his action and his attitudes. Filling in the details of his deliberation, we observe that Jack wants to fetch a pail of water and knows that he cannot lay his hands on one at the base of the hill, where he now stands. He also believes that water is available at the top of the hill, hence, were he to climb the hill – which is something he can do – he could fetch a pail of water. Jack, then, wants to go up the hill (because he believes it is a means to realizing his desire to fetch a pail of water), and he believes it lies within his power to go up the hill (since, for example, he falsely believes that the hill is neither too steep nor too slippery); so straightaway he goes up the hill. Here we see the rational necessity that connects his reasons (his wanting to go up the hill and his believing he can go up the hill) and his action (his going up the hill): if he wants to go up the hill and believes he can, then everything else being equal (e.g. assuming no other desire overrides this wanting), it is irrational for him *not* to go up the hill.
9. A *syllogism* is a deductive argument with two premises and a conclusion. Aristotle develops the theory of the syllogism in his writings on logical theory.
10. See especially Winch (1958: §II.2). Winch quotes and discusses Weber (1956: Ch. 1).
11. For more on this point, see below. A related issue much discussed in the literature is this. John Wilkes Booth killed Abraham Lincoln by

shooting him with a gun, and we should quite naturally say that his killing Lincoln is identical to his shooting Lincoln. However, Booth shot Lincoln in squeezing the trigger of the gun he held in his hand on the evening of 14 April 1865, while Lincoln died on the morning of 15 April. How, then, can Wilkes's shooting Lincoln be identical to his killing Lincoln, since they occurred at different times? (See Thomson 1971: 115.)

One solution is to distinguish between what Arthur Danto calls the *basic act* that Booth performs – roughly, a simple movement of his body – and an act that is an effect of that basic act – namely, Lincoln's dying. (For Danto's conception of a basic act, see Danto (1965: 141–8).) In other words, according to Danto, there are not one, but two things Booth did: he squeezed the trigger, and (consequently) he killed Lincoln. Davidson, though, sees Danto's distinction as an instance of the confusion between *an event* and *how we describe the event*. Booth's squeezing the trigger and his killing Lincoln are one and the same event, according to Davidson, described alternately by mentioning the "basic act" he performed the evening of 14 April 1865, and by mentioning something that occurred the following morning and was the tragic consequence of what he did the night before. This is something we frequently do, as Davidson notes: "we very often identify actions by referring to their consequences" (1987b: 38). Thus the contrast Danto wants to draw between *two actions* (i.e. a basic act and a non-basic act) is, rather, a contrast between *two descriptions* of the same action. Everything we do, Davidson says, is identical to a basic act; "we never do more than move our bodies: the rest is up to nature" (1980a: 59). Certainly, we *do* do more than move our bodies; the point, more carefully put, is that whatever else we do, no matter how complex (giving a speech, marrying one's childhood sweetheart, sending a satellite into orbit), can also be described as our moving our bodies.

12. See Charles (1984: 90–96) and note 14, below.
13. Davidson introduces the notion of a prima facie judgement on analogy with conditional judgements of probability, such as "That the barometer is falling makes it probable that it will rain"; that is, "It is probable that it will rain *in so far as* the barometer is falling". See Davidson (1980a: 37–8).
14. What exactly Aristotle's own view is, we observed above, is a matter of scholarly debate. On one reading, the two premises of a practical syllogism, expressing the agent's desire and belief, constitute her deliberate choice (*proairesis*), and these cause (in the sense of efficient causality) her action, which is the syllogism's conclusion. Alternatively, Aristotle's view may be that the conclusion of a practical syllogism is a judgement that the action is desirable. In describing his own views, Davidson usually speaks as though the conclusion, as well as the premises, of a practical syllogism were judgements, but he writes that "no weight should be given to the word 'judgment'" in such talk. He does not suppose, he says, "that someone who wants to eat something sweet necessarily *judges* that it would be good to eat something sweet", and by

analogy he does not suppose that someone who eats *this* sweet thing necessarily judges that it would be good to eat it (1980a: 97n.) Giving a "propositional expression" to desires and actions by describing them as judgements is, rather, a throwback to the old-fashioned use of the term "judgement" (for this, see Joseph (1916: 14)), wherein philosophers used it in much the same way as today we call many mental states and acts *attitudes*. Thus actions (and desires) are judgements or attitudes in so far as they have propositional contents and can be interpreted; as Winch observes in a remark quoted above, actions are a species of "meaningful behavior" (see note 10). We should read Davidson's account of the practical syllogism as taking an action as its conclusion.

15. In Chapter 6 we saw that, according to Davidson, the relata of causal relations are events, whereas in the context of his action theory he speaks of beliefs and desires – which, we have just noted, are dispositions and thus states, rather than events – as causes. In response to this prima facie inconsistency (pointed out by Stoecker (1993b)) Davidson says that "to call reasons causes doesn't go against [the] common way of speaking or thinking about causes", wherein

> we normally take for granted a great deal of background ... [and] typically want to know what is added to that background to make the occurrence of the effect intelligible. If we take this generous attitude towards the nature of a cause, ... people can be causes, stones can be causes, all kinds of things can be causes.
>
> (Davidson 1993d: 287)

Strictly speaking, then, it is not my belief that Iran is not the second largest Muslim nation (which is a mental *state*, not an *event*) that causes my denying that it is, when queried; having this belief is, rather, the relevant part of the background of my mental economy that makes my speech act intelligible. We can tighten this looser sort of talk, and say that the event that causes my utterance is, perhaps, *the bringing together* of this belief with my desire to inform my questioner that Iran is not the second largest Muslim nation, or *my deriving* that belief from my knowledge that another nation has the second most Muslim citizens. See Davidson (1993d: 288; 1980a: 12–13).

16. Remember that a *causal concept*, for Davidson, is a *dispositional concept*, in the sense that causal concepts define properties of objects in terms of their typical causes and effects. When Davidson (and Quine) describes the advance of science as consisting in a move from causal (= dispositional) to non-causal (= non-dispositional) concepts, that advance is consistent with saying (in that more advanced account) that water molecules *causally* interact with the physical properties of sugar crystals to break the sugar's covalent bonds.
17. Davidson discusses the form of a fully fledged causal law in Davidson (1980a: 158–9).
18. Consider, for example, the economic principle that governs the relationship between the price of labour in a market and the total amount of labour demanded in that market. That relationship is voided if, for example, political conditions interfere with the functioning of the

market, but the nature of those political conditions lies beyond the scope of economic theory.

19. We return to this point in §8.4.
20. Note that (10) covers a sugar cube's dissolving in water however we describe sugar; but we recognize it *as* an inference we can make only if we describe the sugar in a way that connects it with chemical theory. The point is exactly analogous to the one made in §6.3, that Jack's falling causes his crown's breaking however we describe his falling, but we can *explain* that breaking only if we mention that it was a falling with a force of 800 newtons. Adding this detail permits us to draw it under the covering generalization (12), given in that section.
21. Davidson originally dubbed the principle that for every true causal statement there is a covering law the principle of "the nomological character of causality", but in later articles he calls it, more modestly, the "the cause–law thesis".
22. That article is Davidson (1995d); the quoted remark is from Davidson (1999a: 619).
23. For example, the generalization, "All balls in the urn are black" supports the inference that if x is a ball in the urn, then x is black, but we cannot infer that *had* a ball been in the urn, it *would have been* black. Had there been more balls in the urn (but there are not), or were someone now to add a new ball, that ball may have been or would be white. In contrast we can infer from the law, "All balls dropped from a height of 10 feet reach a terminal velocity of approximately 18 feet per second", not only that if x is a ball dropped from a height of 10 feet, it falls with the specified terminal velocity, but also that *were* someone now to drop a ball or *had* a ball been dropped, it would behave or would have behaved as the law describes.
24. Contrast this with the generalization, "All emeralds are grue", where x is grue if we first examine x before 1 January 2010 and it is green; or we do not first examine x before 1 January 2010 and it is blue. If all our observations of emeralds were made before 1 January 2010, and we only came across green emeralds, this would not confirm the generalization. This shows that the generalization "All emeralds are green" is (partly) confirmed each time we observe a green emerald, but "All emeralds are grue" is not. (Goodman introduces the predicate "grue" in his landmark work on induction; see Goodman (1983).)
25. More precisely, a *strict science* is a closed, comprehensive theory, where a theory T is *closed* only if events in the domain of T causally interact only with other events in the domain of T, and T is *comprehensive* only if whenever an event e_1 in the domain of T causes the occurrence of a second event e_2 in T's domain, there is some law of T that covers their causal interaction. A law, then, is a strict law if it is formulated in the language of a closed comprehensive theory or it can be derived from laws formulated in the language of a closed comprehensive theory.
26. Compare Ramsey's definition of belief and desire given in §4.1. Davidson contrasts "pure" causal terms, like solubility, which are

"defined in terms of a single test" (Davidson 1980a: 15), with the attitudes, for which there are usually multiple identifying criteria. See §8.5.

27. This example comes from McLaughlin (1993).
28. See Broad (1925: 472), quoted in McLaughlin (1989: 109).
29. I borrow this example from Guttenplan (1995: 93–5).
30. Davidson's picture of the mental making a difference to the causal order by its supervenience on the physical may still not be enough to meet the richer standard that the mental be causally *efficacious*, as opposed to its being causally *relevant*. For an argument that Davidson is not precluded from meeting this richer standard, see McLaughlin (1989).

Chapter 8. The matter of mind

1. For Aristotle's definition of substance, see *Categories*, Ch. 5.
2. In his 2001 Townsend Lectures, John McDowell observes that it is crazy, too, to say that Socrates' mind believes this or that; the *res cogitans* that does the thinking "is also a *res dormiens*, a *res ambulans*, and so forth", that is, it is the man Socrates who has beliefs, desires and other attitudes, not his mind. The word "mind", properly speaking, "labels a collection of capacities and propensities possessed by minded beings" (McDowell 2001: 18). Davidson fully agrees with these Aristotelian sentiments.
3. The quotations in this paragraph all come from Descartes (1984: 158–9 (AT VII 225–6)). The premises underwriting the inference from conceptual to ontological dualism are (i) his definition of substance and (ii) the claim that "there is no one who has ever perceived two substances by means of two different concepts without judging that they are really distinct" (1984: 159 (AT VII 226)).
4. Descartes (1985: 99–108). Descartes originally composed the *Treatise on Man*, and its companion *The World* (1985: 81–98) between 1629 and 1633, but he suppressed both works after hearing that the Roman Inquisition had condemned Galileo's *Dialogue Concerning the Two Chief World Systems* in 1633. Although he summarizes its views in part five of his *Discourse on Method*, the *Treatise on Man* was not published until 1664, 14 years after Descartes's death.
5. Persons and their mental states are *tokenwise* identical to physical objects and states of physical objects if each person is a physical object, and a state of a person is a state of a physical object. *Typewise* identity is stronger: it implies that the mental state of a person (e.g. doubting that the Red Sox will win the series next year), whenever it occurs, is always identical to the same physical state (such as a certain pattern of neural activity).
6. My discussion of reductionism in this and the following paragraphs draws upon Nagel (1979a); see also Hempel (1966: Ch. 8).
7. Patricia and Paul Churchland coin the term "neurophilosophy" to characterize their project in the philosophy of mind. See, for example, Patricia Churchland (1986) and Paul Churchland (1988: Ch. 7).

With Quine, Davidson is in agreement, or rather vice versa. Quine professes that "I acquiesce in what Davidson calls anomalous monism", although he adds, optimistically, that "efforts [in neurobiology and computer science] to reclaim territory from" mentalistic idioms is "to be encouraged and watched with great interest" (1990: 71–2). Quine's position is subtle and difficult to summarize, owing in part to the fact that he rarely writes on the philosophy of mind *per se*; for the most part, one has to tease out his views on mind from his work on the philosophy of language. For a useful overview, see the article on Quine by Christopher Hookway in Guttenplan (1995: 520–25).

8. This mystery is precisely the impetus for Malebranche's occasionalist thesis that "we see all things in God". See Malebranche (1980: 230ff). More generally, occasionalism is the thesis that in cases of apparent causal interaction, the (apparent) cause does not actually bring about the (apparent) effect, but is, rather, the "occasion" on which some other force, such as God, brings about that effect.
9. Recall from Chapter 7, note 24, that x is grue if and only if we first observe x before 1 January 2010 and it is green; or we do not first observe it before 1 January 2010 and it is blue. Similarly, something is an emerire just in case we first notice it before 1 January 2010 and it is an emerald; or we do not first observe it before 1 January 2010 and it is a sapphire.
10. By this definition, classic psychological phenomena like tasting a pineapple or the experience of what it is like to be a bat (to take the vivid examples from Russell (1938) and Nagel (1979b)) fall outside the scope of the mental. Certainly, we ought not to *deny* that these are psychological states or events; rather, these lie outside the scope of Davidson's theory. This is a reasonable limitation on his project, which is one part of a larger enterprise focused on language and action; and it is *these* mental states, the propositional attitudes, that especially bear on meaning and action. As a consequence, though, Davidson has little to contribute to long-standing puzzles about subjective experience or the nature of self-consciousness.
11. In this section we discuss the relation between the anomalism of the mental, on the one hand, and the indeterminacy of interpretation and dispositional character of mental concepts, on the other; in the next section we focus on the normativity of the mental.
12. Recall from §4.4 that what this rules out is a speaker's *knowingly* contradicting himself. I may believe that a bird I observe is an American kestrel, despite my knowing, too, that these raptors rarely measure more than a third of a metre, and the bird I see is twice that size. In this case, I hold these contradictory beliefs because I fail to bring them together and hence do not realize that they are inconsistent.
13. Dennett's position is widely seen as instrumentalist (see for example Baker (1994)), but he rejects the label and its implication of anti-realism. See Dennett (1991), where he argues for a third way between the standard options, realism and anti-realism.

14. See, for example, Davidson's reserved response (Davidson 1999a: 357) to Bill Martin's efforts to draw out the ethical implications of his philosophy (Martin 1999).
15. See Aitchison (2000: 89–90).
16. In his *Philosophical Investigations*, Wittgenstein gives the following example illustrating the difference between symptoms and criteria:

    > If medical science calls angina an inflammation caused by a particular bacillus, and we ask in a particular case "why do you say this man has got angina?" then the answer "I have found the bacillus so-and-so in his blood" gives us the *criterion* ... If on the other hand the answer was, "His throat is inflamed", this might give us a *symptom* of angina. I call "symptom" a phenomenon of which experience has taught us that it coincided, in some way or other, with the phenomenon which is our defining criterion.
    >
    > (1958: 25, emphasis added)

    Wittgenstein emphasizes that a condition may "fluctuate" between being a symptom or a criterion for the presence of another property, and this defuses worries that the contrast between symptoms and criteria runs foul of rejection of the analytic–synthetic distinction.
17. Notice that if we drop the assumption that (7) states a law, that is, that it implicitly contains the modal operator "necessarily" made explicit in (9), then the argument does not go through, since in place of (10) we would have

    (10′) If $C_{\varphi}(x)$, then x is verbal

    which states an empirical (i.e. *de facto*), rather than nomological, regularity.

Chapter 9. Conclusion: scepticism and subjectivity

1. Davidson's 1973 address (1974a) was later published (and is now reprinted in Davidson (1984a)) under the oft-imitated or parodied title "On the Very Idea of a Conceptual Scheme" (e.g. Quine's "On the Very Idea of a Third Dogma", reprinted in Quine (1981b)); it originated as the sixth of Davidson's 1970 John Locke lectures at Oxford University. Later essays, many reprinted in the third volume of Davidson's collected writings (Davidson 2001a), develop this theme.
2. Hume later extends this to include *all* phenomenal qualities: "If colours, sounds, tastes and smells be merely perceptions, nothing we can conceive is possest of real, continu'd, and independent existence; not even motion, extension and solidity" (Hume 1978: 228).
3. For the relation between possessing a concept and possessing certain abilities, or "know how", related to that concept, see Fodor (1998: Ch. 1).
4. Consider, for example, Benjamin Whorf's famous inference (1978) from an analysis of the characteristics of verbs in the Hopi language to his thesis that Hopis and Europeans have radically different conceptual schemes.

Two languages that fail the test of inter-translatability are often described as *incommensurable*, a way of speaking introduced by Thomas Kuhn (in his widely discussed and cited *The Structure of Scientific Revolutions* (1996)) and Paul Feyerabend; but see note 5, below.

5. See Rorty (1982: 5). Rorty's treatment of Davidson's philosophy is subtle and complicated; in "The World Well Lost" he sees the debate between Davidson and the sceptic as Kantian-style antinomy, although his sympathies ultimately lie with Davidson and not the sceptic.
6. Kuhn's work on the history of scientific revolutions is often cited as presenting some of the best candidates for non-translatability between systems of concepts, and therefore as grounds for conceptual relativism. Gerry Doppelt, though, argues that this misreads Kuhn's position. According to Doppelt, the primary difference between alternative scientific schemes, for example, Daltonian and pre-Daltonian chemistry,

   > is *not* ... that each paradigm is imprisoned within its own concepts ... [Rather] the most revolutionary dimension of a ... new paradigm implies a shift of commitment to a new set of theoretical problems as the "core" of the discipline – substantively different from the problematic which defined the hard core of science under the old paradigm. (Doppelt 1982: 120)

   As Michael Krausz and Jack Meiland put it, on Doppelt's reading of Kuhn the primary difference between Dalton and the phlogiston theorists is in the *cognitive values* to which they are committed, not their *concepts* (Krausz & Meiland 1982: 110).

   Thus, when Kuhn characterizes paradigm debates as necessarily at "cross-purposes", he means that literally. It is not that the rivals lack a sufficient commonality of language to communicate or argue; rather, they lack a sufficiently common definition of the discipline and its criteria of explanatory adequacy to allow their discourse to terminate in rational consensus (Doppelt 1982: 120).

   If this is right, and Doppelt's readings of Kuhn and the scientific history are well-motivated, then these sorts of examples do not give us reason to believe that scientists before and after the revolution have radically different *conceptual* schemes. On this point compare Rorty (1979: 316).
7. Hume overcame this inconvenience, but only by conflating perceptions with perceptual beliefs, but this *is* a confusion (e.g. my perceiving a green apple is neither true nor false, while my perceptual belief that there is a green apple before me *is* true or false). Other philosophers have sought "basic" statements, the contents of which are exhausted by their report of immediate experience, such as Schlick's *Konstatierungen* or the basic propositions of Russell (1940). These moves are ineffective; but see note 8.
8. Sensations connect beliefs to the world by causing those beliefs and by being caused by the things they are sensations of. I see a rose bush outside my window, and I believe I do; since, everything else being

equal, one's sensations of rose bushes are caused by rose bushes' being in the vicinity, the existence of my sensation implies the existence of the rose bush; hence if I believe I see it I ought to believe it is there.

McDowell worries that if our sensations constrain our beliefs only through their causal properties, then they cannot supply the "friction" that prevents our rational agency, including our capacity to form empirical beliefs, from coming adrift of the world. (Indeed, Davidson at one time describes his conception as a "coherence theory of truth and knowledge", which misleadingly suggests – *à la* F. H. Bradley – that *every* comprehensive and consistent theory of the world is true; later, he regrets using that label. See Davidson (2001a: 155).) McDowell's concern derives from what he sees as Davidson's undeconstructed dualism between, on the one hand, sensations as subject to causal relations and, on the other, attitudes ("the conceptual") as subject to rational constraints. This dualism, then, leaves sensations outside "the domain of rational interrelatedness [which for Davidson is] coextensive with the domain of the conceptual" (McDowell 2001: 146–7). The conceptual domain is, in McDowell's Kantian language, the domain of our spontaneity or freedom, hence if "the domain of rational interrelatedness" extends no farther than the conceptual, then that leaves our capacity to judge and to act unconstrained by anything external to it. McDowell's solution is to extend the domain of rational interrelatedness to include sensations that, consequently, belong to both the realm of nature and the realm of the rational. In the end, this undermines the contrast between the "inside" and the "outside" while leaving thought and action constrained by something over which it does not exercise control.

Davidson seeks the same desiderata by pursuing the opposite strategy. Where McDowell constrains our agency by bringing sensations into the realm of the rational, Davidson treats the attitudes and actions, as well as sensations, as subjects of causal relations. We are natural objects, as well as rational agents; as such, we are buffeted by the same forces that affect brutes and inanimate objects. The difference is that some of the causal relations we participate in can be described in terms of final as well as efficient causality, and therein lies our rational agency, that we act for reasons. But being subject, too, to efficient causes, our attitudes bear the mark of a world that lies beyond our will.

9. Davidson's objection to scepticism, therefore, is that our situated causal interactions with other thinkers constitute our concepts, and hence there is no room for those concepts to be radically in error. Our subjectivity emerges only through our intersubjective and objective relations.

Critics have objected that Davidson dismisses the sceptic only by begging the question against him. A Davidsonian interpreter invokes the principle of charity and attributes to a speaker's utterance *S* a content based on his (the speaker's) causal interactions with his environment (plus her knowledge of his personal history, etc.); charity tells her to interpret him in such a way that his utterance correctly reflects that environment.

> But the appeal to charity turns out to involve the idea of unproblematic access to certain causal relations between speakers and objects in the world. If, in the context of the skeptic's question, we grant ourselves this access, the game is over before it begins.
> (Williams 1991: 313)

In her charity the interpreter writes a certain view of the world into her interpretation of *S*. But, the sceptic posits, her view may itself be radically in error, and hence she may attribute to the speaker a set of mostly false beliefs about the world. We were assured that the speaker got most of his beliefs right only by assuming that most of the interpreter's beliefs (e.g. about the speaker's relationship with the world) were already true.

The problem with the sceptic's (i.e. Williams's) objection is that it presupposes that the interpreter's intentional states are all fully constituted before she enters into a dialogue with her interlocutor. Otherwise, the premise that she arrived at their conversation with a set of radically false beliefs makes no sense. However, the interpreter's mental states are constituted *in vivo*, too, through the intersection of her interactions with the world with those of the speaker. This intersection, when it is sufficiently developed – when, in effect, dialogue has emerged – yields thinking and speaking. At that point, then, it makes sense to speak of one or the other's making mistakes, but only against the background of their large-scale agreement with one another and the world. For more on this line of reasoning, see Ramberg (2001).

10. Oscar and his doppelgänger first appear in Putnam (1975). Since then, they have made guest appearances in hundreds of publications. For a selection of responses to Putnam's original article and the issues it raises, see Pessin & Goldberg (1996). Note that, in what follows, twin earth is assumed to be a distant part of the actual universe, and not a different possible world in the Leibnizian or modal logical sense.
11. For a conflicting appraisal of Swampman's linguistic abilities, based on a different set of intuitions about the case, see Fodor (1994b: App. B).
12. That is, computational psychology describes the functional role that mental representations play within a person's mental economy, which in the cases of Oscar and Twoscar are isomorphic; while naturalistic psychology captures wherein Oscar's and Twoscar's psychologies differ.
13. It should be evident that my use of the term "relational model of mind" is distinct from the meaning of that expression in contemporary psychoanalytic theory. (I owe this clarification to Hillary Glick.)
14. See especially Wittgenstein (1958: §§256, 261).
15. On the difficulties associated with that extension, however, see the end of §3.3.

16. Observe that it is the triviality of first-person avowals that accounts for their not being based on evidence (e.g. that I do not ordinarily conclude that I believe that *p* by making any special enquiries, rather, I just *know* what I believe), and yet their being treated as more authoritative than third-person claims that *are* based on (perhaps substantial) evidence.

Bibliography

I. Selected works by Donald Davidson

1952 "Why Study Philosophy?", *View Point* **2**, 22–4.

1955 "Outlines of a Formal Theory of Value", with J. J. C. McKinsey & P. Suppes, *Philosophy of Science* **22**, 140–60.

1956a "A Finitistic Axiomatization of Subjective Probability and Utility", with P. Suppes, *Econometrica* **24**, 264–75.

1956b "Experimental Measurement of Utility by Use of a Linear Programming Model", abstract with P. Suppes, *Econometrica* **24**.

1957 *Decision-Making: An Experimental Approach*, with P. Suppes. Palo Alto, CA: Stanford University Press.

1959 "Experimental Tests of a Stochastic Decision Theory", with J. Marschak. In *Measurement: Definitions and Theories*, C. W. Churchman & P. Ratoosh (eds), 233–69. New York: John Wiley & Sons.

1963a "Actions, Reasons and Causes", reprinted in *Essays on Actions and Events* (1980).

1963b "The Method of Extension and Intension". In *The Philosophy of Rudolf Carnap*, P. A. Schilp (ed.), 311–50. The Library of Living Philosophers, volume XI. La Salle, IL: Open Court.

1966a "Theories of Meaning and Learnable Languages", reprinted in *Inquiries into Truth and Interpretation* (1984).

1966b Review of *The Logic of Preference* by George Henrick von Wright, in *Philosophical Review* **2**, 233–5.

1966c "Emeroses by Other Names", reprinted in *Essays on Actions and Events* (1980).

1967a "The Logical Form of Actions Sentences", reprinted in *Essays on Actions and Events* (1980).

1967b "Causal Relations", reprinted in *Essays on Actions and Events* (1980).

1967c "Truth and Meaning", reprinted in *Inquiries into Truth and Interpretation* (1984).

1969a "On Saying That", reprinted in *Inquiries into Truth and Interpretation* (1984).

1969b "Facts and Events", reprinted in *Inquiries into Truth and Interpretation* (1984).

1969c "How is Weakness of the Will Possible", reprinted in *Essays on Actions and Events* (1980).
1969d "The Individuation of Events", reprinted in *Essays on Actions and Events* (1980).
1969e "True to the Facts", reprinted in *Inquiries into Truth and Interpretation* (1984).
1969f *Words and Objections: Essays on the Work of W.V. Quine*. Dordrecht: D. Reidel.
1970a "Semantics for Natural Languages", reprinted in *Inquiries into Truth and Interpretation* (1984).
1970b "Mental Events", reprinted in *Essays on Actions and Events* (1980).
1970c "Events as Particulars", reprinted in *Essays on Actions and Events* (1980).
1970d "Agency", reprinted in *Essays on Actions and Events* (1980).
1971a *Semantics of Natural Language*, edited with Gilbert Harman. Dordrecht: D. Reidel.
1971b "Eternal Events vs. Ephemeral Events", reprinted in *Essays on Actions and Events* (1980).
1973a "In Defense of Convention T", reprinted in *Inquiries into Truth and Interpretation* (1984).
1973b "Freedom to Act", reprinted in *Essays on Actions and Events* (1980).
1973c "Radical Interpretation", reprinted in *Inquiries into Truth and Interpretation* (1984).
1973d "The Material Mind", reprinted in *Essays on Actions and Events* (1980).
1973e "Psychology as Philosophy", reprinted in *Essays on Actions and Events* (1980).
1974a "On the Very Idea of a Conceptual Scheme", reprinted in *Inquiries into Truth and Interpretation* (1984).
1974b "Paradoxes of Irrationality". Reprinted in *Philosophical Essays on Freud*, R. Wollheim & J. Hopkins, 289–305. Cambridge: Cambridge University Press, 1982.
1974c "Belief and the Basis of Meaning", reprinted in *Inquiries into Truth and Interpretation* (1984).
1974d "Replies to David Lewis and W.V. Quine", *Synthese* **27**, 345–9.
1975a *The Logic of Grammar*, edited with Gilbert Harman. Encina, CA: Dickenson Press.
1975b "Thought and Talk", reprinted in *Inquiries into Truth and Interpretation* (1984).
1976a "Reply to Foster", reprinted in *Inquiries into Truth and Interpretation* (1984).
1976b "Hempel on Explaining Action", reprinted in *Essays on Actions and Events* (1980).
1976c "Hume's Cognitive Theory of Pride", reprinted in *Essays on Actions and Events* (1980).
1976d "Introduction" and "Discussion", *Origins and Evolution of Language and Speech*. Annals of the New York Academy of Sciences **280**, 18–19, 42–5.
1977a "The Method of Truth in Metaphysics", reprinted in *Inquiries into Truth and Interpretation* (1984).
1977b "Reality without Reference", reprinted in *Inquiries into Truth and Interpretation* (1984).
1978a "What Metaphors Mean", reprinted in *Inquiries into Truth and Interpretation* (1984).
1978b "Intending", reprinted in *Essays on Actions and Events* (1980).
1979a "Moods and Performances", reprinted in *Inquiries into Truth and Interpretation* (1984).

1979b "Quotation", reprinted in *Inquiries into Truth and Interpretation* (1984).
1979c "The Inscrutability of Reference", reprinted in *Inquiries into Truth and Interpretation* (1984).
1980a *Essays on Actions and Events*. Oxford: Oxford University Press.
1980b "Toward a Unified Theory of Meaning and Actions." *Grazer Philosophische Studien* **11**, 1–12.
1982a "Rational Animals", reprinted in *Subjective, Intersubjective and Objective* (2001), 95–105.
1982b "Empirical Content", reprinted in *Subjective, Intersubjective and Objective* (2001), 159–75.
1983 "A Coherence Theory of Truth and Knowledge", reprinted in *Subjective, Intersubjective and Objective* (2001), 137–57.
1984a *Inquiries into Truth and Interpretation*. Oxford: Oxford University Press, 1984.
1984b "Communication and Convention", reprinted in *Inquiries into Truth and Interpretation* (1984).
1984c "First Person Authority", reprinted in *Subjective, Intersubjective and Objective* (2001), 3–14.
1984d *Expressing Evaluations*. The Lindley Lecture (monograph). University of Kansas.
1985a "Adverbs of Action" and Replies to Essays. In *Essays on Davidson: Actions and Events*, B. Vermazen & M. Hintikka (eds), 230–41. Oxford: Clarendon Press.
1985b "Reply to Quine on Events". In *Actions and Events: Perspectives on the Philosophy of Donald Davidson*, E. Lepore & B. McLaughlin (eds), 172–6. Oxford: Blackwell.
1985c "Incoherence and Irrationality", *Dialectica* **39**, 345–54.
1985d "Plato's Philosopher", *The London Review of Books* **7**(14), 15–17.
1985e "A New Basis for Decision Theory", *Theory and Decision* **18**, 87–98.
1986a "Judging Interpersonal Interests". In *Foundations of Social Choice Theory*, J. Elster & A. Hylland (eds), 195–211. Cambridge: Cambridge University Press.
1986b "Deception and Division". Reprinted in *Actions and Events: Perspectives on the Philosophy of Donald Davidson*, E. Lepore & B. McLaughlin (eds), 138–48. Oxford: Blackwell.
1986c "A Nice Derangement of Epitaphs". Reprinted in *Truth and Interpretation: Perspectives on the Philosophy of Donald Davidson*, E. Lepore (ed.), 433–46. Oxford: Blackwell.
1987a "Knowing One's Own Mind", reprinted in *Subjective, Intersubjective and Objective* (2001), 15–38.
1987b "Problems in the Explanation of Actions". In *Metaphysics and Morality: Essays in Honour of J. J. C. Smart*, P. Pettit, R. Sylvan & J. Norman (eds), 35–49. Oxford: Blackwell.
1988a Review of W. V. Quine, *The Time of My Life: An Autobiography*, *The Journal of Symbolic Logic* **53**, 293–5.
1988b "Reply to Burge", *The Journal of Philosophy* **85**, 664–6.
1988c "The Myth of the Subjective", reprinted in *Subjective, Intersubjective and Objective* (2001), 39–52.
1988d "Epistemology and Truth", reprinted in *Subjective, Intersubjective and Objective* (2001), 177–91.
1989a "The Conditions of Thought". Reprinted in *The Mind of Donald Davidson*, J. Brandl & W. Gombocz. Amsterdam: Editions Rodopi.

1989b "James Joyce and Humpty Dumpty". Reprinted in *Midwest Studies in Philosophy* 16, P. French, T. E. Uehling & H. Wettstein (eds), 1–12. Notre Dame, IN: University of Notre Dame Press, 1991.

1989c "What is Present to the Mind?", reprinted in *Subjective, Intersubjective and Objective* (2001), 53–67.

1990a "Turing's Test". In *Modelling the Mind*, W. H. Newton-Smith & K. V. Wilkes, 1–11. Oxford: Oxford University Press.

1990b "Representation and Interpretation". In *Modelling the Mind*, W. H. Newton-Smith & K. V. Wilkes, 13–26. Oxford: Oxford University Press.

1990c *Plato's Philebus*. New York: Garland Publishing.

1990d "Meaning, Truth and Evidence". In *Perspectives on Quine*, R. Barrett & R. Gibson, 68–79. Oxford: Blackwell.

1990e "The Structure and Content of Truth", *The Journal of Philosophy* **87**, 279–328. (The John Dewey Lectures)

1990f "Epistemology Externalized", reprinted in *Subjective, Intersubjective and Objective* (2001), 193–204.

1991 "Three Varieties of Knowledge", reprinted in *Subjective, Intersubjective and Objective* (2001), 205–20.

1992a "The Second Person", reprinted in *Subjective, Intersubjective and Objective* (2001), 107–21.

1992b "The Socratic Concept of Truth". In *The Philosophy of Socrates: Elenchus, Ethics and Truth*, K. J. Boudouris (ed.), 51–8. Athens: International Centre for Greek Philosophy and Culture.

1992c "The Third Man." Catalogue *for Robert Morris: Blind Time Drawings with Davidson*. Allentown, PA: The Frank Martin Gallery, Muhlenberg College.

1993a "Method and Metaphysics", *Deucalion* **11**, 239–48.

1993b "Thinking Causes". In *Mental Causation*, J. Heil & A. Mele (eds), 3–17. Oxford: Oxford University Press.

1993c "Locating Literary Language". In *Literary Theory After Davidson*, R. W. Dasenbrock (ed.), 295–308. University Park, PA: Pennsylvania University Press.

1993d Replies to seventeen essays. In *Reflecting Davidson: Donald Davidson Responding to an International Forum of Philosophers*, R. Stoecker (ed.). Berlin: de Gruyter.

1993e "Radical Interpretation Interpreted". In *Reflecting Davidson: Donald Davidson Responding to an International Forum of Philosophers*, R. Stoecker (ed.), 77–84. Berlin: de Gruyter.

1994a "What is Quine's View of Truth?", *Inquiry* **37**, 437–40.

1994b "The Social Aspect of Language". In *The Philosophy of Michael Dummett*, B. McGuinness & G. Oliveri (eds), 1–16. Dordrecht: Kluwer.

1994c "On Quine's Philosophy" and "Exchange between Donald Davidson and W. V. Quine following Davidson's Lecture", *Theoria* **60**, 184–92 and 226–31.

1994d "Foreword". In *The Philosophical Papers of Alan Donagan: Volume II Action, Reason, and Value*, J. Malpas (ed.), vii–ix. Chicago, IL: University of Chicago Press.

1995a "Could There Be a Science of Rationality?", *International Journal of Philosophical Studies* **3**, 1–16.

1995b Entry on Donald Davidson. In *A Companion to the Philosophy of Mind*, S. Guttenplan (ed.), 231–6. Oxford: Blackwell.

1995c "Pursuit of the Concept of Truth". In *On Quine*, P. Leonardi & M. Santambrogio (eds), 7–21. Cambridge: Cambridge University Press.

1995d "Laws and Cause", *Dialectica* **49**, 263–79.

1996 "The Folly of Trying to Define Truth", *The Journal of Philosophy* **93**, 263–78.

1997a "Indeterminism and Antirealism", reprinted in *Subjective, Intersubjective and Objective* (2001), 69–84.

1997b "Gadamer and Plato's Philebus". In *The Philosophy of Hans Georg Gadamer*, L. Hahn (ed.), 421–32. Chicago, IL: Open Court.

1997c "The Centrality of Truth". In *The Nature of Truth, Proceedings of the International Colloquium, Prague, 17–20 September, 1996*, J. Peregrin (ed.), 3–14. Prague: Filosofia.

1997d "Who is Fooled?". In *Self-Deception and Paradoxes of Rationality*, J. P. Dupuy (ed.), 15–27. Stanford: SCLI.

1997e "In Conversation: Donald Davidson." Videotapes organized, introduced, and edited by R. Fara. Preface by R. Fara and summaries by M. Fara. London: Philosophy International. [Nineteen videotapes of Davidson discussing his views with W. V. Quine, Sir Peter Strawson, Nancy Cartwright, Tim Crane, Martin Davies, Michael Dummett, Stuart Hampshire, Jim Hopkins, Jennifer Hornsby, Michael Martin, John McDowell, David Papineau, Richard Rorty, Mark Sainsbury, Gabriel Segal, Barry Smith and Barry Stroud.]

1997f "Seeing Through Language". In *Thought and Language*, J. M. Preston (ed.), 15–27. Cambridge: Cambridge University Press.

1997g "The Emergence of Thought", reprinted in *Subjective, Intersubjective and Objective* (2001), 123–34.

1998 "The Irreducibility of the Concept of the Self", reprinted in *Subjective, Intersubjective and Objective* (2001), 85–91.

1999a "Replies". In *The Philosophy of Donald Davidson*, E. L. Hahn (ed.). The Library of Living Philosophers, volume XXVII. Chicago, IL: Open Court.

1999b "Intellectual Autobiography". In *The Philosophy of Donald Davidson*, E. L. Hahn (ed.). The Library of Living Philosophers, volume XXVII. Chicago, IL: Open Court.

1999c "Interpretation: Hard in Theory, Easy in Practice". In *Interpretations and Causes: New Perspectives on Donald Davidson's Philosophy*, M. De Caro (ed.). Dordrecht: Kluwer.

2001a *Subjective, Intersubjective and Objective*. Oxford: Oxford University Press.

2001b "What Thought Requires". In *The Foundations of Cognitive Science*, J. Branquinho (ed.), 121–32. Oxford: Oxford University Press.

II. References

Aitchison, J. 2000. *The Seeds of Speech: Language Origin and Evolution*. Cambridge: Cambridge University Press.

Antony, L. 1998. "Anomalous Monism and the Problem of Explanatory Force", *The Philosophical Review* **98**, 153–87.

Aristotle 1984. *The Complete Works of Aristotle*, J. Barnes (ed.). Princeton, NJ: Princeton University Press.

Austin, J. L. 1962. *How to do Things with Words*, J. O. Urmson (ed.). Cambridge, MA: Harvard University Press.

Baker, L. R. 1994. "Instrumental Intentionality". In *Mental Representation*, S. Stich & T. Warfield (eds), 332–44. Oxford: Blackwell.

Barwise, J. 1989. *The Situation in Logic*. Stanford, CA: Center for the Study of Language and Information.

Barwise, J. & J. Perry 1981. "Semantic Innocence and Uncompromising Situations". In *Midwest Studies in Philosophy VI: The Foundations of Analytic Philosophy*, P. A. French, T. E. Uehling & H. K. Wettstein (eds), 387–403. Minneapolis, MN: University of Minnesota Press.

Barwise, J. & J. Perry 1983. *Situations and Attitudes*. Cambridge, MA: MIT Press.

Benacerraf, P. & H. Putnam (eds) 1983. *Philosophy of Mathematics: Selected Readings*, 2nd edn. Cambridge: Cambridge University Press.

Bennett, J. 1985a. "Adverb-dropping Inferences and the Lemmon Criterion". See Lepore & McLaughlin (1985), 193–206.

Bennett, J. 1985b. "Critical Notice of Davidson's Inquiries into Truth and Interpretation", *Mind* **94**, 601–26.

Bilgrami, A. 1986. "Meaning, Holism and Use". See Lepore (1986), 101–22.

Bilgrami, A. 1992. *Belief and Meaning*. Cambridge, MA: Blackwell.

Blackburn, S. 1984. *Spreading the Word: Groundings in the Philosophy of Language*. Oxford: Oxford University Press.

Broad, C. D. 1925. *The Mind and its Place in Nature*. London: Routledge & Kegan Paul.

Burge, T. 1983. Review of Davidson's *Essays on Actions and Events*, *Ethics* **93**, 608–11.

Burge, T. 1986. "On Davidson's 'On Saying That'". See Lepore (1986), 190–208.

Carnap, R. 1956a. "Empiricism, Semantics, and Ontology". In *Meaning and Necessity*, R. Carnap, 205–21. Chicago, IL: University of Chicago Press. Originally published 1950.

Carnap, R. 1956b. *Meaning and Necessity*. Chicago, IL: University of Chicago Press.

Carnap, R. 1959. "The Old and the New Logic", I. Levi (trans.). In *Logical Positivism*, A. J. Ayer (ed.), 133–46. New York: The Free Press. Originally published 1930–31.

Carnap, R. 1967. *The Logical Structure of the World and Pseudoproblems in Philosophy*, R. A. George (trans.). Berkeley, CA: University of California Press. Originally published 1928.

Charles, D. 1984. *Aristotle's Philosophy of Action*. Ithaca, NY: Cornell University Press.

Chihara, C. 1975. "Davidson's Extensional Theory of Meaning", *Philosophical Studies* **28**, 1–15.

Chisholm, R. 1970. "Events and Propositions", *Noûs* **4**, 15–24.

Chomsky, N. 1972. *Language and Mind*. New York: Harcourt Brace Jovanovich.

Churchland, P. 1986. *Neurophilosophy: Toward a Unified Science of the Mind-Brain*. Cambridge, MA: MIT Press.

Churchland, P. 1988. *Matter and Consciousness: A Contemporary Introduction to the Philosophy of Mind*. Cambridge, MA: MIT Press.

Collins, J. 1999. "Indeterminacy and Intention". See Hahn (1999), 501–28.

Danto, A. 1965. "Basic Actions", *American Philosophical Quarterly* **2**, 141–8.

De Caro, M. (ed.) 1999. *Interpretations and Causes: New Perspectives on Donald Davidson's Philosophy*. Dordrecht: Kluwer.

Dennett, D. 1978. "Intentional Systems". In *Brainstorms: Philosophical Essays on Mind and Psychology*, Daniel Dennett, 3–22. Montgomery, VT: Bradford Books Publishers. Originally published 1971.

Dennett, D. 1987. *The Intentional Stance*. Cambridge, MA: MIT Press.

Dennett, D. 1991. "Real Patterns", *The Journal of Philosophy* **88**, 27–51.

Descartes, R. 1984. *The Philosophical Writings of Descartes*, vol. 2, J. Cottingham, R. Stoothoff & D. Murdoch (trans.). Cambridge: Cambridge University Press.

Descartes, R. 1985. *The Philosophical Writings of Descartes*, vol. 1, J. Cottingham, R. Stoothoff & D. Murdoch (trans.). Cambridge: Cambridge University Press.

Diamond, C. 1991. "Throwing Away the Ladder: How to Read the *Tractatus*". In *The Realistic Spirit: Wittgenstein, Philosophy and the Mind*, C. Diamond, 179–204. Cambridge, MA: MIT Press. Originally published 1988.

Dilthey, W. 1991. *Introduction to the Human Sciences*, vol. 1, R. Makkreel & F. Rodi (eds). Princeton, NJ: Princeton University Press. Originally published 1883.

Doppelt, G. 1982. "Kuhn's Epistemological Relativism: An Interpretation and Defense". In *Relativism: Cognitive and Moral*, M. Krausz & J. Meiland (eds), 113–46. Notre Dame, IN: University of Notre Dame Press. Originally published 1978.

Dummett, M. 1981. *Frege: Philosophy of Language*, 2nd edn. Cambridge, MA: Harvard University Press.

Dummett, M. 1986. "A Nice Derangement of Epitaphs: Some Comments on Davidson and Hacking". See Lepore (1986), 459–76.

Etchemendy, J. 1988. "Tarski on Truth and Logical Consequence", *The Journal of Symbolic Logic* **53**, 51–79.

Evnine, S. 1991. *Donald Davidson*. Stanford, CA: Stanford University Press.

Field, H. 1980. *Science Without Numbers: A Defense of Nominalism*. Oxford: Blackwell, 1980.

Fodor, J. 1981. "Methodological Solipsism Considered as a Research Strategy in Cognitive Psychology". In *Representations: Philosophical Essays on the Foundations of Cognitive Science*, J. Fodor, 225–53. Cambridge, MA: MIT Press. Originally published 1980.

Fodor, J. 1987. *Psychosemantics*. Cambridge, MA: MIT Press.

Fodor, J. 1994a. "Fodor's Guide to Mental Representation". In *Mental Representation: A Reader*, S. Stich & T. Warfield (eds), 9–33. Oxford: Blackwell, 1994. Originally published 1985.

Fodor, J. 1994b. *The Elm and the Expert: Mentalese and its Semantics*. Cambridge, MA: MIT Press.

Fodor, J. 1995. "Entry on Jerry Fodor". See Guttenplan (1995), 292–9.

Fodor, J. 1998. *Concepts: Where Cognitive Science Went Wrong*. Oxford: Oxford University Press.

Fodor, J. & E. Lepore 1992. *Holism: A Shopper's Guide*. Cambridge, MA: Blackwell.

Frege, G. 1953. *The Foundations of Arithmetic*, rev. edn, J. L. Austin (trans.). Evanston, IL: Northwestern University Press. Originally published 1884.

Frege, G. 1967. "The Thought: A Logical Inquiry", A. M. Quinton & M. Quinton (trans.). In *Philosophical Logic*, P. F. Strawson, 17–38. Oxford: Oxford University Press. Originally published 1918.

Frege, G. 1980. "On Sense and Meaning". Reprinted and translated in *Translations from the Philosophical Writings of Gottlob Frege*, 3rd edn, P. Geach & M. Black, 56–78. Totowa, NJ: Rowman & Littlefield Publishers. Originally published 1892.

Galileo G. 1960. "The Assayer", A. Danto (trans.). In *Philosophy of Science*, A. Danto & S. Morgenbesser (eds), 27–32. New York: Meridian Books. Originally published 1623.

Gamut, L. T. F. 1991. *Logic, Language, and Meaning, Volume II: Intensional Logic and Logical Grammar*. Chicago, IL: University of Chicago Press.

Geach, P. & M. Black 1980. *Translations from the Philosophical Writings of Gottlob Frege*, 3rd edn. Totowa, NJ: Rowman & Littlefield.

Goodman, N. 1983. *Fact, Fiction, and Forecast*, 4th edn. Cambridge, MA: Harvard University Press.

Grandy, R. 1973. "Reference, Meaning and Belief," *Journal of Philosophy* **70**, 439–52.

Grice, H. P. 1967. "Meaning". In *Philosophical Logic*, P. F. Strawson, 39–48. Oxford: Oxford University Press. Originally published 1957.

Guttenplan, S. (ed.) 1995. *A Companion to the Philosophy of Mind*. Oxford: Blackwell.

Haack, S. 1978. *Philosophy of Logics*. Cambridge: Cambridge University Press.

Hacking, I. 1975. *Why Does Language Matter to Philosophy?* Cambridge: Cambridge University Press.

Hacking, I. 1986. "The Parody of Conversation". See Lepore (1986), 447–58.

Hahn, E. L. (ed.) 1999. *The Philosophy of Donald Davidson*. The Library of Living Philosophers, volume XXVII. Chicago, IL: Open Court.

Hale, B. & C. Wright 1997. *A Companion to the Philosophy of Language*. Oxford: Blackwell.

Heal, J. 1978. "On the Phrase 'Theory of Meaning'", *Mind* **87**, 359–75.

Heal, J. 1997. "Radical Interpretation". See Hale & Wright (1997), 175–96.

Heil, J. & A. Mele (eds) 1993. *Mental Causation*. Oxford: Oxford University Press.

Hempel, C. 1966. *Philosophy of Natural Science*. Foundations of Philosophy Series. Englewood Cliffs, NJ: Prentice Hall.

Higgenbotham, J. 1986. "Linguistic Theory and Davidson's Program in Semantics". See Lepore (1986), 29–48.

Higgenbotham, J. 1999. "A Perspective on Truth and Meaning". See Hahn (1999), 671–86.

Hintikka, J. 1980. "Theories of Truth and Learnable Languages". In *Philosophy and Grammar*, S. Kanger & S. Ohman (eds), 37–57. Dordrecht: Reidel.

Hofstadter, D. 1979. *Gödel, Escher, Bach: An Eternal Golden Braid*. New York: Basic Books.

Hookway, C. 1995. "Entry on Willard Van Orman Quine". See Guttenplan (1995), 520–25.

Horwich, P. 1990. *Truth*. Oxford: Blackwell.

Hume, D. 1975. *Enquiries Concerning Human Understanding and Concerning the Principles of Morals*, 3rd edn, L. A. Selby-Bigge (ed.), P. H. Nidditch (rev.). Oxford: Oxford University Press. *ECHU* originally published 1748; *ECPM* originally published 1751.

Hume, D. 1978. *A Treatise of Human Nature*, L. A. Selby-Bigge (ed.), P. H. Nidditch (rev.). Oxford: Oxford University Press. Originally published 1739–40.

Jeffrey, R. 1983. *The Logic of Decision*, 2nd edition. Chicago, IL: University of Chicago Press.

Joseph, H. W. B. 1916. *An Introduction to Logic*. Oxford: Oxford University Press.

Joseph, M. 2000. "Mental Representation and the Metaphysics of Meaning in Wittgenstein's *Tractatus*", *Philosophical Investigations* **23**, 122–46.

Kant, I. 1977. *Prolegomena to Any Future Metaphysics*, P. Carus & J. W. Ellington (trans.). Indianapolis, IN: Hackett. Originally published 1783.

Kant, I. 1990. *Fundamental Principles of the Metaphysics of Morals*, T. K. Abbott (trans.). Amherst, NY: Prometheus Books. Originally published 1785.

Kenny, A. 1963. *Action, Emotion and Will*. London: Routledge & Kegan Paul.

Kim, J. 1976. "Events as Property Exemplifications". In *Action Theory*, M. Brand & D. Walton (eds), 159–77. Dordrecht: Reidel.

Kim, J. 1985. "Psychophysical Laws". See Lepore & McLaughlin (1985), 369–86.

Kim, J. 1993. "Can Supervenience and 'Non-Strict Laws' Save Anomalous Monism?" In *Mental Causation*, J. Heil & A. Mele (eds), 19–26. Oxford: Oxford University Press.

Kotatko, T., P. Pagin & G. Segal (eds) 2001. *Interpreting Davidson*. Stanford, CA: Center for the Study of Language and Information Publications.

Krausz, M. & J. Meiland 1982. *Relativism: Cognitive and Moral*. Notre Dame, IN: University of Notre Dame Press.

Kripke, S. 1982. *Wittgenstein on Rules and Private Languages*. Cambridge, MA: Harvard University Press.

Kuhn, T. 1996. *The Structure of Scientific Revolutions*, 3rd edition. Chicago, IL: University of Chicago Press.

Leeds, S. 1978. "Theories of Reference and Truth", *Erkenntnis* **13**, 111–30.

Lemmon, E. J. 1962. "Comments". In *Logic of Decision and Action*, N. Rescher (ed.), 96–103. Pittsburgh, PA: University of Pittsburgh Press.

Lemmon, E. J. 1978. *Beginning Logic*. Indianapolis, IN: Hackett.

Lepore, E. (ed.) 1986. *Truth and Interpretation: Perspectives on the Philosophy of Donald Davidson*. Oxford: Blackwell.

Lepore, E. 2000. *Meaning and Argument: An Introduction to Logic through Language*. Oxford: Blackwell.

Lepore, E. & B. Loewer 1989. "You Can Say that Again". In *Midwest Studies in Philosophy*, P. French, T. E. Uehling, Jr. & H. Wettstein (eds), 338–56. Notre Dame, IN: Notre Dame University Press.

Lepore, E. & B. McLaughlin (eds) 1985. *Actions and Events: Perspectives on the Philosophy of Donald Davidson*. Oxford: Blackwell.

Loar, B. 1976. "Two Theories of Meaning". In *Truth and Meaning: Essays in Semantics*, G. Evans & J. McDonell (eds), 138–61. Oxford: Oxford University Press.

Loar, B. 1981. *Meaning and Mind*. Cambridge: Cambridge University Press.

Locke, J. 1975. *An Essay Concerning Human Understanding*, P. H. Nidditch (ed.). Oxford: Oxford University Press. Originally published 1689.

Mackie, J. L. 1974. *The Cement of the Universe*. Oxford: Clarendon Press.

Malebranche, N. 1980. *The Search After Truth*, T. Lennon & P. Olscamp (trans.). Columbus, OH: Ohio State University Press. Originally published 1712.

Martin, B. 1999. "Interpretation and Responsibility: Excavating Davidson's Ethical Theory". See Hahn (1999), 345–56.

Mates, B. 1972. *Elementary Logic*, 2nd edn. Oxford: Oxford University Press.

Melden, A. I. 1961. *Free Action*. Oxford: Routledge and Kegan Paul.

McDowell, J. 1976. "Truth Conditions, Bivalence and Verificationism". In *Truth and Meaning: Essays in Semantics*, G. Evans & J. McDowell. Oxford: Oxford University Press.

McDowell, J. 1998a. "Anti-Realism and the Epistemology of Understanding". In *Meaning, Knowledge and Reality*, J. McDowell, 314–43. Cambridge, MA: Harvard University Press. Originally published 1981.

McDowell, J. 1998b. "Putnam on Mind and Meaning". In *Meaning, Knowledge and Reality*, J. McDowell, 275–91. Cambridge, MA: Harvard University Press. Originally published 1992.

McDowell, J. 1998c. *Meaning, Knowledge and Reality*. Cambridge, MA: Harvard University Press.

McDowell, J. 1998d. "Meaning and Intentionality in Wittgenstein's Later Philosophy". In *Mind, Value and Reality*, J. McDowell, 263–78. Cambridge, MA: Harvard University Press. Originally published 1992.

McDowell, J. 2001. "Naturalism in the Philosophy of Mind". Townsend Lecture in Philosophy, presented at the University of California at Berkeley, 7 March 2001.

McGinn, C. 1976. "A Note on the Frege Argument", *Mind* **74**, 422–3.

McGinn, C. 1986. "Radical Interpretation and Epistemology". See Lepore (1986), 358–86.

McLaughlin, B. 1989. "Type Epiphenomenalism, Type Dualism, and the Causal Priority of the Physical", *Philosophical Perspectives* **3**, 109–35.

McLaughlin, B. 1993. "On Davidson's Response to the Charge of Epiphenomenalism". In *Mental Causation*, J. Heil & A. Mele (eds), 27–40. Oxford: Oxford University Press.
McLaughlin, B. 1995. "Epiphenomenalism". See Guttenplan (1995), 277–88.
Mill, J. S. 1950. *Philosophy of Scientific Method*, E. Nagel (ed.). New York: Macmillan. [Originally published as *A System of Logic* in 1881.]
Miller, A. 1997. "Tacit Knowledge". See Hale and Wright (1997), 146–74.
Modrak, D. 2000. *Aristotle's Theory of Language and Meaning*. Cambridge: Cambridge University Press.
Morris, C. 1938. *Foundations of the Theory of Signs*. Chicago, IL: University of Chicago Press.
Mulhall, S. 1987. "Davidson on Interpretation and Understanding", *Philosophical Quarterly* **37**, 319–22.
Mulhall, S. 1993. *On Being in the World: Wittgenstein and Heidegger on Seeing Aspects*. London: Routledge.
Nagel, E. 1979a. *The Structure of Science: Problems in the Logic of Scientific Explanation*. Indianapolis, IN: Hackett.
Nagel, T. 1979b. "What is it Like to be a Bat?" In *Mortal Questions*, T. Nagel, 165–80. Cambridge: Cambridge University Press. Originally published 1974.
Ogden, C. K. & I. A. Richards 1946. *The Meaning of Meaning*, 8th edn. New York: Harcourt, Brace and Company.
Olson, K. R. 1987. *An Essay on Facts*. Cambridge: Cambridge University Press.
Peacocke, C. 1995. "Content (1)". See Guttenplan (1995), 219–25.
Pessin, A. & S. Goldberg 1996. *The Twin Earth Chronicles*. Armonk, NY: M. E. Sharpe.
Pettit, P. & J. McDowell 1986. "Introduction". In *Subject, Thought and Context*, P. Pettit & J. McDowell, 1–15. Oxford: Oxford University Press.
Plato 1980. *Collected Dialogues*, E. Hamilton & H. Cairns (ed.). Princeton, NJ: Princeton University Press.
Putnam, H. 1960. "Minds and Machines". Reprinted in Putnam (1975), 362–85.
Putnam, H. 1975. "The Meaning of 'Meaning'". In *Mind, Language and Reality: Philosophical Papers*, vol. 2, H. Putnam, 215–71. Cambridge: Cambridge University Press.
Putnam, H. 1978. *Meaning and the Moral Sciences*. London: Routledge & Kegan Paul.
Putnam, H. 1981. *Reason, Truth and History*. Cambridge: Cambridge University Press.
Putnam, H. 1983. "Mathematics without Foundations". In *Philosophy of Mathematics: Selected Readings*, 2nd edn, P. Benacerraf & H. Putnam (eds), 295–311. Cambridge: Cambridge University Press. Originally published 1967.
Quine, W. V. O. 1960. *Word and Object*. Cambridge, MA: MIT Press.
Quine, W. V. O. 1961. "Two Dogmas of Empiricism". In *From a Logical Point of View*, 20–46. New York: Harper & Row. Originally published 1951.
Quine, W. V. O. 1969. *Ontological Relativity*. New York: Columbia University Press.
Quine, W. V. O. 1976a. "Truth by Convention". In *The Ways of Paradox and Other Essays*, 77–106. Cambridge, MA: Harvard University Press. Originally published 1936.
Quine, W. V. O. 1976b. *The Ways of Paradox and Other Essays*. Cambridge, MA: Harvard University Press.
Quine, W. V. O. 1980. *Elementary Logic*, rev. edn. Cambridge, MA: Harvard University Press.

Quine. W. V. O. 1981a. *Mathematical Logic*, rev. edn. Cambridge, MA: Harvard University Press. Originally published 1940.
Quine, W. V. O. 1981b. *Theories and Things*. Cambridge, MA: Harvard University Press.
Quine, W. V. O. 1981c. "Things and their Place in Theories". In *Theories and Things*, 1–23. Cambridge, MA: Harvard University Press.
Quine, W. V. O. 1985. "Events and Reification". See Lepore and McLaughlin (1985), 162–71.
Quine, W. V. O. 1986. "Reply to Charles Parsons". In *The Philosophy of W. V. Quine*, L. E. Hahn & P. A. Schilp, 398–403. LaSalle, IL: Open Court.
Quine, W. V. O. 1990. *Pursuit of Truth*. Cambridge, MA: Harvard University Press.
Ramberg, B. 1989. *Donald Davidson's Philosophy of Language*. Oxford: Blackwell.
Ramberg, B. 1999. "The Significance of Charity". See Hahn (1999), 601–18.
Ramberg, B. 2001. "What Davidson said to the Skeptic or: Anti-Representationalism, Triangulation and the Naturalization of the Subjective". In *Interpreting Davidson*, T. Kotatko, P. Pagin & G. Segal (eds), 213–36. Stanford, CA: Center for the Study of Language and Information Publications.
Ramsey, F. 1931a. "Facts and Propositions". See Ramsey (1931c), 138–55. Originally published 1927.
Ramsey, F. 1931b. "Truth and Probability". See Ramsey (1931c), 156–98.
Ramsey, F. 1931c. *The Foundations of Mathematics and other Logical Essays*, R. B. Braithwaite (ed.). London: Kegan Paul, Trench, Trubner & Co.
Rorty, R. 1979. *Philosophy and the Mirror of Nature*. Princeton, NJ: Princeton University Press.
Rorty, R. 1982. "The World Well Lost". In *Consequences of Pragmatism*, 3–18. Minneapolis, MN: University of Minnesota Press. Originally published 1972.
Rorty, R. 1999. "Davidson's Mental-Physical Distinction". See Hahn (1999), 575–94.
Rosenberg, A. 1985. "Davidson's Unintended Attack on Psychology". See Lepore and McLaughlin (1985), 399–407.
Ryle, G. 1949. *The Concept of Mind*. Chicago, IL: University of Chicago Press.
Russell, B. 1912. *The Problems of Philosophy*. Oxford: Oxford University Press.
Russell, B. 1931. Critical Notice of Frank Ramsey's *The Foundations of Mathematics*, *Mind* **40**, 476–82.
Russell, B. 1938. *Principles of Mathematics*, 2nd edn. New York: W. W. Norton. Originally published 1903.
Russell, B. 1940. *An Inquiry into Meaning and Truth*. London: Allen and Unwin.
Russell, B. 1984. *Theory of Knowledge: The 1913 Manuscript*, K. Blackwell & E. R. Eames (eds). New York: Routledge.
Schlick, M. 1959. "The Foundation of Knowledge". In *Logical Positivism*, in A. J. Ayer (ed.), 209–27. New York: Macmillan. Originally published 1934.
Searle, J. 1969. *Speech Acts: An Essay in the Philosophy of Language*. Cambridge: Cambridge University Press.
Segal, G. 1989. "A Preference for Sense and Reference", *The Journal of Philosophy* **86**, 73–89.
Sher, G. 1974. "On Event Identity", *Australasian Journal of Philosophy* **52**, 39–47.
Shiffer, S. 1982. "Intention-based Semantics", *Notre Dame Journal of Philosophy* **43**, 119–56.
Shiffer, S. 1987. *Remnants of Meaning*. Cambridge, MA: MIT Press.
Smart, J. J. C. 1971. "Sensations and Brain Processes". In *Materialism and the Mind Body Problem*, D. Rosenthal (ed.), 53–66. Englewood Cliffs, NJ: Prentice-Hall. Originally published 1962.

Stich, S. & T. Warfield (eds) 1994. *Mental Representation: A Reader*. Oxford: Blackwell.
Stoecker, R. 1993a. "Reasons, Actions and their Relationship". In *Reflecting Davidson: Donald Davidson Responding to an International Forum of Philosophers*, 265–86. Berlin: de Gruyter.
Stoecker, R. 1993b. *Reflecting Davidson: Donald Davidson Responding to an International Forum of Philosophers*. Berlin: de Gruyter.
Strawson, P. F. 1960. *Introduction to Logical Theory*. London: Methuen.
Strawson, P. F. 1967. *Philosophical Logic*. Oxford: Oxford University Press.
Swarz, R. 1965. *Perceiving, Sensing and Knowing*. Berkeley, CA: University of California Press.
Tarski, A. 1944. "The Semantic Conception of Truth", *Philosophy and Phenomenological Research* **4**, 341–75.
Tarski, A. 1967. "Truth and Proof", *Scientific American* **220**, 63–77.
Tarski, A. 1983. "The Concept of Truth in Formalized Languages". In *Logic, Semantics, Metamathematics*, 2nd edn, J. Corcoran (ed.), J. H. Woodger (trans.), 152–278. Indianapolis, IN: Hackett. Originally published as "Pohecie prawdy w jezykach nauk dedukcyjnych" in 1933.
Thomson, J. J. 1971. "The Time of a Killing", *The Journal of Philosophy* **68**, 115–32.
Travis, C. 1997. "Pragmatics". See Hale and Wright (1997), 87–107.
van Heijenoort, J. 1967. *From Frege to Gödel: A Sourcebook in Mathematical Logic 1879–1931*. Cambridge, MA: Harvard University Press.
Vermazen, B. & M. Hintikka (eds) 1985. *Essays on Davidson: Actions and Events*. Oxford: Clarendon Press.
Weber, M. 1956. *Wirtschaft und Gesellschaft*. Tübingen: Mohr.
Weinstein, S. 1974. "Truth and Demonstratives", *Noûs* **8**, 179–84.
Whorf, B. 1978. "The Punctual and Segmentative Aspect of Verbs in Hopi". In *Language, Thought and Reality: Selected Writings of Benjamin Lee Whorf*, J. B Carroll. Cambridge, MA: MIT Press. Originally published 1936.
Wiggins, D. 1997. "Meaning and Truth Conditions: From Frege's Grand Design to Davidson's". See Hale and Wright (1997), 3–28.
Williams, M. 1991. *Unnatural Doubts: Epistemological Realism and the Basis of Scepticism*. Oxford: Blackwell.
Wilson, N. 1959. "Substances without Substrata", *Review of Metaphysics* **12**, 529–39.
Wilson, N. 1974. "Facts, Events and their Identity Conditions", *Philosophical Studies* **25**, 303–21.
Winch, P. 1958. *The Idea of Social Science and its Relation to Philosophy*. London: Routledge.
Wittgenstein, L. 1933. *Tractatus Logico-Philosophicus*, C. K. Ogden (trans.). London: Routledge. [German edition 1921.]
Wittgenstein, L. 1958. *Philosophical Investigations*, G. E. M. Anscombe & R. Rhees (eds), G. E. M. Anscombe (trans.). Oxford: Blackwell.
Wittgenstein, L. 1960. *The Blue and the Brown Books*, 2nd edn. Oxford: Blackwell.
Wittgenstein, L. 1974. *Philosophical Grammar*, R. Rhees (ed.), A. Kenny (trans.). Berkeley, CA: University of California Press
Xunzi 1963. *Hsün Tzu: Basic Writings*, B. Watson (trans.). New York: Columbia University Press.

Index

actions
  autonomy 139
  choice behaviour 2–4, 49–52
  indeterminacy of translation 75–6
  normativity of the mental 164–7
  theory of truth 46–7
action theory 1, 10, 117–43, 218
adverbial modifiers, logic 103–6
agents
  mental events 138–43
  volition 117–22
analytic statements 7
analytic tradition 1, 25, 106
anomalism of the mental 156–64, 169–70
anomalous monism 1, 148, 152–6
Antony, Louise 166
Aristotle 2–3
  action theory 117–18
  meaning 78, 80
  practical syllogism 123–6
  relational theory of mind 195
  substances 145–6
  virtue 62
atomic sentences 28–9
attitudes
  actions 123–31, 137–8
  correspondence principle 66–70
  externalism 186–96
  indeterminacy of translation 75–6
  interpreter's evidence 52–8
  normativity of the mental 164–7
Austin, J. L. 4

autonomy
  actions 139
  morality 169–70

Barwise, Jon 19–20
behaviourism
  indeterminacy of translation 74–5
  interpreter's evidence 53–4
  mental states 151
beliefs
  actions 120–2, 124–31, 137–8, 161
  choice behaviour 3–4, 49–52
  coherence principle 64–6
  correspondence principle 66–70
  externalism 186–96
  interpreter's evidence 52–8
  l'homme machine 148–9
  meaning 79–80
  normativity of the mental 164–7
  subjectivity 176–85
  theory of truth 46–7
Blackburn, Simon 16–11
body, Cartesian dualism 145–53
bridge principles 150–2

Carnap, Rudolf 6–7, 198, 213
Cartesian dualism 145–53, 154–5
causal concepts
  action theory 119
  generalizations 137
causal explanation 109–16
causal relations 102–16, 218
causality

action theory 118–21
mental concepts 161
mental events 153–6
ontological monism 153–6
cause–law thesis 135, 155–6, 219
causes 102–16
actions 128–31, 137–43
concepts 176–85
epiphenomenalism 138–43
laws 131–8
ceteris paribus clause 132–3, 137
charity, principles of 9, 62–70
meaning 79–80
normativity of the mental 165–7
theory of interpretation 100–1
Chisholm, Roderick 110–12
choice 2–4, 49–53
actions 117–22
see also rational choice theory
Chomsky, Noam 15
Church, Alonzo 18
closed sentences 29, 31–2
coherence
actions 121
principle of 62–6
coherence theory of truth 45
collateral information 59–61
communication, conventions 88–95
compositionality 200
compositional theory of meaning 13–25
compositional theory of truth 24–47
computational psychology 189–90
concepts, subjectivity 176–85
conceptual dualism 145–8, 152–3, 163–4
conceptual monism 148, 152
conceptual relativism 177–85
conditional judgements of value 127
context principle 71–2, 77–8
continence, principle of 128, 164
Convention *T* 27–32, 95–101, 204, 212
conventions 85–95
correspondence principle 58, 63, 66–70
correspondence theory of meaning 17–21, 200
correspondence theory of truth 45
covering laws 135–8, 153, 155–64
cranial morphology, language 170–4

Danto, A. 217

decision theory *see* rational choice theory
deductive inference 69
deflationary theory of truth 45–6, 207
deliberation 2–4
demonstratives 35–6, 38–42
Dennett, Daniel 55, 166–7
Descartes, R. 145–9, 162–3, 210, 229
doubt 175–6
dualism 145–53, 154–5
first-person authority 190
subjectivity 195–6
desires
actions 118, 121–2, 124–31, 137–8, 161
choice behaviour 49–52
l'homme machine 148–9
normativity of the mental 164–6
theory of truth 46–7
Dilthey, Wilhelm, actions 120
dispositions to behaviour 74–5
Doppelt, G. 223
dualism 145–53, 154–5
Dummett, Michael 89, 197, 211

efficient causality 128
empiricism 209
Quine 6–9
epiphenomena, actions 138–43
ethics 2–3, 169–70
event sentences 103–6
events 102–16
actions 117
see also mental events
evidence 52–61
coherence principle 64–6
correspondence principle 66–70
existence, events 106–7
extensional contexts 17, 202
extensional theories 17–22, 97–8
actions 123
paratactic theory 41
schema *T* 24
externalism 186–96

facts 17, 45, 57, 75, 112, 155, 200, 201, 202, 203, 206
false propositions 13
fictionalism 214
Field, H. 214
figurative language 82–8
final causes, actions 121–2, 128

first meanings
  conventions 89
  metaphor 82–8
first-person authority, principle of 190–5
Fodor, J. 208
  meaning 78, 80–1
  naturalism 163
  philosophy of mind 144
  psychology 189
folk psychology 150, 155, 159, 166, 168
formal languages, compositional theory of truth 27–32
Frege, G. 1
  compositional theory of truth 13, 14–15
  context principle 71–2, 77–8
  correspondence theory of meaning 20
  extensional theories 18, 201, 202
  identity criteria 108
  indirect discourse 37–8
  propositions 46
  Quine 6
  semantics and natural language 34–5
  truth 25, 65

Galileo, subjectivity 176
Gamut 200
generalizations
  psychophysical 155–64
  reasons 131–8
Gödel, K. 6
Goodman, N. 219
Grandy, Richard 69–70
Grice, Paul 4–5

Hacking, Ian 89
Heal, Jane 54–5
heteronomic generalizations 157
Higgenbotham, James 41, 84, 206
Hintikka, Jaakko 21
holism
  indeterminacy of translation 74–5
  meaning 77–82
  normativity of the mental 166
  observation sentences 60–1
  Quine 8–9
Homo erectus, cranial morphology 170–4
homonomic generalizations 157
Horwich, Paul 45
human sciences, generalizations 134, 137
Hume, David 210–11, 223
  covering laws 135, 136
  necessary truths 7
  Quine 6, 7
  science of Man 6
  subjectivity 176–7

ideas, Locke 78
identity, events 107–9, 112–14, 220
idiolects 205
  compositional theory of truth 34
  existence of a language 90–1
  holism 81
illocutionary acts, metaphor 84–8
illocutionary forces
  intentions 92
  metaphor 84–8, 211
indeterminacy 80
  interpretation 70–6
  meaning 82
  mind 161
  reference 72–5
indexical elements 36, 100
indirect discourse 36–42
instrumentalism 166–7, 221
intelligibility 69–70
intensional theories 96–7
  actions 123, 125
  correspondence theory of meaning 20–2
  events 111–12
  indirect discourse 37–8, 39–40
intentionality 156–64
intentions 166–7
  actions 122–5
  externalism 188–96
  interpreter's evidence 52–8
  meaning 79–80, 91–5
  normativity of the mental 165
  theory of meaning 4–6
interpretation
  choice behaviour 49–52
  coherence principle 64–6
  compositional theory of truth 34
  correspondence principle 66–70
  evidence 52–8
  indeterminacy 70–6
  intentions 4–6
  meaning 77–101

normativity of the mental 167–8
rational choice theory 4
theory of truth 49
see also radical interpretation

Kant, Immanuel
covering laws 135–6
metaphysics of morals 169
necessary truths 7
subjectivity 176–7
synthetic truths 198
Kim, Jaegwon 140–1, 171–2, 214
knowledge
objectivity 175–6
Quine 7–9
sense-datum theories 56
Kripke, Saul 93–4, 211
Kuhn, Thomas 223

language 1
cranial morphology 170–4
meaning 12–47
radical interpretation 48–76
theory of meaning 4–6
language of thought 80–1
languages
existence of 88–91
translatability 178–85
langue 90
laws
causes 131–8
cranial morphology 170–4
psychophysical 153, 155–64
Lemmon, E. J. 214
Lepore, Ernest 80–1, 104
Lewis, David 21
l'homme machine 147–52
liar paradox 26, 33–4
Loar, Brian 4
Locke, John
correspondence theory of meaning 20–1
meaning 78, 80
private mental entitities 181
Quine 6, 7
locutionary acts
intentions 91–5
metaphor 84–8
logic
coherence principle 64–6
event sentences 103–6
necessary truths 6–7
ontology 106–7
radical interpretation 63–4
theory of truth 46–7
logical consequence 213
logical empiricism 1, 6–7
logical equivalence 18–20, 202
logical forms 35
logical positivism 6, 175
logos 211

McDowell, John 57, 144, 220, 224
McGinn, Colin 180
McLaughlin, Brian 139
malapropism 91–2
material equivalence 202
materialism 147–52, 158
mathematics, ontology 106–7
meaning 1
compositional theory of 13–32
conventions 88–95
correspondence theory of 17–21
externalism 186–96
intention-based approach 4–6
interpretation 77–101
l'homme machine 148–9
metaphor 82–8
relational theory of 17
truth 12–25, 26–47
mental
anomalism of the 156–64
definition 157
normativity of the 164–74
mental concepts 1, 160–4
mental events
actions 138–43
normativity of the mental 167
ontological monism 153–6
mental states
externalism 186–96
materialism 148–52
meaning 78–82
normativity of the mental 166–7
ontological monism 153–60
metalanguage 203
metaphor, meaning 82–8
metaphysics 106–7
Mill, J. S. 7, 110
mind 144–74
relational theory of 186–96
modality 197
monism 148, 152–6
Montague, Richard 21

morality 138–9, 169–70, 216
Morris, Charles 199
Mulhall, Stephen 56

natural languages
  compositional truth theory 27, 32–6
  event sentences 103–6
natural meaning 4–5
naturalism 162–4, 208
Neanderthals 172
necessary truths 6–7
neologism, metaphor 87–8
neurosciences, psychology 151–2
nihilism, linguistic 89–91
nominalists 106
nomological character of causality 219
nomological regularity 135, 155, 160
normativity of the mental 164–74
number, ontology 106–7

objectivity 1–2, 175–6
observation sentences 59–62, 70–5
occasion sentences 59
ontological dualism 145–8, 152, 162–4
ontological monism 148–9, 153–60, 162
ontology
  actions 118
  events 106–7
  mind 144
open sentences 29–31

paradoxes 26, 33–4
paratactic theory 39–42
parole 89–90
partial belief 50
particulars 106
perceptual sentences 61, 70–5
Perry, John 19–20
Plato 2, 13–14, 198
possible worlds 21, 203
practical reason 124, 165
practical syllogism 122–8, 217, 218
pragmatics 199
  metaphor and meaning 83–8
primary reasons 122–8
principle of coherence 62–6
principle of compositionality 15
principle of continence 128, 164
principle of correspondence 58, 63, 66–70
principle of first-person authority 190–5
principles of charity 9, 62–70, 210
  meaning 79–80
  normativity of the mental 165–7
  theory of interpretation 100–1
private language argument 93–4
pro-attitudes 123–5, 129
properties, Aristotle 145
propositional attitude expressions 201
propositions, deflationary theory of truth 45–6
psychology 144–74
psychophysical generalizations 153, 155–60
Putnam, Hilary 84, 179, 186–90

Quine, conventions 92
Quine, W. V. 1, 6–9, 208, 209, 210, 213, 218, 221
  conceptual relativism 181–2, 184
  experience 176
  indeterminacy of translation 70–5
  intensionalist theories 22
  interpreter's evidence 53–6
  ontology 106–9
  radical translation 58–62
  theory of truth 49
  use–mention 203
quotation-mark name 203

radical interpretation 48–76
  absence of conventions 92–3
  correspondence principle 66–70
  illocutionary acts 86
  indeterminacy of interpretation 70–6
  normativity of the mental 165
  principle of coherence 62–6
radical translation 58–62, 70–5
Ramberg, Bjørn 92, 135–6
Ramsey, Frank 64, 206, 207
  choice behaviour 49–53
  decision theory 10
  redundancy theory of truth 43
rational choice theory 2–4, 47, 49–53
  coherence principle 64
  correspondence principle 69
rationality
  actions 120–2, 128, 137–8

coherence principle 64–6
correspondence principle 68–9
interpreter's evidence 52–8
meaning 79–80
normativity of the mental 164–74
theory of interpretation 100–1
realists 106
reality, subjectivity 176–85
reason explanations 122, 128, 131, 134, 138, 164, 165, 168, 171, 172
reasons
actions 117–22, 128–31, 137–43
laws 131–8
primary 122–8
reductionism 149–51
redundancy theory of truth 43–5
reference
correspondence theory of meaning 18–21
externalism 188–9
indeterminacy of translation 72–5
theory of truth 48
relational model of mind 225
relational theory of meaning 17
relational theory of mind 186–96
relations, Aristotle 145
relativism 1–2
conceptual 177–85
reported speech 35, 36–42
Rorty, R. 177, 179–80, 223
Russell, Bertrand 1
choice behaviour 50–1
correspondence theory of meaning 17–19, 20–1
correspondence theory of truth 200, 201
objectivity 175
Quine 6
theory of meaning 97

samesaying 39–42
satisfaction
compositional theory of truth 29–32
indeterminacy of translation 72
theory of truth 48
Saussure 89, 90
sceptical solution 210
scepticism 1–2, 175–96
conventions 94–5
indeterminacy of translation 74–5
problem of other minds 144
Schlick, Moritz 175
Scholastics, substances 145
scientific laws, reasons 131–8
scientific psychology 189–90
Searle, John 4, 212
Segal, G. 206
semantic primitives 13, 198
semantics 198, 199
compositional theory of truth 26–32
conventions 88–95
intention-based approach 4–6
sense-datum theories of knowledge 56
sentences, events 110–11
sets, identity criteria 108–9
Shiffer, Stephen 4, 198, 199, 200
singular causal statements 109–10
slingshot 19–20, 112
Smart, J. J. C. 148
speech acts, metaphor 84–8
standing sentences 59
stimulus meaning, observation sentences 60–1, 208, 209
Strawson, P. F. 4, 205
strict laws 137–8
strict science 155–6, 219
subjectivity 1–2, 175–96
substances 145–6
supervenience 141–3
syllogism 216
synonymy, samesaying 39–40
syntax 198, 199
synthetic statements 7

T-sentences 25, 36, 39–40, 44–9, 95–101, 212
Tarski, Alfred 12
Convention *T* 95–101
meaning and truth 42–7
theory of truth 26–36, 48–9
teleological theory of action 121–2, 129, 138, 216
Thales 106
theory of interpretation
choice behaviour 49–52
coherence principle 64–6
correspondence principle 66–70
indeterminacy of interpretation 70–6
meaning 77–101
rational choice theory 4
T-sentences 95–101
theory of meaning, composition 199
token-epiphenomenalism 139

translation
conceptual relativism 178–85
interpretation 209
radical 58–62, 70–6
truth 1–2
coherence theory of 45
compositional theory of 24–47, 26–47
correspondence theory of 45
deflationary theory of 45–6
events 110–16
interpreter's evidence 52–8
meaning 12–25, 26–47, 79–80, 95–101
radical interpretation 63–4
redundancy theory of 43–5
truth-conditions 23–5
coherence principle 64–5
demonstratives 35
meaning 77
radical interpretation 63
"twin earth" thought experiment 186–95, 225
type-epiphenomenalism 139

unified theory 6, 46–7, 102
unity of a proposition 201
universals 106
use, metaphor and meaning 82–8
utterances, compositional theory of truth 35–41

verificationist arguments 179
vitalism 162
volition, actions 117–22, 128–9

Whitehead, Alfred North 2, 6
Wiggins, David 82
Winch, P. 120, 122, 128
Wittgenstein, Ludwig 203, 222
actions 117, 121
Carnap 6
conceptual relativism 179
dualism 149
natural language 12
private language argument 93–4, 191–2
sceptical solution 211
truth-conditions 25